Mass Replacement Migration: The Example of Greece

"The purpose of this importation (labour) is the same as that of the importation of Indian COOLIES to Jamaica, namely, perpetuation of slavery."
K Marx '*A Warning*' 1866

"What does 'Down with frontiers' mean? It is the
beginning of anarchy.... Only when the socialist revolution has become a
reality, and not a method, will the slogan 'Down with frontiers' be a correct slogan."
Lenin 'April 1917 on *the National Question*'

"Human history has witnessed the epoch of great migrations on the basis of barbarism. Socialism will open the possibility of great migrations on the basis of the most developed technique and culture. It goes without saying that what is here involved is not compulsory displacements, that is, the creation of new ghettos for certain nationalities, but displacements freely consented to, or rather demanded by certain nationalities or parts of nationalities. The dispersed Jews who would want to be reassembled in the same community will find a sufficiently extensive and rich spot under the sun. The same possibility will be opened for the Arabs, as for all other scattered nations. NATIONAL TOPOGRAPHY WILL BECOME A PART OF THE PLANNED ECONOMY"
L Trotsky '*On the Jewish Question*'

VN Gelis
Athens, London
Oct 2016

Contents

Introduction   **p.5**

Neo Liberal Globalisation and Mass Migration: The
Example of Greece   **p.7**

NGOs in Greece: Balkan Re-Colonisation as a NWO
Project?   **p.22**
Old Imperialisms Die Hard   **p.27**
Immigrant Crisis: Facts, Myth or Plot?   **p.33**

Can US Style 'Multiculturalism' Apply to EU Nation
States?   **p.51**
Greece is Being Filled With Economic Migrants, Not
Refugees, While Merkel Orders More   **p.65**

When the Left Hated Mass Migrations and Didn't
'Welcome All Refugees'   **p.70**

Greek Women against the Mass Importation of Cheap
Labour Migrants   **p.91**
How Europe was Stolen   **p.99**

Reaction and Resistance to Migrant Hotspots in Greece:
One Year On   **p.112**

British Trade Union Solidarity and Greece: Aiding
Reaction Then and Now   **p.119**
Euro 32billion Cost of Illegal Migration in Greece **p. 137**

Appendix

Articles and Historical Information on Population Substitution in Greece

Parliamentary Committee on Mass Immigration into Greece 1993 **p.140**

Greece under the Path of the New World Order **p.145**
Debate on the State of Greek Labour
Olympics Bonanza 2004 **p.174**
The End of Greece **p.184**

Citizens Campaign in central Athens
Ag. Panteleimonas Against Illegal Immigration **p.202**

The Left Covers the Illegal Low Lifes **p.204**

New Democracy Builds Illegal Migrants Reception Centres all over Greece **p.206**

Leaflet 'WE HAVE BECOME IMMIGRANTS IN OUR AREA' **p.208**
Call for Action for the Unemployed **p.210**
Greece: A Nation State in its EU Death Throes **p.214**
Vietnam: Those Who Leave **p.217**
US/British 'far left' Groups on Greece **p.237**

Weekly Worker (Globalists par excellence) in an ad hominem attack **p.247**
Complaint: Marx Memorial Library, London **p.254**

Introduction

The purpose of this collection of articles is to provide to a wider audience the issues related to mass migration and the labour movement in Greece. How for instance what initially appeared to be a case of aiding dispossessed from the collapse of the Berlin Wall with the mass influx of Albanians to an actual programme of displacement and replacement of the indigenous population under the guise of 'humanitarianism'.

Illuminating in this analysis is the UN studies on replacement migration for all EU nation states where the main argument isn't that the bosses want an even playing field under globalization with Asia in terms of wages, non-existent pensions and rights that are sometimes over a century old but the allegedly low birth rates which are as much to do with the economic crisis and the wages paid that lead to a very low level of birth rates and the eventual erasure of European nation states.

Various authors have contributed providing a different perspective and eyewitness reports such as Romanos, Slobodan, Tartakovsky, the Saker as they have become involved in the issue of mass migration into the EU.

The second part of the book uses various sources from the past and the present to analyse how the issue of mass migration has been viewed by parliamentarians, citizens committees and how it has changed over time.

This book isn't here to provide answers to the issue but to document the issues analyse their impact and conclude that only the people themselves in each EU nation in the end will provide an answer to what is going on right under their noses. The oligarchy that rules believes inherently that it can ship in any number of migrants without having local and national resistance to the process and as such indicates to all that it wants to depart the historical stage, for never before can one really govern a globalized population and have national support, it is a contradiction in terms, which eventually will eject this same oligarchy from the national terrain and bring back a semblance of control of the nations that make up each country.

The globalist project is unravelling and this is a race against time. They require as many migrants as locals in each country to ensure they have parity and then they can sit back and relax for a generation, but as has been seen with various Referendums, the Greek OXI, the Dutch referendum on Ukraine's visa free travel to the EU, the Brexit vote, the Hungarian Referendum etc. the EU is unravelling and imploding. This book aims to aid in the process of unravelling the EU.

We will not be replaced and displaced and we will not become like the American Indians in the USA living on reservations having lost everything or dispersed to the four corners of the planet.

VN Gelis
October 2016

Neo Liberal Globalisation and Mass Migration: The Example of Greece

'Hope is Arriving' (Syriza Electoral Slogan) Migrants arriving in Athens

Any serious analysis of mass migration as a phenomena has to provide an in depth study as to the effects of the process, of who benefits and who gains and whether it is a natural phenomena[i] or an organised movement[ii] which serves the neo-liberal agenda.

Greece once more is in the eye of the storm. During 2015 around 750,000 have passed through Greece on their way to Northern Europe. The borders have essentially become non-existent. Another 3 million are expected to arrive in 2016. Is this a natural phenomena (product of wars or economic displacement) or something more sinister? A new world order agenda to reduce wages in the EU as it is now in stark competition with the USA and China? Replacing a century and a half of unionised labour?

Greece suffered extensively as a result of two decades of wars, in the first half of the 20th century as a consequence of the collapse of the Ottoman Empire and World War I and as a result of World War II and the subsequent Cold War (Truman doctrine was inaugurated in Greece) and civil war. As such it has been prone to mass movements of populations from abroad to Greece and vice versa and two examples stand out. The population transfers as a result of the Asia Minor expedition of the early 20's that saw a couple of million arrive in Athens from Attaturk's Turkey and the tens of thousands of Greeks that emigrated after the end of the civil war to find work in the factories and mines of Germany, Belgium and France.

From the mid 1960's to approximately 1990 no large population movements occurred apart from the displacement of Greek Cypriots from Turkey's invasion into Cyprus. What did occur and what isn't mentioned ever is the first wave of globalisation created by the Greek merchant ship owners who had Greek flagged crews on their fleet which was mainly used to carry goods East to West and who developed enormously during the period of the embargo on Saudi Arabia in the 1950s.

They were closely linked to the City of London in terms of insurance and financing of loans for developing the merchant fleets and were at the cutting edge of labour reform. With the advent of new technology and the reduction in manning on merchant shipping, alongside the creation of schools for shipping in the Philippines and Central America, Greek flagged ships became a rarity. Most of the personnel were from the 'third world,' unless they were the captains or port engineers. Labour costs were driven to the ground way before the fall of the Soviet Union and in the 1990's this essentially became the blueprint for neoliberal labour relations worldwide.

The military junta of the late 1960's early 1970's pioneered the first wave of cheap labour from Pakistan for agriculture but this was regulated and at the time the Drachma wasn't a convertible currency so the export of currency was minimal and controlled by the government of the day.

Entrance into the EEC

Greece's entrance into the EEC in 1981 occurred under the guise that it would develop both its agriculture and its heavy industry. Nearly four decades later its agriculture has been decimated and its heavy industry destroyed. Instead of Greek agricultural products being protected in the EU wide market the opposite occurred. Greek supermarkets were taken over by larger chains and they started to import produce the world over. This destroyed agricultural labour costs which led directly to the mass importation of cheap labour. We recently had the odious situation of Asian farmers living with animals to pick strawberries in Greece and being shot for asking for wages. [iii]

Fall of the Soviet Union

When the Soviet Union fell there was a mass wave of illegals that arrived from Albania.

Statements alluded to the recent leader of New Democracy Samaras, made at the time when Greeks had two homes and multiple cars led to a massive wave of Albanians to arrive. Initially they were few but then they kept on coming and the crescendo reached the Olympic Games building projects of the early 2000.

Greek bosses started to prefer and select Albanian immigrant workers for cost as well as hours worked. Insofar as there was a building boom, they were needed and older Greek workers became foremen. Just as mechanisation in shipping led to smaller shipping crews required with more simple instructions, so the changes in building construction led to less workers required with a smaller skill set. By 2000 there were allegedly around 800,000 Albanians alone, but official figures always underestimate. According to estimates by the police there are currently 94 different nationalities present in Greece. In the first decade of the 21st century around 1.5 million Albanians gained legal status in Greece and this year all children born in Greece can gain nationality.

A Greek Parliamentary Committee was set up in 1993 to analyse the issue of mass migration and the demographic crisis. All the major parties signed it (PASOK, New Democracy, KKE and Sinaspismos - Syriza's precursor [iv]).

Olympics Building Boom

Between 1999 and 2004 a mass building program of works occurred for the Olympic games. Thousands of companies were created and tens of thousands of new immigrant workers came. "The entrance of the new immigrants in the labor movement, which covers now around one third of the total number of laborers who are occupied in Greece," explained the Greek TUC Report[v] in 2002.

In other words 33% of the working people are immigrants. From this many have concluded that the borders of Greece are hermetically sealed. Greece is a Fortress inside a European fortress! Someone could ask what percentage should the 33% of cheap laborers be, so as to theoretically accept that borders are open? 100% of all laborers, 200%, 500%, an endless figure? Not that we expect a reply to this question.

'Whoever continues to talk about open borders is either consciously lying or doesn't have a consciousness of reality' was a common refrain at the time alongside what was written on walls all over Athens: 'Worker, the bosses like racism.'

Just think about it. More than two million (and more) immigrants who live in Greece, a number which represents 20% of the total population, is a 'conscious lie'! Whilst truth is that Europe closed its borders a long time ago, stopped immigration, became a Fortress. The simple Greek worker who believes in the opposite doesn't have a consciousness of reality! As this reality isn't one which is witnessed daily in their journeys on public transport, in factories, on ships, on building sites and public works, but that which exists in the realms of fantasy.

Is there competition for work amongst Greeks and immigrants?

'No, jobs are not taken by immigrants.' That is what we are told by the anti-racist globalists. Greek capitalists didn't bring them to replace the more expensive and demanding Greek workers but for them to do the jobs which the well fed locals refuse to do! The foreign workers who work in Greece apparently occupy positions that are exclusively those of unskilled laborers such as cleaning duties, cleaners or building work and agricultural work for men.

Allegedly new migrant workers were required for work in occupations that were new in the expanding labor market, such as building sites. Even if we assume that was the case, building sites aren't new occupations and unemployment always existed between 7-10% during the first decade of the 21st century.

As the 'reality' for which we don't all have a 'consciousness' is that before the immigrants arrived in Greece there were no house servants, no building workers, fishermen, no one dug any fields or worked in making furniture!

Let us contemplate the 'logic' of the ahistorical globalist: that before 1990 the Greek worker didn't work; he knitted and waited for the arrival of immigrants to stand upright and become a new labor aristocracy. Now he has found a new occupation: 'managers of consumerism,' avoiding every labor intensive activity, just like the writers on immigration in the neoliberal era avoid every intellectual activity, with the end result of creating paper-thin arguments, full of contradictions.

Greek labor fought for labor standards. Ship owners destroyed them.

The whole of the history of the Greek labor movement and of every country is based primarily on one-two militant sections of workers with a history and tradition, with a socialist tradition and perspective for another world. The dockworkers and building workers before they were globalised were the advanced guard of class struggle. They were the example to be copied by all the other sections. Whoever sits to read a little history will see that the dockworkers and sailors were the first in Greece during the 2nd world war that created Workers' Committees which decided and forced the ship owners onto their regime on the ships. They reached such a level of class militancy and dynamism that the bosses couldn't recruit or sack who they wanted or when they wanted. Their fame spread in all the significant shipping fleets around the world and the dockers and sailors in many countries followed the example of the Greek dockworkers.

Greece occupied around 25% of the shipping fleet of the Western world and it is no coincidence that the ship owners tried to break the power of the dockworkers and ships crews. This was finally achieved by the rise of PASOK in power (in the early 1980's) and the policies of the KKE who wrote off the leadership of the dockworkers and supported the party of 'change' (which is how PASOK called themselves). The ship owners created schools of sailors in the Philippines and slowly but surely started to replace Greek crews with hungry, politically subdued and educationally backward workers so as to escape from the high labor contracts, and the special provisions regarding unhygienic and dangerous labor, pre-determined hours of work and introducing on the ships a regime of the Roman galleys, once more.

The ship owners from their base in the City of London have in store a future identical to the one above for the whole of the working class. With the use of foreign crews they achieved what they hadn't in four decades. They gained from the paltry wages they paid. More significantly they achieved a significant strategic defeat on the whole labor movement in Greece opening the path to the subjugation of all sectors, using as a lever neoliberal mass immigration. This task will be undertaken when every relationship with militant and revolutionary traditions of the Greek labor movement are broken with the replacement of the natural carriers of these traditions not by the 33% of the Greek TUC report but by 100%, with the support of the 'leftist' globalists.

People don't ask to whom do the jobs belong. To the Greek workers or to their bosses? If the Greek boss had 5 Greek workers on an X wage and he sacks them recruiting 15 immigrants, he didn't create 10 new positions but divided 5 wages to 15 people. With such logic (if anyone can call it that) they claim with all honesty that unemployment in Greece has remained stable and during certain periods even been reduced!... What a nice picture for Greek capitalism.[vi]

With 1/3 of the labor force being immigrants, with only 2,000 Greek seafarers left out of an estimated 100,000 in 1970, everything is going fine. For whom? This isn't really the issue. Due to the immigrants the wages on the building sites –as everywhere else in the private sector – are now under the level of the 1980's. Hours of work have gone through the roof. Thus the beggar became a 'strong Greece.' Greece from being at the bottom of the EU, due to the expansion of immigrant labor, is now somewhere in the middle. First among last, great is its glory (but these borders keep on closing whilst the EU keeps expanding).

We are told that the use of immigrants hasn't occurred due to the profit collapse of gross sales by companies, but because of the expansion of the market. We needed immigrants in booming capitalism. You see, without them the Greek worker would be lazy. He wouldn't get off the couch to pick a grape (despite doing this for thousands of years) or to clean a hospital.

Foreign workers do not take jobs from Greeks, this is the common refrain, as the market has developed and unemployment remained the same. But if the market truly developed, would unemployment remain the same? The unemployed remain unemployed in a period of growth of the economy? So who takes all the new jobs (if they truly exist) as they aren't being taken by Greeks? Whilst some economists present a picture of economic boom of capitalism and the appearance of new jobs, unemployment remains static. In other words development doesn't equal a drop in unemployment. Immigrants don't then take the jobs of Greeks. Or are they taking the new jobs and therefore a drop in unemployment is impossible, despite development?

Trying to justify the unjustifiable and to state that the presence of immigrants has no social, political or economic consequences in the neoliberal era, but only brings to the surface the racist nature of Greek people, globalists who justify mass immigration are being led by mathematical precision into the camp of the apologists of capitalism, in its greatest crisis of history, which is attempting to survive transforming the planet into an arsenal of racial conflicts and planetary slavery. The industrial bourgeoisies in globalised capitalism will try to replace the hands it uses with cheaper and cheaper pools of labor, using the endless pools of illegal labor wherever it can on the planet. Not to improve the standard of life of the hungry and dispossessed but to destroy whatever was achieved by struggle by Western workers and to globalize immiseration.

Riots over Illegal Immigration

Two areas, one in the central Athenian working class district of Ag. Panteleomonas, and another in the port town of Patras, have finally broken center-stage in political life. Starting off by people living in the areas, they protested against the mass invasion, occupation and enforced 'multiculturalism' of the Greek globalist oligarchy whose starting point is the City of London.

Initially unable to know what to do and frightened of being blamed for racism they complained to the official authorities about the squatter camps of hundreds of illegal immigrants camped in town squares, in children's play areas, outside churches. The mass number of illegals meant that not having any work, crime skyrocketed in these areas, people were frightened of moving about in their areas, local businesses were forced into closure, property prices catapulted downwards and communal areas were being used by people to defecate, take drugs, drink, even have sex in full public view. Globalization had finally arrived.

The press initially started a mass wave of criticism blaming the victims for the crimes. The authorities provided no facilities for the hundreds thousands of illegals. Why should they? They don't live in working class areas. After all multiculturalism is for the poor, not the rich. Over a sustained period of six months the protestors were vilified by all: by the media, by the government, by the leftists, but not by the Greek people. They stood on their side, in every conversation on the street, in the markets, even by the first large wave of immigrants. There were Albanians who signed petitions against the multicultural wave from Afghanistan, Somalia, Morocco, Pakistan, Nigeria, Chad, Bangladesh etc. The numbers are now currently standing at around 4 million new immigrants in a country of 10 million, in 2009.

The government's loyal followers in the form of the leftists started a mass campaign to brand the citizens of the central Athens district of Ag. Panteleomonas as 'racists,' 'fascists,' and 'Nazis.' They held demo after demo in the area trying to hound out the hundreds of local protestors.

The focal point was the biggest Orthodox Church in Greece and the children's play area in its garden. They would not be cowed or browbeaten though. They fought back, with posters, leaflets, petitions leading up to a national protest in Omonia Square central Athens. After 9 months of struggle and after the disastrous Euroelections for the ruling parties of both right and left, they have finally achieved half their aims.

The square has been cleared and the illegal immigrants have been forced to move on. Of course they haven't gone to the northern rich suburbs of Athens where the businessmen and politicians live, but the whole country has heard about them now. It's become a national issue where before, it was a side issue. The KKE and the leftists in tow have stood on the opposite side of the class war with the government.

The fake Left has refused to participate or take up any of the issues. They have been forced to admit like the government that there is a problem. The 3,500-strong petition that was gathered (in November 2008) was of course ignored when circulated.

It will be extremely difficult to justify the current mass waves of sustained illegal immigration that currently number around 200,000 a year (2010 onwards). When we had Muslim protests in Athens, this further weakened the position of illegal immigration. The Greek working class has no reason to accept wave upon wave of migrants when it itself cannot survive.

By 2009, the percentage of votes going to extreme rightwing parties was minimal and their representation in the Athens council elections (central districts where most of the immigrants congregated) was minor. The arrival of the Troika meant the parties of the extreme centre (PASOK, New Democracy) which adopted the economic genocide of Greece started to fragment and from a high point of combined votes of 85% of the electorate dropped to around 30% (in the 2012 elections) and the political vacuum created meant people voted for parties of the alleged extreme left and right. Retro-fascists in the form of a party called Golden Dawn gained national prominence and the myth created around this party was that it was fighting for state power, when it had no such intentions. It arrived on the scene due to the political vacuum created.

Just as most of the heavy industries of the EU went to Asia due to high labour costs, so the high cost of Greek labour led to the importation of wave upon wave of immigrants who took over whole industries: farming, catering, building, home care, hotel work and so on. Many bosses preferred cash in hand work with no contractual ties and achieved what they always wanted: a labour movement with no history and zero memory. This they achieved in a majority of sectors and wherever there is some industry left, Greeks remain at most 20% of the labour force.

When New Democracy took over the elections in 2012, it was under pressure, due to another round of riots in central Athens after the murder of a Greek by lumpen Afghanis for a video camera as he was taking his wife to give birth. This forced New Democracy to take emergency measures to limit the globalist inflows of migrants who congregated with nothing to do in all the central town squares. This forced Manolis Glezos (historic leader of the Left who helped tear down the German flag from the Akropolis during the occupation) to make a statement against the Left stating it has adopted mass immigration without any criticisms. [vii]

Anyone visiting Athens between 2008 and 2012 would have noticed the total absence of tourist police (they never existed), hundreds of unlicenced immigrant street sellers everywhere, tens of migrants going round in shopping trolleys taking old metal, hundreds involved in daily muggings and in particular many crimes against old people who couldn't defend themselves, whilst we also had the arrival of teenage prostitutes from Africa pushed by pimps 50 meters from a central police station, just south of Omonia Square.

This in a country that suffered extensively during the German occupation losing around 10% of its overall population, with such violence being unknown against old people by hungry and starving Greeks. These were the social effects of neoliberal globalisation on the immigration side. It would also be absurd to believe that so many people could survive in an era of de-industrialisation just by arriving in Greece. The export of the Euro (hard currency) is of course the pull factor, but this would have a detrimental effect on the actual economy as wages were pinned to the floor and local companies would face the full weight of global competition as was witnessed by the mass importation of low priced goods from Asia. A return to a national currency would reduce the presence of such large numbers of migrants only because the currency of the country would no longer have a global trading status.

Dublin II and Frontex

Throughout the first decade of the 21st century an agreement was reached called Dublin II which stated that all new immigrant arrivals would have to be registered in the first country of arrival. For a decade this was argued against by the parties from the Left. The argument was that Greece could not become a depository of lost souls. In other words, once in, new migrants should be free to travel anywhere within the EU. So why even bother paying fig leaf to borders. Why not just set up direct flights to Pakistan, Bangladesh and the Congo for example, and ask who wants to fly to Europe? There would a lot less stress and a lot less corporate propaganda, but how could the powers at be sell this process?

Brussels has a no pushback policy implying that at anytime one is in the territory of the EU one has to be processed forwards, everything else is illegal. That also implies that the navy of each country which is in the Mediterranean has to accept anyone at sea. As the states don't want to openly admit they desire the mass movement of populations from Asia and Africa into the EU, they like the fact that this is organised on a for profit basis by smugglers and hundreds drown every now and again. It serves their globalist agenda.

The unregistered process serves big business well, as a section of workers has no papers, and bosses can use them as a way of lowering wages across the board.

At around the same time another organisation Frontex was set up, based in Poland, whose aim was to process and register the hundreds of thousands that would arrive in the EU.

Syriza's rise to power with Independent Greeks

If Turkey does not accept repatriation Greece cannot be the EU's reservoir of lost souls. This was the new common refrain. Without officially abolishing Dublin II, Germany gave the green light for millions to arrive in the EU. Syriza complied.

Tens of thousands have arrived and there seems to be no let up in the situation.

What is the real agenda? Solving Germany's demographic problem or weakening European elites? Evidence exists for both[viii] options.[ix]

There were indications that this was Syriza's actual program: opening the borders and facilitating the mass importation of labor. It works insofar as tens of thousands don't stay in Greece. Each new migrant is given a travel document to leave Greece within 30 days. Priority is only given to Afghanis, Iraqis and Syrians. The non-EU countries bordering Greece like the former Yugoslavia, have been targeted perhaps to bring it into the EU. Immigrants could in theory just go to wherever they wanted via Bulgaria as there are no borders with Greece. Merkel wanted Brussels to centralize the mass movement of migrants and for each member state to receive constant flows and for Frontex to decide who is registered as an asylum seeker so individual states lose control of their own territory.

The future will be explosive, just like the past.

One cannot argue the political elite did not understand the issues related to mass immigration and the demographic problems of Greece or the fact that neighbouring states have laid claim to Greek land. A whole parliamentary committee was set up and it produced a report in 1993 signed by all the major parties.

The open borders regime introduced with the election of Syriza has meant around 1 million have entered the EU via Greece (officially 740,000) in 2015. The EU commissioner on immigration who happens to be Greek (another 'natural' phenomenon) Dimitris Avramopoulos stated that "the end of the Schengen Treaty will mean the beginning of the end of Europe. We have thrown down the walls and we are seeing that some people are putting them up again," reported Kontra Newspaper on December 4, 2015.

Turkey is expected to receive 3 billion Euros in order to ship across 3 million more migrants in 2016 whilst Greece has agreed to house and feed 50,000 and set up another 4 processing centers on top of the 11 reception centers created in 2012.

The plan is to reintroduce Dublin II whereby migrants are kept in country of arrival for 18 months before being allowed to leave. The expulsion of Greece from Schengen is the new propaganda tool, just like Grexit before it, to force Greece to accept joint naval operations in the Aegean sea with Turkey, to accept sole responsibility of borders to Frontex and lose all rights of national sovereignty.

A weak state with porous borders: a new - found banana republic, without taking into account the host nation. How will they be housed and fed? Various programs are mentioned with respect to this, housing benefits and a minimal food subsidy. So do they have as an aim to house tens of thousands in empty properties that have been abandoned by owners due to the financial crash in Greece. Who will fix up these properties that are in decay? They will house thousands provisionally in old Olympic stadiums or ones still functioning eg. Galatsi, Faliro or the old Olympic Airport in Athens. Four new processing centres are to be set on Aegean islands but only one so far is functioning. No private housing has yet been set up, reported the ProtoThema Newspaper on December 6.

The EU is founded on four core principles: freedom of movement of capital services, capital, and goods. Any logjam in any of them implies the EU starts to unravel. This is what the globalist elites want to avoid at all costs and will try their hardest to achieve.

We had before movements of populations into the EU that were related to decolonization, with Algeria and Vietnam being the two most prominent cases at stake.

Over 100,000 Algerians arrived who were part of the security services of occupied Algeria and a similar situation developed when up to 2 million Vietnamese left Vietnam in the mid-70s when the US occupation collapsed there. Parallels with our times exist in the departure of Iraq's Kurds in the early 1990's organized by the then Secretary of the Conservative Party of Great Britain Jeffrey Archer. Nowadays for Western imperialism to gain influence in each society it occupies, priority is given to all these local quislings like the campaigns to allow Afghani translators free access to the UK by the British Army. [x]

All these issues are pie in the sky schemes without taking into account local reactions. One cannot relocate Asia and Africa into the EU under 'humanitarian' guises or 'welcome all refugees' to justify a globalist neoliberal free for all. One can start a process, attempt to control it by using riot police to stop people's reactions, but in the long term there will be civil wars. The USA is a special case. It was created from scratch as an area whereby each successive wave of migrants replaced another, creating multi-ethnic ghettoes in a period where stability was guaranteed by America's global status. In declining capitalism only ethnic ghettoes can be created which are in conflict with each other over declining resources and the idea that a new order can be created which doesn't resemble the old order of the past is indeed a fantasy by those who have given up hope in another world and support the neoliberal order of the current one.

In John Kerry's recent visit to Athens, his only visit was to an NGO serving mass immigration called Melissa. There were zero protests against his visit.

Sources
[i] George Soros on EU expansion, free trade zones and mass immigration: http://www.project-syndicate.org/commentary/rebuilding-refugee-asylum- system-by-george-soros-2015-09,

[ii] Hungarian PM blames Soros' NGOs for refugee crisis:
https://www.rt.com/news/320192-soros-orban-hungary-usa/

iii] Greece's migrant fruit pickers: 'They kept firing. There was blood everywhere'
http://www.theguardian.com/world/2014/sep/01/greece-migrant-fruit-pickers-shot-they-kept-firing

[iv] Greek Parliamentary Committee on Mass Immigration:
http://imfoccupationgreece.blogspot.gr/2013/08/the-left-knewparliamentary-committee-on.html

[v] Debate on State of Greek Labour 2004
http://imfoccupationgreece.blogspot.gr/2015/12/debate-on-state-of-greek-labour-2004.html

[vi] Illegal Immigration and the NWO in Greece

http://imfoccupationgreece.blogspot.gr/2015/12/illegal-immigration-and-nwo-greece-1999.html

[vii] Manolis Glezos: The Left covers the Illegal Low Lifes:
http://imfoccupationgreece.blogspot.gr/2014/05/manolis-glezos-left-covers-illegal-low.html

[viii] Report states why population of EU which is 6% of global population has to become around 14%

http://www.un.org/en/development/desa/population/publications/ageing/r eplacement-migration.shtml

[ix]Russian politician on EUs alleged refugee crisis: http://russia-insider.com/en/politics/top-russian-politician-explains- who-behind-europes-refugee-crisis-nikolai-starikov-video

[x] Jeffery Archer and Kurds
http://www.theguardian.com/uk/2001/jul/26/iraq.archer 25 years later same * different people...
http://kurdistantribune.com/2013/john-major-lord-archer-and-real-story -of-how-british-people-backed-kurds-in-1991/

NGOs in Greece: Balkan Re-Colonisation as a NWO Project?

The Greek Minister for Migration Mouzalas announced that Greece has spent 1.5 billion euros on migrant flows into the country using state and private providers ranging from the Navy to the commercial shipping fleet.
25 December 2015

The Experience of Mitilini (Lesvos)

The common refrain is that the movement of refugees and economic migrants is a natural phenomena due to the capitalist wars around the world. Another popular refrain is that nongovernmental organisations (NGOs) aren't funded by imperialist governments. But NGOs have been involved in countless coups, counterrevolutions and reactionary social movements, from Serbia, to the Ukraine and now in Greece. Yet NGOs are promoted, encouraged as being 'alternative,' 'progressive,' enhancing the position of the world's dispossessed. Who funds them? What agenda are they serving? How do they function? Are they not part of a sinister agenda to weaken nation states, nations themselves and centralise geopolitical authority under the guise of …'humanitarian assistance'?

Originally in Mitilini the propaganda was that there were no NGO's. So it was claimed as evidence in articles appearing in a variety of Greek papers in the Greek Left Review. The reception meted out to the hundreds of thousands arriving wasn't as great as expected in a country with now more than 30% of the population below the poverty line after years of IMF 'shock treatment.' This propaganda was created of course to ensure that when the NGO's arrived in their hundreds no one would complain.

The Princess from the Arab Emirates

According to a report in 'Rizospastis' (the KKE (Greek Communist Party) newspaper), an NGO called WAHA was seen to be advertising itself with a banner at the regional health centre that it is in cooperation with the 2nd Health District of Mitilini. Public property has been granted to it from which paid 'volunteers' function to provide health surgeries. This has occurred in the country which has seen hospital budges collapse by around 40% and cancer patients demonstrating in public for lack of medicine, whilst 2 million Greeks have lost the right to basic health care due to the absence of work (health care occurs via work insurance and lack of work equals no health insurance). All new migrants arriving are given free access to Greece's ESY (Health Care system). It's also strange how a Princess from a fellow Arab country is aiding the relocation of Arabs to the EU, when no Arabs have been relocated to the Gulf states.

As with Doctors without Borders which was founded by high ranking French politicians (Bernard Kouchner who is now part of the pro-American civil war regime of Ukraine) so WAHA has as its base France and was set up by a Princess from Abu Dhabi, called Sheiksa Samsa. They are active in Afghanistan, Nigeria, Cameroon, Ethiopia, Kenya, Senegal, Sudan, Zambia, Somalia, Tanzania, Benin, Guinea and Yemen. They set up health centres in many of these countries and they are funded by private donations or by charity and they also collaborate with the airline ETIHAD.

The UAE has intervened indirectly in the Yemen war on behalf of Saudi Arabia and is allegedly giving relief to women from war zones. Are these women the wives/sisters of those fighting Saudi Arabia or are they those who are collaborating with Saudi Arabia to crush resistance in Yemen? There have been reports of the UAE shipping in paid mercenaries from Latin America to do a job on the Yemenis and the fact that a Princess runs WAHA does imply its motives cannot be anything other than sinister.

From October 2015 WAHA has expanded exponentially in the Balkans, in Serbia, Croatia, FYROM [Macedonia] and Slovenia. In the borders of these states they have set up mobile units of 'defence and saviour.' In Serbia as in Mitilini they have access to government health centres as stated in their website.

On November 10, the French deputy Minister of European Affairs Harlem Dezir accompanied by the French Ambassador in Serbia visited the reception centre for migrants in Belgrade. There WAHA has set up health clinics to look after migrants.

NGO's funded by Governments

There is another NGO in Mitilini which is functioning under the title 'Danish Refugee Council' (DRC). This organisation collaborates with WAHA on the programme it enforces in the Balkans which we referred to previously. It is self-characterised as a humanitarian organisation and it has been set up in 1956. It functions in more than 30 countries. It offers help to refugees and disposed people. 'Our aim is to help those who have been hit hard from wars and conflicts and have been expelled due to racial, religious, ethnic, social or marginalized reasons.'

This organisation cooperates fully with official governments and other national organisms and its main source of funding is the Danish Ministry, the EU and the UN, alongside government donations and sponsors.

It is also extremely strange that British citizens have had an area in Mitilini named after them for these mass migration inflows, Kempsons place for example. Everyone knows Molyvos doubles up as a tourist site in the summer months but this seems to be second place now thanks to the demands of the European elites. Local resistance to these schemes finally boiled over when Kammenos (the Greek Defence Minister of Independent Greeks) visited the island, was pelted with eggs and abuse was shouted at him for allowing the destruction of parts of Mitilini.

Reports in the media (Proto Thema) have circulated that Greek shipowners have got government contracts for shipping migrants to Athens (regular price was 80,000 euros but these contracts were signed for 140,000 euros). Anyone who knows Greece knows that government contracts are always issued with kickbacks and despite all protestations to the contrary it is impossible to believe Syriza is a break with the past on these issues when everyone knows it is just more of the same.

Another NGO called One Nation produced a video which created a lot of questions. It shows members of this organisation in small speed boards directing migrant flows to the strait between Skala and Sikemia and the Turkish coast greeting the migrants in English and telling them where to land.

The video on the speedboat of 'One Nation' shows a label 'Team Humanitarian' and in their Facebook info about themselves they are seen giving out water and the migrants must receive it with their ...right hand! This NGO is active in Bosnia, Bangladesh, Gaza and Syria and they raise money for their aims. It also supports a Turkish NGO 'IHH' which is active in the border between Greece and FYROM [Macedonia].

Occupation of Public Property by NGO's

A number of black cladded pseudo anarchists stormed the Mitilini Labour Centre and occupied it alleging it now belongs to 'migrants' and 'refugees'. Without asking those whose representatives use it (KKE militants) they expelled them from these offices in a building in Lesvos, capital of Mitilini. Property acquired by the labour movement through years of struggle (the guerilla resistance in Mitilini continued a long time after the formal end of conflict in the rest of Greece) was now taken over by dubious individuals who hide their faces so as to not be known. One night the local chapter of the KKE with bats took it back. As retribution black clad 'anarchists' beat up another bunch of leftists in the annual parade for the fall of the Junta (November 17) and allegedly thought they were ...KKE when they weren't, sending a couple to hospital. They then apologized for this turn of events via the pages of the so-called Soros funded alternative media site, Indymedia. New global reception centers are planned for Lesvos.

On the December 17 Tsipras flew to Leros island and visited a disused factory site that will now house thousands of illegals. The EU has passed a decision due to the 'refugee crisis' to bypass national borders and override nation state decisions using Frontex no longer simply as a means of registering migrants but as a means of allegedly ...defending borders. In practice this will mean reorganizing even bigger shipments for 2016. Germany is now threatening to sue EU countries which aren't accepting migrant quotas. Enforced globalism is key to the 4th Reichs survival.

Greece has now started a world wide propaganda campaign on behalf of Germany alleging that they have spent according to Mouzalas, the Minister for Migration (a new Ministry set up by Syriza!), 1.5 billion euros for these migrant flowswhilst at the same time stating they have abandoned for a second time in less than a year their 'alternative programme' to alleviate gross poverty in depression hit Greece.

2015 was a trial run. If Germany is to get the numbers right and aim to double the EU's population within the next generation it needs to up the game and treble the migrant flows for 2016. This appears to be the primary role of the 'non-state' state funded NGO's…as described in a prescient piece by F. William Engdhal, titled Soros Plays Both Ends in Syria Refugee Chaos. Angela Merkel has been warning of a new Balkans. 2016 will become a make or break year as migrant flows of this level will be difficult to justify.

Notes

http://www.ibtimes.com/refugees-feuds-fake-ngos-volunteers-doing-humanitarian-work-international-aid-2110739

http://sibilla-gr-sibilla.blogspot.co.uk/2015/12/blog-post_210.html

http://www.waha-international.org/?what-we-do=1838

http://www.balkaneu.com/concern-activity-ngo-one-nation-lesvos-2/

https://greekleftreview.wordpress.com/2015/09/09/refugee-crisis-lesvos-is-a-waiting-hell/

http://www.statewatch.org/news/2015/aug/greece-camp-Kara-Tepe-report-and-proposals.pdf

http://journal-neo.org/2015/12/18/soros-plays-both-ends-in-syria-refugee-chaos/

https://www.theguardian.com/commentisfree/2015/nov/05/angela-merkel-euro

Old Imperialisms Die Hard

Whilst old imperialisms die hard and some dream about the glory days of bygone eras, like the Austrians in the Balkans or the Germans in Greece.

16 February 2016

Austria threatened to send in the army to the borders of Greece, NATO to send warships to the Aegean, Greece is alleged to be expelled from Schengen, enforced Hotspots of migrants are to be created from one end of Greece to the other, growing calls for a European army - a week becomes a long time in Balkan politics. A game of pass the parcel has started for show. Once more as in the past, Greece is to blame for all the sins of modern capitalism in disarray. The Greeks are responsible for crashing the global economy and now they are responsible for the mass migrant inflows to the EU to serve the big businesses appetites for an endless pool of cheap labour. The reality is far more complicated than first meets the eye.

In a week where Merkel was in London taking part in an alleged conference on the Syrian 'refugee crisis' but in reality militarily preparing behind the scenes the next stages of the conflict and a way of finding a new excuse to sell the arrival of millions more migrants into the EU, her anti-Russian statements show the direction the new situation is going. For over two years the US/EU has been pushing Turkey to invade Syria and divide the country up and after covering for them when they shot down a Russian fighter jet allegedly on their territory, they are pushing Turkey once more into conflict with Russia and Syria. All of a sudden the migrant flows from as far afield as sub-Saharan Africa are Russia's and Greece's fault. Merkel sensing the ground giving up under her feet with many demonstrations and protests against her infamous proposals that the planet could essentially arrive in Germany is on a downward spiral and like a cornered rat is lashing out in every direction.

What is really behind the statements of various EU ministers who on the one hand criticise EU member states for not doing enough to accept 'refugees' and on the other of not 'closing the borders' - in other words two sets of contradictory and self-conflicting statements? Without asking the Greek population, the EU decided to create migrant Hotspots to park anything between 400,000 and 1,000,000 people in various areas around Greece. They have chosen as one among many places the 4th most populous in terms of tourism, an island in Greece called Kos. They have chosen one of the most depressed suburbs of the port town of Piraeus in Athens called Perama. None of the rich suburbs has ever been selected and they never will.

When Syriza came to power they made a big hue and cry in closing 13 detentions centres for migrants. Allegedly the conditions were inhumane and they should all be let loose, which they were. They then organised their mass removal to the northern countries of the EU on the quiet. When the migrant flows started and signal was given that the borders between Greece and Turkey were essentially open and illegal smugglers wanted deaths every so often in the Aegean sea to sell the concept of the 'refugee' escaping death destruction and willing to die in an ocean crossing, they set the scene for the arrival of tens of state-sponsored NGO's who organised this process alongside the corporate globalist media which sold the event as if it was a Hollywood movie; only the popcorn was missing. Initially, people took for granted what was being sold especially on the Greek islands. Now they have woken up and smelt the coffee.

Imposing punitive tax rates on the islands of the Aegean sea from 13% to 23%, they want to park hundreds of thousands of people on them and turn them into dumping depots for cheap labour so the EU can assign people depending on how they divide up their transportation to the EU's 28 member states. The local police aren't strong enough to do this, so they are militarising the conflict, talking about bringing in NATO to allegedly stop the migrant flows, but, in reality, organise them better and crush all opposition to this NWO hidden agenda.

In Kos, people protested outside an area assigned by the Greek military to be a dumping ground. They were obviously concerned that if it wasn't policed and 100,000 arrivals would stay there for months on end, the island would be unable to cope, security would be non-existent and the new image of the island that deteriorated since last year would have a detrimental impact on tourism. This is already occurring on the Turkish side with the Russian sanctions causing tourism to plummet. Why not have it occurring on the Greek side also? The local authorities in Kos responded in the way they know best, cracking heads open, arresting people and firing tear gas on them. But they didn't expect such a resistance in defiance of truckloads of riot police from Athens. According to the Police Federation Representative, people fired guns above the police heads, threw grenades at them which they use for fishing, the Town's Mayor used council road diggers and filled the streets with sea rocks blocking transport to the disputed site. The mayor has now called a referendum for the islanders regarding the Hotspot. The Regional Prefecture of Greece's Supreme Court said this cannot occur and void it. Brussels decides, Greece has to agree; democracy once more in the EU goes out of the window.

Even if the EU blocks Greece's borders, even if NATO arrives in the Aegean, even if the Syriza government has decided to turn Greece's tourist islands into Merkel's 4th Reich cheap labour camps, without the agreement of the local people, imposing these things will be very difficult as the island communities are tight knit and labelling them all as being Nazis - as the local Syriza MP Kamateros did - weakens their arguments as questions aired need to be addressed.

Thousands are now arriving from the Maghreb countries via Turkey and it has been revealed that visa restrictions have been abolished between Turkey and North Africa so anyone can fly into Istanbul, then go to the coast by bus and come across by dinghy. Local people know this and the concept of the war-torn refugee is wearing thin in Greece. Hence, the campaign by the same corporate shipowners' media that sold the IMF roadshow in Greece, asking for the islanders of Lesvos to be given a Nobel Peace Prize.

Whilst old imperialisms die hard and some dream about the glory days of bygone eras, like the Austrians in the Balkans or the Germans in Greece, the bottom line is that without tonnes of troops with boots on the ground, most of these visions are pie in the sky dreams which get overturned at the first serious hurdle. Imperialism's new humanitarianism under the guise of helping the migrants and the drowning babies in the Aegean is just an up to date excuse to play the old divide and rule conquer game. The problem is the world moved. People ain't falling for it.

ΟΡΓΗ ΛΑΟΥ ΟΡΓΗ ΘΕΟΥ... ΟΙ ΚΑΤΟΙΚΟΙ ΤΗΣ ΜΟΡΙΑΣ ΔΙΑΔΗΛΩΝΟΥΝ
ΓΙΑ ΤΟΝ ΤΟΠΟ ΤΟΥΣ... «ΜΑΥΡΟ ΠΡΟΒΑΤΟ» Ο ΔΗΜΑΡΧΟΣ ΣΠΥΡΟΣ
ΓΑΛΗΝΟΣ (ΒΙΝΤΕΟ)

📅 Σεπτέμβριος 19, 2016   👤 Lesvosnews.gr

Citizens of Morias in Lesvos demonstrating
against the dumping of migrants on their island.
Syriza Mayor Spiros Galinis nowhere to be found. Sep 2016

Notes

https://www.rt.com/news/331551-austria-military-balkans-refugees/

http://www.iefimerida.gr/news/250329/kammenos-dehomai-tin-emploki-toy-nato-sto-algalo

http://www.abc.net.au/news/2016-02-09/germany-criticises-russian-airstrikes-in-syria/7150868

https://www.rt.com/news/329942-austria-greece-schengen-exclusion/
http://patari.org/forum/viewtopic.php?p=57167

http://uk.reuters.com/article/uk-europe-migrants-germany-idUKKBN0UA09420151227

http://www.hurriyetdailynews.com/greece-offers-to-send-migrants-directly-back-to-turkey-via-aegean-sea-.aspx?pageID=238&nID=94949&NewsCatID=351

http://www.bloomberg.com/news/articles/2016-02-08/merkel-expresses-outrage-over-russian-air-strikes-in-syria

http://edition.cnn.com/2015/11/24/politics/obama-francois-hollande-white-house-meeting/

https://www.neweurope.eu/article/putin-is-no-ally-against-isis/?utm_content=buffer3787c&utm_medium=so
https://www.rt.com/news/331586-pegida-anti-migrant-demonstrations-europe/

http://uk.reuters.com/article/uk-europe-migrants-germany-idUKKBN0UA09420151227

https://euobserver.com/migration/132181

http://www.reuters.com/article/us-greece-politics-immigrants-idUSKBN0LI0MJ20150214

http://imfoccupationgreece.blogspot.co.uk/2015/12/ngos-in-greece-balkan-recolonisation.html

Immigrant Crisis: Facts, Myth or Plot?

February 09, 2016

The designed, created and carefully articulated immigrant flow to Europe, generating one of the biggest crises in after the Cold War as the byproduct of US waged wars in the Middle East, is rolling out according to the already written screenplay. As the pretext for rising extreme right sectors within the EU boundaries, revival of nationalism, racism and fascism, dramatic changes to European societies bring to the reality inter-ethnic and inter-religion confrontations which painfully remind Europeans to some previous Apocalypses which took out over 60 million lives killed just in WWII.

Decades long, war mongering politics of US and NATO satellites, their role in creating and backing various insurgent and terrorist groups from Afghanistan to the Levant and North Africa, brutal neocolonial politics of the Western "corporate governments", guided from the shadows by the huge corporate business, every present hunger and greed for influence, markets and resources; brutal regime changes by the means of "color revolutions"; breaking all agreed international standards and laws, forcing UN to surrender and capitulate under the enormous pressure of US administration are destroying already fragile balance and security system established...after the WW2.

Refugees on Serbian-Hungarian border

As the result of such militant politics, wars, stimulated coups, creation and backing of terrorist and insurgent groups and organizations, entire regions in Asia, Middle East and sub-Saharan parts of Africa are practically destroyed, leaving barely sustainable conditions for survival for millions of people in war zones. Destroyed, impoverished countries with new puppet regimes controlled and loyal to their murderers and occupiers, are incapable to control own territory with various ethnic and religion entities which sink into the ocean of never ending conflicts, becoming the colonial Eldorado for the western multinational corporation, stealing their resources, oil, gas, organizing narcotics production and distribution, human and child trafficking.

It was expectable, of course, that the flows of refugees will start moving like the huge river, fleeing from their homelands, seeking for the safe Heavens, away from the horror of war zones in Libya, Syria, Iraq, Yemen, Afghanistan and other countries. War masters are fully aware of the arising crises and their outcomes. What's more, it seems that they counted it as the inevitable collateral damage and even more: they articulated and directed crises to serve their purposes and aims.

The most of refugees, which are almost neglected and underreported were dislocated from their homes inside the own countries, making the situation even worse for the legally elected governments to help own people in refugees camps while in the same time they have to wage war against DAESH and US/NATO backed, so called, "moderate rebels", who are everything else but "moderate".

Small neighboring countries like Jordan and Lebanon also accepted a large number of Syrian and other non-Syrian refugees, while the rest of them keep moving further to Turkey and through Turkey to – Europe.

What is weird in this dramatic situation is that actually not a single wealthy Arab country, bonded to US and being their loyal ally, accepted any Syrian refugee. The most obvious situation is with oil rich Saudis who accepted literally zero refugees from the region, although there are reports documented by photographs about thousands of air conditioned tents raised near the Riyadh which purpose and use is a but unclear, where over hundreds of thousands refugees could be settled without the problem.

http://www.washingtontimes.com/news/2015/sep/15/saudi-arabia-has-100000-air-conditioned-tents-sitt/

It seems that refugees are allowed to flee only through those countries which are actively opposing American influence and domination. These facts raise serious concerns that a huge refugees flow is somehow articulated, directed and regulated by the same countries responsible for the wars, regime changes, destruction of their countries, economies, and generation of the huge refugee's crisis destroyed their homelands (US, UK; Turkey Saudi, Israel, Qatar, and other EU countries selling weapons and arming the region)

With the most of the rich, US-allied Arab countries around the Syria and Iraq which are ultimately refusing to accept war refugees, the only path out of the war zone, except Jordan and Lebanon, is Turkey or an extremely dangerous sea route across the Mediterranean.

The most of refugees from Syria, and other Muslim countries previously or still burning in war flames, are fleeing to Turkey where huge refugee camps were organized. But why Turkey? It is one of the strongest and most loyal US/NATO partners in the region and wider and somehow, at the first glance it doesn't fit the recognized schema of refugee's path.

We are getting to the point now. Turkey is trying to access EU for decades and it was denied by the most influencing EU members all the time along. They are the NATO member and the most important US/NATO ally but yet, still not a member of EU? This situation really bothers Turkey which still dreams their old Ottoman imperial dreams of returning to Balkans, increasing their influence in the region as well as in Europe.

Besides indisputable evidences provided by Russia of illegal oil trade between Turkey and ISIS who is supplying stolen Syrian oil to Erdogan's regime, providing huge profits to Turkey, while in the same time Turkey backs ISIS by delivering smuggled arms and weapons, military and medical support, instructors in exchange for oil, Turkey founds ideal excuse in this situation to benefit itself, concerning her unsuccessful attempts to access EU.

Refugee crisis and a huge human immigration flow to and trough Turkey is the key point for future Turkey aspirations to join EU, using refugee/immigrant swarms as crisis generator and blackmail of European countries that were refusing Turkey's accession to EU.

By accepting hundreds thousands refugees and economic immigrants, under excuses that Turkey cannot handle anymore such pressure, Erdogan is channeling thousands of refugees daily through Balkans region to EU countries.

Interestingly, the most of those immigrants are seeking asylum in Germany, which accepted so far, about one million immigrants. Is it just a coincidence? Is it a kind of coercing of Germany to refrain from approaching to Russia? Is it perhaps American deadly grip around the European neck to keep EU countries in obedience? Or Merkel had her own agenda, planning to obtain numerous, low cost labor power?

It seems that Erdogan's plan is succeeding so far: EU countries trying to stop or slow down the influx of immigrants from Turkey agreed to help Turkey with billions Euro worth package. Money is already flowing to Turkey which economy is suffering badly from sanctions imposed by Russia, after Turkey in irresponsible and deliberate act, downed Russian fighter jet when Russian pilot and one serviceman lost their lives.

Nevertheless, since Turkey is not EU member despite her attempts to access union, Erdogan is not obliged to keep and protect his borders as the outside EU borders under the common EU politics, and Greece due to its location, numerous islands and long borders is actually hollow and transparent to illegal immigration. Various NGOs, mostly financed by George Soros, are taking active role in funneling the overfilled glass by financing and directing huge human flows towards Europe. Immigrants are instructed, financially helped and their movement is articulated with carefully prepared instructions:

(http://news.sky.com/story/1551853/sky-finds-handbook-for-eu-bound-migrants).

When the EU members started to worry and openly complain, Turkey just swayed the head and said- we cannot handle them anymore. We need help from EU. And suddenly, billions of EU tax payer's money has been sent to Turkey overnight?

But immigrants are still coming. Of course – Turkey is not EU member and is not obliged to protect the outer EU borders. They will let them go to the old enemies: Greece, Bulgaria and Serbia? Again a coincidence? I wouldn't say so. Mentioned countries together with Montenegro allied in the Balkans alliances, expelled weakened Turkey entirely during the Balkan Wars 1912-1913 and there are almost no traces of Turkish presence in the area from that time. It is the nice opportunity today for a Turkish payback for the shameful defeat and in the same time for a strong pressure on EU to accept Turkey into the EU.

(http://encyclopedia.1914-1918-online.net/article/balkan_wars_1912-1913)

In this process, US is actively backing Turkey in all these dirty games in order to keep the most important NATO ally satisfied and compensated for their concessions.

Although accepting the most of the immigrants and advocating in EU flexible and generous immigration quotas plans, Germany is not the only host country. Large number of immigrants arrived to France, Sweden, Finland, UK, Denmark, Hungary and other EU member states, while the millions of people are still en-route to Europe arriving from Asia and Africa.

Heartwarming pictures in host countries of people waiting arriving immigrants with huge signs and welcome messages are fading away, and new, disturbing images of clashes in the streets of European countries emerge. Violence in the streets of European towns, caused by ethnic and religious animosities as the result of the immigration is rising daily, changing the pictures of Europe.

European rightists are raising voice and reviving against illegal immigration and immigration at all. Particular concerns are about the rising of extreme right sectors and revival of old nightmare of fascism, racism, and white supremacists who build their identity and presence on the European scene on serious concerns about "artificial and forceful demographic engineering", "security and national interest threats", "violence and demands for Sharia laws in the areas where Muslim population is present in the larger numbers etc. Islamophobia is in the full swing and rising up daily with every new wave of immigrants arriving.

With the increased power of right sectors, European member states will respond by issuing more and more restricting laws and regulations, narrowing so far achieved human rights and liberties. We are witnessing this process already started in France, where emergency state is declared, with the considerable presence of military and police forces particularly after the bloodshed in Paris, which was done by infiltrated Muslim extremists and Wahhabi militants.

Many fear that Francois Hollande this situation could extends to the election in 2017 to prevent the coming to power of forces that voters want (such as, for example, the National Front).

The European Union is in a state of emergency. Germany is conducting it in silence and under a different name. German media are strictly controlled. Officials of almost all parties in the federal parliament conducted wholeheartedly same policy of pushing the nation into chaos and open dictatorship. The salvation can only expect citizens of countries that have not yet been "blessed with" membership in EU.

http://www.dailymail.co.uk/news/article-3397860/Anti-immigrant-Soldiers-Odin-raise-concernFinland.html

In the same time Denmark issued regulations allowing seizure of immigrant properties and/or money above the certain allowed amount under the excuse that such values will be used to cover their accommodation and other costs. This measure for sure will not be hailed by immigrants and will increase already present tensions and rage.

The European Union is founded on the proclaimed high principles of equality, freedom and prosperity. From these ideals, two decades after the establishment has all come to nothing, except relative concept of well-being, given that the GDP per capita is among the highest in the world – 21,400 Euros annually.

With the increased influence and strength of right sector, including revived (but never distinguished) fascists, racist and white supremacists in Europe, it is expectable that further conflicts and clashes with immigrants will be inevitable. Europe is facing two opposite sides, both equally extreme in their nature: right sector with their well-known ideologies which will attract more members or fans with each conflict, and on the other side, undefined but unsusceptible high number or radicalized Muslims among which there are DAESH and radicalized Islamist mercenaries, infiltrated into the European countries within the huge and continuous influx of immigrants.

http://www.infowars.com/norway-oslo-police-we-have-lost-the-city/

https://www.rt.com/news/328851-finland-soldiers-odin-migrantpatrol/?utm_source=browser&utm_medium=aplication_chrome&utm_campaign=chrome

It seems that the underlying plan of neocon powers and New World Order (NWO) promoters is rolling out as planned without bigger obstacles, all covered under the slogan of "political correctness" which, as the relatively new approach, is absolutely unacceptable due to its tendency of hiding or overstepping the truth in the name of "higher goals of ethnic tolerance multi culture and multi confessional pluralism".

"Wikileaks founder Julian Assange believes that the mass exodus from Syria is part of the US strategy against the government from Assad: The depopulation of the country will bring the country to the brink of collapse because especially the educated middle class is being driven out. Europe's strategy of open borders plays to the US interests in the hands."

("South Front" 29.10.2015)

In the same time, let's take a look on the role of Israel. Israel is illegally expanding its territory over Palestinian lands over decades.

https://en.wikipedia.org/wiki/List_of_villages_depopulated_during_t
he_Arab%E2%80%93Israe_li_conflict

They are performing active politics of genocide and de-population of Palestinians and other Arabs in their surroundings. New founding of gas/oil on occupied Syrian Golan Height is a sweet cake for them but there is a problem: there are Iraqis and Assyrians living around. Proxy war with the most brutal force in the recent history will swiftly depopulate huge areas which will be the nice expansion area for the Greater Israel.

So Israel is actively supporting ISIS, channeling and articulating this way refugee's crisis and depopulation of Syria and Iraq. How convenient at the same time. Who is the supporter backing up Israel? Well US again!!!http://www.examiner.com/article/europe-taking-a-stand-against-israeli-religious-basedaggression

What was the imminent reaction upon first problems with immigrant swarm: a significant support and uprising of the right sectors in the most of EU countries along with extreme rightists and fascists emerging? Fascism is evil! It is the nightmare. It is the dusk of the civilization. Yet, it is rising again and authors of the crisis knew it EXACTLY that this will happen, but they didn't do a thing to prevent it. Why?

Of course there is the reason. Europe still didn't abolish and exterminate fascism from her roots. The first NATO gen. secretary was – German Nazi WWII officer. US accepted and pulled huge number of Nazi scientists as well as officers after the WWII, Germany had also former Nazi officers as the high ranking army officers after WWII. Roots of Nazism are still burning in Poland, Ukraine, Germany, Finland, Sweden, France, Austria, Hungary, even UK, Spain and Italy. Somewhere it is stronger somewhere weaker but ever-present.

(https://www.facebook.com/patriotischeeuropaeersagennein/videos/1659493604302159/)

EU members, faced with the increased threats of conflicts between anti-immigration oriented groups, pro immigrant oriented groups and immigrant groups itself, will soon be enforced to gradually introduce more restrictive measures and regulations until they finally declare a kind of emergency states further restricting rights and liberties of own citizens by tightening control over the internet, restricting or even banning free speech, controlling and oppressing alternative and free media, banning mass rallies, and other measures that could seems to be appropriate for the government administration.

https://www.rt.com/news/330419-germany-small-arms-sales/

This could be the pretext and introduction to more totalitarian regimes which could easily turn the European countries to the right and ultimately to the fascism within the EU boundaries.

Fascist and Nazis just needed a food to grow up and get strength. And they are offered such food, a huge immigrant influx: different culture, different religion, different philosophy, heritage, language, lookout, lifestyle, laws. It is the rich feast for the small but still alive fascist groups. With so much food they are growing fast and become more and more dangerous. You can see the example of Islamophobia and rise of nationalistic and racist intolerance in UK media for example:

https://www.facebook.com/OfficialBritainFirst/videos/945859365559325/

And yet, that was all known to the creators of the NWO! So we could only conclude that it was the part of the plan, a well defined and performed agenda. This brings now, more restrictive laws and less so far achieved liberties, less human rights, stronger and more aggressive police, more military on streets, somewhere declared emergency states, all as I have already described.

All these issues happened already and are happening RIGHT NOW! Indeed, what is going on now in Europe? Schengen is partially abolished. It seems very probably that will be abolished at the certain period of time. Citizens all over the Europe are rising against governments and refugees acceptance. There are new proposals to set military to the borders, – each country 1000-1500 troops that is EU army of 30.000 troopers! Is this the attempt of EU to create own army besides NATO?

Greek crisis still hangs over the heads of EU member states. If EU decide to close and seal the borders and to stop receiving more immigrants, or even to start deportations, Greece will soon have the number of immigrants exceeding 50% of own population? We could call it as artificial and violent demographic engineering. It is an invasion in fact, whether you like that term or not. The same fate could expect Macedonia, Bulgaria and Serbia.

The logical outcome of the conflicts which already started between immigrants, authorities and local population, as well as particular steps that some EU countries already made will ruin EU unity and mechanisms established so far.

EU will start crumbling and falling apart over the internal borders: border controls will be reintroduced, more and more EU countries will be strictly opposing acceptance of new immigrants and will demand deportation of already received immigrants. If denied by the EU administration, EU member states will be soon on their way out of EU, (Hungary, Poland, UK and others to follow them).

EU monetary system will start rolling down and some countries in order to protect themselves from the inevitable collapse will reconsider the return of their national currencies. Collapse of Euro zone will even more degrade and ruin the poorest EU member like Greece which is on the brinks of default, Portugal, Bulgaria,

Romania, but even the Italy is not far away from that scenario and others will follow them EU members will be faced with more rigorous terms to pay their debts and to achieve arrangement to prevent their defaults.

Weakening of EU institutions or eventual collapse of Euro zone common monetary system will artificially strengthen US dollar, prolonging for a while the collapse of US economy and banking system deeply dependent on military sector, (in other words on the continuous state of war in the large number of regions). This will purchase some additional time to US bankers and Wall Street and FED, but with collapsing oil prices, the degrading situation in EU, the rising and strengthening BRICS, it will be the short run, the safe Heavens will not last forever for the economy which is approximately 18 trillion dollars in debt.

Faced with the imminent danger of the civil wars, or at least, wide spread clashes and conflicts, with already present and pretty large Muslim population in Europe, radicalized with the fresh influx of immigrants and disguised Islamist, which would soon be armed by the illegal arms smuggling, EU citizens will remain more or less silent on all of those governmental measures, voluntarily giving up from their liberties. The fear and feelings of insecurity will just gain US will gain more influence on their vassals in American dictated anti-Russian politics.

http://thesaker.is/sexual-terrorism-in-the-heart-of-europe/

The model for destabilizing Europe and ignite war on the European continent was tested on the former Yugoslavia, and later in 1999 with the illegal bombing of Serbia against all international laws. The same concept was used to the number of Arabic countries as well as in Ukraine. The blindness and deafness of EU leaders and countries acting like obedient pawns of US will lead to the final and ultimate dissolution of EU and breaking the most of achieved bonds, leaving only NATO as the top administration which will dictate American interests to vassal European countries.

US are brutally enforcing EU partners to raise and keep holding sanctions against Russia although it is huge measure against the interest of each EU member. Some members openly shout about that, but must be humiliated and obey what boss said. Nevertheless, this situation could not be expected to last forever. France already announced that they could vote against sanction renewal soon, but what happened as the result?? Paris attack, Calais clashes, chaos all over the France, state of emergency, restrictive laws, armed military and police forces on the streets and French towns, mass arrests ...

Merkel and Germany wanted to build North Stream. They are ever ready to break the wall and start dealing business with Russia; of course they had tremendous exchange with Russia...Than suddenly... Cologne mass raping happened. And not only Cologne clashes with radicalized Muslim immigrant groups are all over the Germany ... and it will be more; much more...

The EU will be crucified between vital economic and political interests in favor of Russia and humiliation and obedience towards the Empire. How long it will last? Is it better for EU to be united and strong and independent of US will and to do what is in her interest? Would each particular country in the dissolved EU, have enough strength and courage to resist the pressure from US?

(http://www.globalresearch.ca/are-the-us-elites-attempting-to-destroy-europe-bytriggering-a-flood-of-immigrants-and-refugees/5502526)

Let's be reasonable and frank: Americans still need NATO. But US do not need EU. That is the fact. And we are looking the outcomes.

It is clear that those who are responsible for conflicts, wars and refugees crisis have moral and legal obligations to handle the refugees crisis and that they have to settle down all the problems arose upon their irresponsible actions. But instead of licking the wounds, Europeans should look back to the own politics towards African and Asian countries, they should stop supporting American imperial interests and work together in preventing the causes of the crisis- they should immediately return to the international standards and laws, stop proxy wars in the region, weapons and arms delivery, forcing other countries like Turkey, Saudi Arabia, Israel, Qatar and others to stop supporting ISIS and other militant Islamic terrorist organizations and to recognize legally elected governments and regimes.

Without the proper identification of the causes and roots of this huge crisis, there would be no proper measures and medicaments to solve the problem.

The disastrous US imperialistic and war mongering politics created still burning war battlefield zone in Ukraine and one lose and easily destabilizing zone with the great potentials for new conflicts in the Balkans countries.

Failed recent attempt of color revolution in Macedonia in order to oust legally elected government and Mr. Gruevski, who should be replaced with American puppet clown Zaevski, several terroristic attacks or attempts in Bosnia and Herzegovina, continuous attempts to abolish Republika Srpska, criminal fake so called state Kosovo,

Turkish attempts to gain influence in the Balkan countries reviving dreams of Ottoman empire, announced arming of Croatia by US government with the missiles capable to target the most of Serbia and Republika Srpska are just some of those activities in creating incandescent state of the powder barrel where arriving Muslim immigrants will be just as a wick ready to ignite the huge explosion of conflicts, not only in the Balkans.

Who and when will light up the wick… we are going to see.

Muslims immigrants, who are already distressed and pissed with their fate, humiliation, suffer, poverty, human loses, but also with religious hatred and intolerance which at least a portion of them keep in their hearts, could be; and probably would be used as a cannon fodder and as the same excuse for the inevitable war, as the Jews were used by Nazis in the years prior to WWII.

You need someone to blame for the social, monetary and political collapse, and you need urgently to find, or – *create* the "enemy". This is what is happening right now.

Immigrants and refugees will for sure represent a real threat to the European stability. They are already a threat, disrupting established political relationships and stability; this is indisputable, with a lot evidences and issues emerging daily.

http://medzicas.sk/potomkovia-fasistov-v-nemecku-sa-prebudzaju/

But they are not a threat because on they own, or because they are "barbarians" due to the different religion, civilization or cultural norms or whatever… they will be a threat because of the conflict of interests within the European borders; between the left and right sectors; between rich and poor European countries; between EU members who are actually responsible for the entire crisis by their erroneous politics to the Levant and Mid East and those EU

members not feeling responsible in any way for the crisis; because of inherit feelings of Europeans towards ethnically, culturally, religion dissimilar population which probably have the same feelings towards Europeans, which they hold responsible for the situation they have faced; because the swarms of uncontrolled immigration will for sure cause the reaction of hosts and there is NOTHING that EU or particular member states could do to stop it or prevent it.

Imperialistic war mongering politics of US backed by the UK, France, Turkey, and other European countries, along with the allies like Israel, Saudi Arabia, Qatar and others who helped creating ISIS as the US, proxy army; Talibans as US proxy army; "Moderate rebels" in Syria as the US proxy army. That KLA (UCK) in Kosovo was US/NATO proxy army against Serbia; Mujahidin terrorists in Bosnia were NATO proxy army.

We should be aware that enormous immigrant swarms of young solely men of conscripted age infiltrated purposely among refugees and immigrants are future proxy army in the heart of Europe. Evidences of ISIS members photographed in the battlefield and then again in the cities of Germany, France and other countries as asylum seekers are all over the internet, face recognition software are easily do their work and evidences are indisputable. Authorities on the EU member states are fully aware of these evidences but are not willing to admit it publicly. Why? What they are hiding? Which agenda they are following?

Some of the answers could be found in this excellent article describing the new ways of the modern wars and methods of coercion:

http://www.rand.org/pubs/rgs_dissertations/RGSD189.html

The only thing that spoiled and to some extents delayed the evil axis plan is Russian extremely efficient action in Syria combined with coalition against US mercenaries (ISIS) engaged in that US proxy war. Faced with the inevitable defeat in Syria, US government already shifted their plans and ambitions toward the Afghanistan and Libya where they are actively transporting fleeing Jihadists from Syria.

This is particularly dangerous for escalation of conflicts since Libya is just nearby across the Mediterranean to Italy, and Afghanistan is once again the potential hot spot on the Russian borders.

Firm evidences exist about US involving in evacuating, backing transporting ISIS members to Libya, Yemen, and Afghanistan. Why Libya? Of course, oil again, but from Libya to Italy is a short run… a nice and easy path to import Jihad to EU.

Afghanistan should be again a hotspot at the very border of Russia. US provocations in the South Chinese Sea against China are aimed to create mini NATO in Asia which would surround Russian Far East, as well as China and N. Korea. Battleground for the WWIII is almost complete.

The entire EU is actually in the vassal position to US. Although it might sound insane, the only logical outcome to return of national sovereignty and independence is: European Union must die. It should be disassembled and dissolved. EU is the most effective tools to keep EU member states in the vassal position pushing them towards the New World order agenda with one leader in rule.

EU is the tools in the hands of US administration for crushing national states sovereignty with one shot and without a single bullet fired; it is the worst totalitarian system with officials and administration which is not elected or loyal to the own countries, but rather as the self-sustaining parasitic organism is sucking blood and life from the European countries and citizens. EU bureaucrats are loyal to themselves only, neglecting national interests of their own countries. Two administrations – EU and NATO are in the most effective control over the life of every European citizen.

European countries actually have opposite interests to Americans, Europe needs a large and open market for their products, EU need resources and trade exchange of enormous values with Russia and

Euro-Asian countries, EU needs energy, gas, oil, and long term stability peace and security for own development.

There is nothing of mentioned now due to the long term overseas pressure; friendly and mutually beneficial relations between Russia, BRICS countries and Euro Asian territory is in direct confrontation with US imperial interests. Whenever Europeans are starting to wake up and get sober, Americans start the engine of already prepared underlying future crises igniting blazes which destroy any such attempts (Former Yugoslavia civil wars, Ukrainian civil war, Greek financial crisis, immigrant crisis…) keeping Europeans quiet and… obedient.

Wake up Europe until it is too late.

By Solajic Slobodan
Serbia

No to the 4th Reich banner on demo in Greece

Can US Style 'Multiculturalism' Apply to EU Nation States?

The issue that confronts every thinking person today regarding globalisation and its effects in every society is the question of multiculturalism.

26 February 2016

In trying to analyse why America never really had a mass movement for equality (or socialism), Steinbeck noted that "we didn't have any self-admitted workers. Everyone was a temporarily embarrassed capitalist.[i]" What made America different from Europe?

The collapse of the feudal order i.e. the system that was based on monarchies and land, and the emergence of a system based on markets and products, occurred for roughly 500 years, from around 1500 to the early 20th century. Throughout this period of history we had in Europe the emergence of capitalist nation states, the creation of a uniformity in language, and culture to the extent each specific country developed, and to the extent it was integrated within larger economic and political zones created by the growth of Empires (sterling, francophone etc.) The emergence of the USA as the dominant world power due to the collapse of the European powers in two world wars led inadvertently to the adoption of the American multicultural system as the role model for the rest of the world.

Mass Immigration, Private Armies and Multiculturalism

The issue that confronts every thinking person today regarding globalisation and its effects in every society is the question of multiculturalism. Alongside globalisation, from nowhere suddenly appeared, millions of people from many countries in nearly every

European metropolis. Are there historical examples for this event? Is it an organised plan? Without history as a guide for what is occurring no one is able to find a serious answer to the questions and concerns many have. The problem though remains: which particular history are we going to research? Where will we find answers for today?

The American state is the prototype as it wasn't created from scratch due to some racial, national or cultural rebellion of a certain nation against another. Instead, it was a product of the expansion of European colonists on a new geographic plateau. The reasons as to why the Europeans went there aren't part of this brief analysis. But the fact that they travelled from many European countries of different tongues and cultures does have some historical weight, when the original Americans, were those called 'Indians' and were erased by the pogroms of the colonialists and the importation of disease during the various phases of the expansion on the soil of the USA. Based on this experience and on what occurred in South Africa, the European would be global neo-colonialist was full of praise for the methods of concentration camps and reservations.[ii]

What distinguishes therefore a state of settlers from the indigenous development of a nation? That is the question that needs analysing. The settler doesn't try to develop a country, on the contrary, he wants to survive firstly in his new surroundings, and the general wellbeing is subsumed into individual advancement. That is why when the colonists arrived in the USA, they sent the Indians to 'paradise,' and then they imported black slaves so as to continue the

productive relationships with Old Europe - by creating their own version of heaven on earth: a society based on slavery. Many colonists were funded by European governments to create businesses in the USA and to send back their produce for a monetary gain. Thus the colonists were an extension of Europe, but without anyone essentially in charge and without a national coordinator. It is essentially like that in our days as well.

The development of the USA in the 19th century and the rise of the labour movement contained within it many new phenomena that weren't the same as the rest of Europe. Three basic characteristics show a particular development:

- Firstly migrants were leaving Europe en masse and going to the US in the latter half of 19thcentury. No such movement was happening towards Europe.
- The use of private armies for the confrontation against strikes-popular demands was unique to the USA.
- The non-existence a labour movement during the period of industrialisation of the country was specific to the USA.

No other advanced capitalist country had such an exceptional history. Bourgeois historical analysts had identified the historical peculiarity of America, but they had never focused on explaining how the country with the most advanced technology has the most backward civil rights movement for two centuries now? This historical contradiction is one that I will try to analyse, but not fully, as history is a work in progress and reality may disprove this basic analysis.

The creation of industrialised national companies in transportation, electricity, oil etc. created the so-called robber barons, arch-sharks and the American version of Aristotle Onassis (Rockefellers, Carnegies, Morgans etc.) Whole cities belonged to a single

company. The American factories, the housing, the food distribution centres and, in parallel, the creation of private armies which supported the interests of the owners. Even the Federal Reserve

Bank became a private concern. Politics became a vehicle for business and overt corruption as exemplified by Mark Twain's novel The Gilded Age were everyone was on the make and the take (Tammany Hall), as the population boom after the end of the US civil war increased by an amazing 25% in a single decade…

The Creation of the USA: Multiculturalism Without Limits

The arrival of immigrants from the USA in the 19th century was the following:

- 1841-50 - 1.7 million people
- 1851-60- 2.6m
- 1861-70-2.3m
- 1871-80-2.8m
- 1891-00-3.7m
- 1901-10-9m
- 1911-20-5.8m

In the 1850-60s the first unions of workers were created (Knights of Labour) with the result being to try to maintain their work, as there was a mass immigrant flood. The fact that America hadn't as yet industrialised and hadn't been occupied from one end to another meant that many movements could occur from area to area. In the first 40 years of the period we are analysing, immigrants came from Germany, England, Ireland, China and the Scandinavian countries. After the 1880's immigrants came from Italy, Greece, Korea, Japan, Mexico, the Philippines. No other country on earth in that period of history had such a migrant flow from all the corners of the earth. No country since either.

The right of the bosses to recruit whomever they wanted, whenever they wanted, under a regime of permanent importation of foreign-born labour, made the creation of real unions almost impossible. A characteristic example is a not too well publicised book in Greece, but one that is very important for our days, which was printed in Greece by the KKE (the Greek Communist Party), The Unknown History of the Labour Movement in the USA' (1993).

There we see a description as to how the American bosses functioned in the 19th century (bold mine):

The contractors make their appearance as representatives of the American flag in the most impoverished parts of Hungary, Italy, Denmark, they say stories about fantastic wages in America, they lie to the impoverished souls and they get them to sign contracts which aim to provide funds for the trip which very few understand. When they arrive at the pre-agreed destination of the contracts, they discover that their golden dreams have turned into a nightmare as they make them work in mines factories or railroads, with even lower wages than their compatriots, whose place they take. (p.121)

John   Swinton's   Newspaper,   30th December   1883

In the publication of 18th May 1884, Swinton recounted that thousands of Hungarians were imported into the areas of Connellsville in Pennsylvania where the young Frick made millions. Here sixteen men and women were placed in small huts, each the size of 2.5 to 3m. This was a usual phenomenon. The owners "turned the English against the Irish and the opposite... the Germans against both... they maintained a constant war amongst the tribes... The harshness was described openly by the words of an owner: "It's better to lose two men, than a cow."

These industrialist slaves were also used as strike breakers... They were recruited so as to go into work, without knowing their rights... Honest working men... these poor souls, from poor Italy, would never play the role of a strike breaker if they could choose. Butthey couldn't. From the ships they were received like herds in scenes of frightening violence, they passed them via the lines of strikers who fought throwing stones and swearing towards the gates of the closed factories or the mines whilst everywhere there were battles.[iii]

The first unions tried to block the importation of foreign born labour as contracts were signed in other countries, but they weren't able to defeat the bosses on this crucial issue.

Multiculturalism: The Main Reason for the Backwardness of the American Labour Movement?

The question that arose is as follows: whilst America had the most advanced technology on earth in relation with Old Europe (despite that it almost always used Europeans for its technological advancement!) why did the labour movement remain so backward in relation to the European one? In contrast to all other industrialised metropolises the USA never created a pan-national labour movement with parliamentary representation. The closest it came to this was the growth of the Socialist Party[iv] prior to WW1 and the emergence of the CIO[v] (Congress of Industrial Organizations) via the sit-down strikes of the 1930's.

Whenever there was a strike, a security company with arms in hand was called to defend the interests of the bosses. The characteristic of the era was that due to the unlimited number of immigrants, one strike could easily be replaced by newly arrived immigrants who got work as the spies-grassers of the security company of the bosses and then they stole the work of those who came before them. Until, of course, their time came up for firing and then the same thing happened to them. The most famous company was called Pinkertons and it was created so as to help the bosses maintain low wages. The strike-breakers were given prominence.

Victor Serge, a revolutionist in the time of Lenin, had written this about this period:

In the United States, the participation of the private police in the conflicts between labour and capital has grown fearfully. The offices of famous private detectives provide the capitalists with discreet informers, expert provocateurs, riflemen, guards, foremen and also totally corrupt "trade union militants". The Pinkertons, Burns and Thiels detective agencies have 100 head offices and about 10,000 branches: they supposedly employ 135,000 people. Their annual budget comes to $65 million. They have set up industrial espionage, factory-floor espionage, espionage in the workshop, the shipyards, offices, and wherever there are workers employed. They have created the prototype of the worker-informer.[vi]

From the Marxist tradition people have grappled with the issue. Examples are Engels and Trotsky, who each in their way and their own period of history tried to find answers. Engels tried to do so towards the end of the 19th century, Trotsky during the period of Roosevelt's New Deal[vii]. US exceptionalism alone cannot explain the phenomena. In an article just before he was murdered, the Russian Revolutionary Leon Trotsky tried to outline the differences

between the European labour movement and the American one[viii], by making the observation that in every European country we had the creation of national unions and political parties of the working class, but not in the USA. We have one party with two names:

Democrats and Republicans. On this issue very few have paid attention, assuming that America is simply an extension of Europe and the same with Europe, but in reality it is an abortion of it.

Reduction of the Immigrant Cataclysm-Rise in Peoples Power

Up until the First World War, the Americans didn't have a national Labour Party, nor did they have national unions. Their rise occurred after the end of WW1, with the ending of the importation of foreign-born labour, in particular after 1924. The 1929 crash led to one in three Americans becoming unemployed and this destruction led those remaining in work to fight to maintain their jobs by engaging serious struggles. Thus were formed the national unions. The rise of the post-war labour movement of equality with blacks in America (CIO allowed black members in 1935), almost led to the creation of a national labour party as the one that existed in England (Labour Party) or Germany (Social Democratic Party). Almost.

But it never occurred, even after the global meltdown following 1973 that hit the advanced capitalist countries. In the 1980's decade we had a new round of foreign born labour being imported into the USA which led to 10% of the population coming from one country, Mexico, whilst the total volume of immigrants became equivalent to more than 40-50 million during the last 25 years[ix].

The creation of a state-excrescence with many nationalities where each lived in its own ghetto while the state had the supra-national role of overseeing 'good behaviour' of the ghettoes, led to the creation of an infamous theory of progressive 'multiculturalism', which isn't related to the peaceful co-existence of the various nationalities, but to a society whose aim is a race to the bottom and where relationships are based on backs against the wall in various ghettos. From here comes the common refrain that trying to say anything political that does not cause offence is like walking on eggshells. The police and the state security services became the final arbiters.

The national products of America in food for instance, are of a worse standard than anything produced by the nation states of Old Europe, as America is forced to produce products of low quality so that they can be acceptable across the board for all the various nationalities. Thus they have neither any taste nor any characteristic, nor any particular quality. In the final analysis that is the aim of the 'multicultural' melting pot. For every peoples/nation to lose their history, their traditions, their diet and their historical means of survival. All of this is done not to replace a given with something of a higher standard. An industry of fast food, with the imported junk of low cost is therefore directly related to the rot of intellectual thought for those who are apologists of "multiculturalism". Those who propagate that American multiculturalism is the highest standard achieved by humanity - at a time when we all recognise that it is a system in dissolution of a perpetual race to the bottom with the aim of getting people to fight each other so a higher power can manipulate and control them better - will be defeated by the nations that want to survive. Assuming, of course, there are any. TTIP, GM foods and Monsanto are in no way the high point of human civilisation we must all emulate.

It's no coincidence that as noted in the passage below by a US General Thomas P. Barnett in his book Blueprint for Action that:

"We will rarely find societies adequately prepared – either intellectually or emotionally – for the travails that lie ahead. Instead the elements most prepared will be those most willing to wage bloody resistance against this process: educated, worldly young men who are familiar with the future we offer and have already decided that it is corrupting beyond all reason. So yes I do account for non-rational actors in my worldview. And when they threaten violence against the global order, I say Kill them'[x].

Industrial scale 'Multiculturalism'

There is obviously a difference between countries that had modern colonial empires in the recent historical past, such as Britain, France, Germany, Spain, Portugal etc. and those that were parts of other Empires, like Greece or Serbia. They aren't the same. Creating mini-USA's in every country cannot but create a justified nationalist backlash, as the independence of small states was gained through battles sometimes beyond human comprehension as the example of Serbia shows when it lost 75% of all its adult males during WW1 in its independence struggle against the Austro-Hungarian Empire. Nowadays we have organised NGO's helping millions relocate, labour agencies offering work contracts in countries other than the ones the applicants are residing in (widespread in Eastern Europe for workers to work in Western Europe), electronic spying on all employees via CCTVs, the monitoring of emails etc. A recent European Court ruling held that workers have no right to privacy. The massive growth of globalised non-union labour in every major metropolis and the massive overwhelming retreat of labour rights is evidenced by plans to introduce 1 Euro an hour wage for newly arrived migrants to Germany[xi].

This shift towards the 19th century labour practices of the USA started forcefully in Europe after 1989. It began in the UK and France (the two countries with large ex-colonial empires). The role model was then adopted to a lesser or greater degree by those politically tied to these centres of imperialism. 'Antiracist' laws have been passed in a series of countries making it a criminal offence to criticise either 'multiculturalism' or any ethnic group, despite the evidence of ghettoes in schooling, living accommodation and social-cultural outlooks[xii].

The level of integration of the nation state

Greece had around 98% homogeneity achieved in over 70 years of a rigid school curriculum, one national religion, one language (with regional dialects), and a national cuisine. This resulted in a uniformity where a 'multinational' existence created by the presence of different foreign-born migrants didn't grow organically over a period of decades - as in America - but grew in the space of 25 years - at a breakneck speed. Just as assimilation was going to occur - as for instance in the case of the large Albanian community within Greece (their offspring went to Greek schools while the parents did not) - the rug was pulled under their feet with the collapse of the building trade where a majority of Albanians worked. Many have been forced to emigrate once more.

American multiculturalism grew throughout the 19th century and in the latter half of the 20th century on solid foundations even ghettoised ethnic communities existed. That's what's unique about America. It's no coincidence that Americans greet themselves with the prefix Irish-American, Italian-American or African-American. Greece on the other hand, had to fight tooth and nail over a period of around 150 years to first of all secure its land and sea borders (from the 1821 Greek Revolution to the incorporation of the Dodecanese Islands e.g. Rhodes, Kos etc. in 1948). No Albanian greets himself as Albanian-Greek neither does any Bangladeshi that resides in Greece greet himself as Bangladeshi-Greek.

The agenda therefore is not only to have a globalised labour movement, but to have a globalised society, a melting pot of inter-ethnic ghettoes. If anyone raises his heads above the parapet, he will be crushed. The mean can vary. From fines and imprisonment up to targeted assassinations. The form which is being created mirrors the large transnationals that rule the world as they can operate in any country, have a multinational managerial administration and utilise whatever labour force they see fit. The old nation-states of Europe are now on suicide watch. They will be blown apart if the people that reside in them don't organise to stop this globalist NWO agenda.

---

[i] "Except for the field organizers of strikes, who were pretty tough monkeys and devoted, most of the so-called Communists I met were middle class, middle aged people playing a game of dreams. I remember a woman in easy circumstances saying to another even more affluent: "After the revolution we will have more, won't we dear?" Then there was another lover of proletarians who used to raise hell with Sunday picnickers on her property".

"I guess the trouble was that we didn't have any self-admitted proletarians. Everyone was a temporarily embarrassed capitalist. Maybe the Communists so closely questioned by the Investigation Committee were a danger to America, but the ones I knew – at least they claimed to be Communists – couldn't have disrupted a Sunday-school picnic. Besides, they were too busy fighting among themselves". Steinbeck, J., A Primer on the '30s, Esquire, June 1960: 85-93https://en.wikiquote.org/wiki/John_Steinbeck

[ii] "Hitler's concept of concentration camps as well as the practicality of genocide, so he claimed, to his studies of English and United States history. He admired the camps for Boer prisoners in South Africa and the Indians in the wild west; and often praised to his inner circle the efficiency of America's extermination –by starvation and uneven combat – of the red savages who could not be tamed by captivity," Toland, J., Adolf Hitler, p. 202https://espressostalinist.com/genocide/native-american-genocide/

[iii] John Swinton https://en.wikipedia.org/wiki/John_Swinton_(journalist)

[iv] The Socialist Party founded in 1901 once received 6% of the national votehttps://en.wikipedia.org/wiki/Socialist_Party_of_America#Early_history

[v] CIO https://en.wikipedia.org/wiki/Congress_of_Industrial_Organizations

[vi] Victor Serge: What everyone should know about repressionhttp://www.marxists.org/archive/serge/1926/repression/ch2.htm

[vii] Engel's Letter to Sorge about US Labour:

"Then, and more especially, immigration, which divides the workers into two groups: the native-born and the foreigners, and the latter in turn into (1) the Irish, (2) the Germans, (3) the many small groups, each of which only understands only itself: Czechs, Poles, Italians, Scandinavians, etc. And then the Negroes. To form a single party out of these requires quite unusually powerful incentives. Often there is a sudden violent élan, but the bourgeoisie need only wait passively and the dissimilar elements of the working class fall apart again".http://classicalmarxismvsimmigration.blogspot.co.uk/2011/02/engels-letter-to-sorge-why-no-us-labour.html

[viii] Discussions on US Labour Party https://www.marxists.org/archive/trotsky/1938/04/lp.htm

[ix] US Immigration figures http://cis.org/immigrant-population-record-2013

[x] Barnett, Thomas, P., Blueprint for Action, p. 282

[xi] http://www.breitbart.com/london/2016/02/13/german-government-to-create-100000-subsidised-migrant-jobs-that-pay-just-e1-an-hour/

[xii] German Historian to be prosecuted by Greece in anti-racist lawhttp://www.avgi.gr/article/6076832/antiratsistikos-nomos-vs-xaints-rixter

Bibliography
Robert Michael Smith, From Blackjacks to Briefcases
Vernon Briggs, Mass Immigration and the National Interest

Greece is Being Filled With Economic Migrants, Not Refugees,

While Merkel Orders More

It is time to speak openly on the migration crisis: they are not refugees, they are migrants

10 March 2016

First we had the Hotspots, where Greece was ordered by the EU to create locations where refugees and migrants will be placed. Greece was told the Hotspots would be there for a short period, and a government minister said refugees would be placed there for 72 hours only. But reality proved otherwise. A fence was constructed along the border with Macedonia and Merkel said the migrants must remain in Greece. The Slovak Prime Minister said Greece must be "sacrificed" and blamed it for not stopping the refugee flood from Turkey as if it could do anything.

Now, the Greek islands are now full with migrants, chaos is the name of the game and tourism has been sinking for months. Migrants are arriving at 5,000-7,000 a day and growing. But that was not enough. On Saturday, came the order. Chancellor Merkel, who refused to compromise with Greece on its debt despite the fact that it cannot ever recover economically without a stimulus and is sinking deeper and deeper into depression, said that Greece is not doing enough to accept refugees although the country cannot even provide for its own. Merkel ordered Greece to work at a "lightening speed." An Order is an order, when the Führer decides something, it must be carried out.

Lebanon also accepted refugees. In fact, 25% of the total population are now refugees. But Lebanon is a good member of the global society. It abides by international law. In Lebanon, migrants and refugees have freedom of movement. Not the EU. Migrants and refugees in the EU are confined not to international law but to EU law serving corporate profit. They do not enjoy a freedom of movement, but must remain in Greece. In Germany migrants will be paid one euro per hour for their work, with the government supposedly paying 7.5 Euro more. In Greece, migrants will be used as slave labor by corporations, explained Greek socialist economist Mr. Dimitris Kazakis.

The discourse regarding the refugee crisis has been very misleading. Many people feel bad for the refugees, myself included. But a visit to Victoria Square in Athens where the "refugees" are stranded revealed very quickly that almost of all of them if not all, appear to come from Central Asia, not Syria. They were not fleeing a war. That they could afford to come all the way to Greece and pay for the high smuggling feeds meant either that they are not poor, but middle class or that someone paid for them to come. A woman I spoke to wondered how the migrants had the money to make such a long journey. She said that following the wars in Iraq and Syria refugees did not rush to Greece. "What has changed?" she wondered

aloud.

Victoria Square exhibits children along with their mothers, young men and families. Of course, every sentient human being will feel bad for people without a home, especially for the children. But what will the migrants do in Greece? Greece's economy has 48% of unemployment among youth. What kind of long-term solution does Greece have for these people? None.

Greeks, however, long accustomed to migrating themselves, feel bad for the migrants. A "Refugees Welcome" protest was held in Athens by well-meaning liberals over the weekend. A petition to this effect was organized by Trotskyists and pseudo-socialists. But in a country that already has severe unemployment, what is the solution of those who signed the petition for the migration crisis? For the large companies the solution is simple: Fire the Greek and hire the migrant. But why would the Left advocate such a thing?

The European Left has truly lost it. Socialism means working hard for a better society and ensuring fair rights for one's own people first and foremost. It is not welcoming everyone when the economy is bad, giving free hand-outs, and not thinking about tomorrow – at a time when one cannot even take care of one's own. This is not the 1950s and the German Wonder Years. The economy is in a structural crisis and unemployment will expand. Emptying countries of their middle class inhabitants, increasing unemployment in Europe for locals and employing migrant for slave labor, is a receipt for disaster and social conflict. Of course, migrants must be taken care of by the UN but as long as Greece is a member of the EU, migrants will be exploited by transnational corporations as they do not enjoy freedom of movement.

The Western Left forgot that before one can help others, one must help oneself first. That local conflict and sexual attacks may ensue at an unscreened acceptance of millions of Muslim migrants should be obvious when one looks at the examples of Sweden and Germany. And what kind of a solution is it to absolve oneself of responsibility for causing wars in other countries by accepting migrants who left their wives and mothers behind who will then be employed as cheap labor while locals become unemployed? A holistic solution to the problem would require a policy of non-interference and allowing countries to develop without exploitation. But such a solution does not match the vision of those who seek endless profit and do not mind destroying more and more countries. Such a solution would also not allow war-mongering liberals as Barack Obama and Hillary Clinton to feel good about their "humanitarianism" for accepting Syrian refugees into the US while they support terrorism in Syria and Palmyra is destroyed forever. No people should be forced to accept economic migrants when their own economy is in shambles.

The hypocrisy of Merkel is particularly noteworthy. Not only has she been taking an active part in the destruction of Syria and refused to accept Greece's modest proposals for alleviating the economic crisis, she now calls on Greece to accept more "refugees" at an even faster pace. The EU gave 3 billion euro to Erdogan, who has been sending migrants across the Aegean. Greece, an EU member, is supposed to get just 700 million euro for accepting the migrants.

It is time to speak openly on the migration crisis: they are not refugees, they are migrants. Of course, the financial elite would love to see more conflicts on European soil which is why people should not blame the migrants who likely were misled into coming into Europe based on false promises. In Germany some migrants already expressed their wish to return to Iraq after finding Germany not as idyllic as they thought. People should not fall into the "Refugees Welcome" fantasy. It will end badly.

Joshua Tartakovsky

Interestingly enough, it is precisely at times as these when a Marxist analysis can prove useful. For example, Press TV and other Muslim leftists, sympathize with the migrants and appear to encourage more migration, while they fail to understand that the migrants will be used as slave labor and as pawns in a civil war. Similarly, many supposed leftists feel bad for "refugees" and call for accepting more when Greece's economy is destroyed and when it is clear there can be no employment for newcomers. While Marxism can rightly be attacked for looking at the external framework while ignoring man's inner condition, at times as these it can also prove essential for understanding the broader framework.

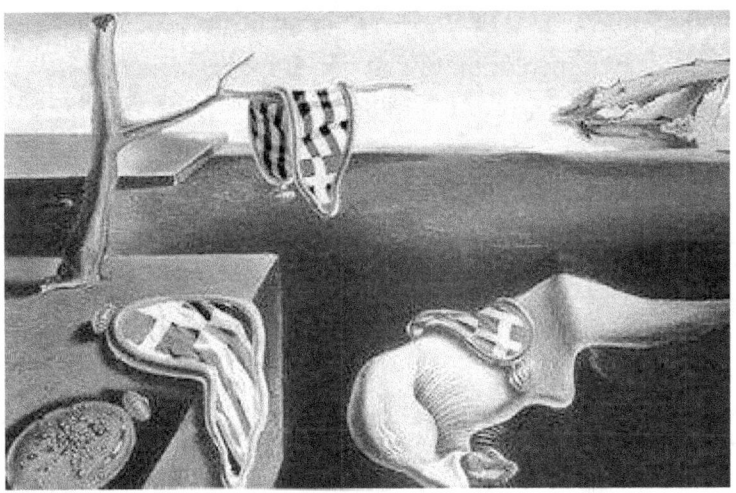

When the Left Hated Mass Migrations and Didn't 'Welcome All Refugees'

There was a time in the past when the Left hated immigrants and didn't 'Welcome All Refugees'. Since the Soviet Union collapsed, it became fashionable in the West to support mass migration in the name of helping the 'poor', promoting 'diversity' and combatting hate crimes all in the name of 'tolerance'.

20 March 2016

"The purpose of this importation (of labour during a tailoring strike in Britain) is the same as that of the importation of Indian coolies to Jamaica, namely the perpetuation of slavery. If the masters succeeded through the import of German labour, in nullifying the concessions they had already made, it would inevitably lead to repercussions in England."

-Karl Marx, 1866

Globalist pseudo-humanitarianism has now fully gone mainstream.

Never a day stops when bleeding heart humanitarians are on TV, in the media, on talk shows, towering above all and sundry selling us drowned or crying babies, people in tents on muddy and wet campsites, showing us images of boat people either drowned or with life jackets whilst at the same time supporting the militarisation of everything. It's as if the world has turned on its head and suddenly the migrant is now viewed as a new Promethian god recreating a new and better humanity from its old rotting corpse[i]. The core essence as to whom they are and why they are coming has been lost. No one questions the corporate propaganda campaign, journalists or politicians. The Left just repeats it.

But there was a time in the not too distant past when the migrant flows were deemed to bedubious and reactionary. Insofar as the Soviet Union existed the Left kept at arms bay from imperialist 'humanitarianism', now it's as if all other issues no longer exist and this is their raison d'etre. Three historical cases from the recent past come to light: Cuba, Algeria and Vietnam. It's the political equivalent of Goldman Sachs doing charity and donning a philanthropic costume, while at the same time looting pensions, destroying nations and exporting real economic and social genocide. Let no one be fooled times may have changed but the core essence of mass migration in the imperialist era remains the same. We will look at the first two in Part One and at Vietnam and the implications of 'Welcoming All Refugees' in Part Two.

The Example of Cuba

The Cuban Revolution, which initially was more about agrarian land and democratic reforms against the hated neo-colonial Batista regime and eventually turned into a full blown Russian style revolution with the adoption of communism by Fidel Castro, had seen a two decades long period of a mass exodus by certain sections of the population. Initially, those that fled were close to Batista's regime and after the failed US invasion in the Bay of Pigs thousands more fled. In total around 10% of Cuba's population, 1m people fled. They mostly went across in boats to Miami USA.

The Heritage Foundation writes (emphasis added): "Since 1959, Cubans have been engaged in one of the most significant migrations, proportionally, in modern times. Over eight percent of the island's population has gone into exile with around 700,000 coming to the U.S. prior to 1980 in several phases. Between January 1, 1959 and the October 22, 1962 Missile Crisis, 248,070 migrated to the United States. In early 1959 members of the political and military elite fled, followed by members of the propertied and professional sectors, who by 1961 comprised 45 percent of the registrants with the Cuban Refugee Program"[ii].

Fidel Castro labelled all those fleeing as gusanos (worms), which is what in reality they were. They supported the re-invasion of Cuba, the overthrow of the revolutionary regime, and the return of the hated Batista dictatorship. Failure to achieve the overthrow of the Revolution they became involved in terrorist activity against Cuba and all those that traded with it. The assistance of the American security services was obviously invaluable.

Throughout the 1960s and 1970's they went around bombing various targets even to the extent of bringing down a Cuban Airliner killing everyone on board[iii]. It was only with a change of US strategy towards Cuba, after it was clear that the Revolution couldn't be overthrown by force, that the US sponsored terrorist activity dried up in the 1980's.

Nowadays with the large mass migrant flows into the EU, it is easy to entrap them into your own security service agenda as they are migrants. If they don't do as you say, you can threaten to send them back to where they came from. Also, if they are on the margins of society and are dodgy characters back home, if they are caught by the police of the new country they are residing in, they can be turned and used by the security services for their own narrow agenda. So let no one be fooled that US/EU security services aren't going to use migrant patsies to further their NWO agenda as after all some of them were recipients of US-EU aid in their respective countries, and have ulterior motives which may not be progressive, but doubly reactionary. Without any checks or balances, any independent controls, any cross verification of stories anyone can claim anything about their past as they most certainly do, gaining an asylum status brings in a certain number of privileges, not least to those who profit from this (rental agencies, politicians in kickbacks, businesses in the form of cheap labour etc.) and ensures that the right of permanent stay becomes the norm[iv].

Algeria

The example of Algeria, France's main colony for decades, is illuminating for we have a mass exodus after independence of the old colonial settlers and as it illuminates the role of the French Left. While both Vietnam and Algeria were French colonies, Vietnam became half independent first but soon fell to neo-colonialism due to America's intervention, and Algeria became fully independent. Yet they are both interrelated in terms of strategy and occupation.

Once the French lost Vietnam, withdrew and handed over the reins to American imperialism, they focused on Algeria. What Vietnam taught them was that they had to be doubly tough against the Algerian struggle for independence. At the time (1950's) the French Communist Party wasn't in government and there were two resistance groups in Algeria against the French occupation. Which one did the CP support? The one of course that ended up collaborating openly with the Occupation under De Gaulle's France. Below we see the role of the French PCF:

"Nor was the French Communist Party's record on Algeria any better. From the PCF's original positive involvement in setting up the Algerian immigrant labourers' organisation L'Etoile du Nord Africaine it was all downhill. The PCF described the revolt in Constantine as 'fascist', even after the natives had been bombed into submission. In 1956 it voted special powers to Guy Mollet's socialist government to repress the Algerian revolution.[1] The PCF had opposed Algerian independence since Massali Hadj first proposed it in 1937. In 1955 the PCF complained against charges of disloyalty to the Algerians: 'Have we not already shown that we support a policy of negotiation with the peoples of North Africa for the creation of a true "Union française"?'[2] — as if the Algerian people were demanding a true Union française! But with the outbreak of war, the PCF faced some criticism for this uncomradely betrayal of the Algerian people. Rather than take responsibility for the policy outright, they sought to deflect responsibility by shifting the blame onto the working class. In a speech to students, the PCF spokesman Laurent Casanova asked them to take into account 'the spontaneous attitude of the French popular masses on the question'.[3] Writer Francis Jeanson, who undertook clandestine work for the FLN, remembers Casanova speaking more bluntly. 'He used to say, "The working class is racist, colonialist and imperialist."'[4] In fact it was the Communist Party above all that was responsible for spreading chauvinist attitudes towards the Algerian struggle amongst working class people. 'Victims of the myth of French Algeria,' wrote Fanon, 'the parties of the Left create Algerian sections of the French political parties on Algerian territory'. The truth was that it was they, before it was the working class, who assumed the right of France to rule over Algeria. In fact, the Communist Party of Algeria (PCA) recruited heavily amongst white settlers in Bab el Oued and Belcourt, according to Michael Farrell, who also charges that many PCA members were later active in the reactionary OAS[v].

It was left to an obscure Greek Michel Raptis (Pablo) who was in exile in France to organise a solidarity movement with the Algerian revolution, organise tens of engineers around the world to go set up mobile arms production factories in neighbouring countries and to smuggle weapons in for the resistance[vi]. He was eventually caught trying to overthrow the Algerian economy by flooding it with fake French currency, was put on trial in Amsterdam, and had his French residency withdrawn being put in prison in Holland for two years. Between 1962 and 1965 he became a core minister of Ben Bella's first liberation government and was instrumental in forcing the mass exodus of the over one million French settlers in Algeria those who became known as Pieds Noir[vii].

Pablo was put in prison and had his status revoked by Holland, and only a sole British Labour MP came to his defence. This is what he said in justifying his support for Algerian Independence:

"I will limit myself to a few words on the Algerian drama, which is at the heart of the affair that you are judging, Monsieur President, Messieurs Judges. I wonder if the Christian and civilized men and women of Western Europe, wallowing in their current relative material comfort, realize deep down what has been going on for the past seven years in Algeria, what is currently happening in the hell of Angola, or the drama, for example, of the Congolese children dying of hunger in the thousands. If they realize to what point our civilization is only a matter of an epidermis that it suffices to scratch for an incredible potential for cruelty, violence and injustice toward our brothers – the people of color cruelly oppressed and exploited – to escape".

"Have we in Western Europe truly realized the horrors of the colonial war in Algeria, that fact that there have been seven years of massacres and torture, around a million deaths on the Algerian side, more than two million poor peasants chased from their villages, displaced, "regrouped" in temporary camps, more than 250,000 Algerian refugees in Morocco and Tunisia, most of whom are elderly, women, and children who are war orphans, more than 300,000 Algerians in prisons and concentration camps in France itself? Yet these figures appear in the official French press and the countless literary and other documents that have been produced by this colonial war, the most atrocious of our century[viii]."

Once Pablo joined the Ministerial Department of Agriculture, 1m French settlers fled the country out of a population of 10m Algerians by FMLN policy of land distribution. Agriculture was returned once more to its rightful owners, and food production was geared to the needs of the domestic economy as a priority, not to serve solely the interests of imperialist France[ix].

No subsequent French Left organisation led campaigns for the poor refugees from Algeria nor did they go round in a mass hysteria of 'welcome the refugees'. This was obviously logical as they didn't do much to support the anti-colonial resistance despite having a Parliamentary representation and commanding a significant percentage in elections (being the number one party in 1945 with 5m votes!). After betting on the wrong horse in Algeria (and supporting Mejj Hadji) they sure as hell didn't want to be seen supporting the Pieds Noir so they kept silent, as opposed to the experience in our times where supporting every last migrant is evidence of …socialism and the revolution around the corner! The Algerian events led to deep turmoil in many of the French PCF militants, as they were formally against imperialism but in practice defenders of colonial France.

Indeed, all the way till the early 1980's the French Communist Party maintained a position of strict intransigence to waves of immigration to France and one could argue that this position predated the conflicts in East Germany today, with many attacks noted by towns with Communist Party mayors against the resettlement of migrants in their districts. The 1980's French elections under the leadership of George Marchais was partly fought on the platform of No Open Borders. Up until early 2000 in Calais where the PCF had electoral strength, closing of the Sangatte migrant squatter camp was one of its priorities. As indeed it did[x].

The Algerian exodus was one of a pattern of post-colonial societies. They had to go through the motions of getting rid of the settlers just to develop as societies on a human level. Without that, they could go nowhere. Imperialism, of course, tried to put every hurdle in the way, but we didn't live in the era where they would be labelled openly as 'racists'. That came much later as evidenced when Mugabe got rid of white farmers who allegedly had their land …stolen from them, land which they acquired at the point of a gun.

Bibliography

Ian Birchall, Revolutionary History: European Revolutionaries and Algerian Independence 1954-1962

[i] Prometheus https://en.wikipedia.org/wiki/Prometheus

[ii] http://www.heritage.org/research/reports/1980/07/the-cuban-refugee-problem-in-perspective-1959-1980

[iii] http://cuban-exile.com/doc_051-075/doc0073.html

[iv] Stuart Monk http://www.dailymail.co.uk/news/article-3407885/Asylum-seekers-forced-live-houses-red-doors.html

[v] Algeria and the Defeat of French Humanismhttps://www.marxists.org/reference/subject/philosophy/works/fr/defeat-french-humanism.htm#n28

[vi] Pablo https://en.wikipedia.org/wiki/Michel_Pablo

[vii] Pieds Noir https://en.wikipedia.org/wiki/Pied-Noir

The War in Algeria 1961 Declaration of Michel Raptis at the Amsterdam Trial

Source: Sylvain Pattieu, Les Camarades des freres. Aris, Syllepse, 2002;

First Published: Quatriéme Internationale no. 14, November 1961; Translated: for marxists.org by Mitch Abidor.

[viii] Pablo role as Minister of Agriculture https://books.google.co.uk/books?id=_eUtQjseKaIC&pg=PA34&lpg=PA34&dq=michel+raptis+algerian+revolution+french+left&source=web&ots=AdNRSZ1JQI&sig=tMRKjdnqFOcvhBdkrdlnxHgSiyY&hl=en&sa=X&oi=book_result&ct=result&redir_esc=y#v=onepage&q=michel%20raptis%20algerian%20revolution%20french%20left&f=false

[ix] Alain Krivine and Algeria https://www.marxists.org/archive/krivine/1956/algeria.htm

[x] French Elections https://en.wikipedia.org/wiki/French_legislative_election,_1945

George Marchais, On Immigration https://www.youtube.com/watch?v=LG2BA9SxClM

Vietnamese boat people....
When the Left Hated Mass Migrations

Continuing the story of how leftists became protecting illegal immigrants and why immigration is not necessarily a consequence of war.

27 March 2016

"Human history has witnessed the epoch of great migrations on the basis of barbarism. Socialism will open the possibility of great migrations on the basis of the most developed technique and culture. It goes without saying that what is here involved is not compulsory displacements, that is, the creation of new ghettos for certain nationalities, but displacements freely consented to, or rather demanded by certain nationalities or parts of nationalities."
L. Trotsky [i]

Vietnam

Vietnam was the story of a country, which, unable to become independent with the collapse of the European empires, ended up in a liberation war with the world's strongest power on earth at the time, the USA, which led to millions of deaths, near absolute devastation of its land and infrastructure and showed that a country which seeks independence can fight until the end and come out victorious whomever the enemy happens to be. Its tenaciousness, integrity and self-sacrifice have only been matched by the Serbs' struggle for independence in the 20th century.

The French Left had an abysmal record when it came to anti-colonial struggles. It was in government (1945-1947) when a revolt occurred in Vietnam after the collapse of the Japanese occupation. The Parti Communiste France (PCF) didn't support the anti-colonial struggle, it voted for war credits and agreed to an expeditionary force going to Vietnam to put down the independence struggle. It's also absurd to believe that whilst participating in France's imperialist government from 1945-47, that the PCF had an interest in anti-imperialism when it was in government with the imperialists themselves! Here is what they wrote:

"Are we, after having lost Syria and Lebanon yesterday, to lose Indochina tomorrow, North Africa the day after?" (L'Humanité (24 July 1946)

As early as September 1945, the Saigon committee of the French CP "warned [the Viet Minh] that any 'premature adventures' in Annamite independence might 'not be in line with Soviet perspectives.'" That same month the French government (including several CP ministers) proposed a military budget of 193 billion

francs, including 100 billion for the Expeditionary Force in Indochina; the CP voted for the bill. [21] In July 1946, smelling a victory in the next elections, the Communists took up a virulent nationalist stance: "Are we, after having lost Syria and Lebanon yesterday, to lose Indochina tomorrow, North Africa the day after?" wrote L'Humanité (24 July 1946). Two days later the CP deputies voted for a constitutional definition of the French Union which made Vietnamese "independence" purely fictional! [ii]

Once the French were defeated in Vietnam and the country was divided up at the 54th parallel, the Americans initially sent in advisers who then became military personnel and by the time LBJ had taken over as President in the USA, 500,000 troops were stationed there. Vietnam witnessed all sorts of wars - land, air based, chemical warfare, you name it, and more bombs were dropped on Vietnam than on any other place in the whole of WW2, apparently. Yet they didn't give up. They only went abroad to neighbouring countries to re-group and fight anew. They didn't leave their country en masse in boats and ask for refugee status. Nixon became infamous for carpet bombing in a secret war in Cambodia where the Viet Minh ran to regroup. Neither did 80% of their adult males leave as is happening in our times. So in what way can one explain the mass movement nowadays?

In analyzing what happened in Vietnam and what the US strategy was we see clearly that it was related to ensuring food independence was at zero and pushing people into cities that couldn't cope. Let's see in this statement called 'Those That Leave' issued by the Republic of Vietnam, what occurred:

"The American strategy aimed at killing two birds with one stone: on the one hand, to weaken the Vietnamese by 'draining away the water', i.e. the people; on the other, to turn those same people into mercenaries of Washington. For those men who roamed the pavements of the towns had no other recourse than to enlist in Thieu's army and police. In this way 1,200,000 men were pressed into that army and police commanded by more than 50,000 officers, well-trained, indoctrinated and supervised by tens of thousands of American advisers. If one adds to these numbers the civil servants, political agents, and leaders of various anti-communist parties and organisations, one will find that at least 1.5 million people were living from salaries paid by the American budget — not to mention the taxes paid by the local population.

To serve that war machine, a whole commercial network to import luxury goods consumed by the Americans and the privileged strata - a 'tertiary' set-up of banks, insurance companies, coffee-houses, bars, hotels, brothels, and drug traffickers - mushroomed.

On liberation day, 300,000 Saigon households were registered as 'traders' at least twice the number of factory workers. American military aid averaged 1.3 billion dollars a year, economic aid 600-800 million dollars; not to mention the on-the-spot expenditures of the American expeditionary corps and services, the CIA for instance, which maintained at least 30,000 'pacification agents', not to mention, too, aid from other capitalist powers: France, Japan, Great Britain, West Germany. All that money — 2 billion dollars a year on average — allowed several million people to live without participating in any productive work. One understands why there were in South Viet Nam on the day of liberation:

— More than 3 million unemployed people;

— Several hundred thousand prostitutes and drug addicts;

— Several dozen thousand gangsters and other criminals, whose number later increased with the release of the former Thieu police, paratroops and rangers;

— One million tubercular people;

— Several hundred thousand people affected by venereal diseases;

— Four million illiterate people." [iii]

So the US occupation economy was based on two factors: removing agricultural independence(so the guerrillas could be starved out) and utilising the urban unemployed to become a coercive collaborationist tool in implement US war aims. In what way is any of the above different in Greece today? The farmers are being evicted and destroyed to not be able to provide any form of resistance to the economic genocide unleashed by 6 years of the IMF-ECB by ensuring an independent food supply, and tens of thousands of migrants are being imported to become a reactionary social force to be used against Greeks if resistance becomes armed (indications are that it has started in some isolated areas)[iv]. It was inevitable therefore, when the US occupation ended that a whole layer of Vietnamese society was left exposed and retributions would start, so they made a run for it.

If there were militant solidarity movements in opposition to imperialist interventions abroad in the Western countries, it would have stopped them from invading so quickly. The anti-war movement grew in America in opposition to the Vietnam War, primarily as a consequence of military conscription, and for almost two decades after America's defeat in Vietnam, there were no significant direct military interventions until the Soviet Union collapsed.

The first big such intervention was for the oil-igarchs of 'poor little Kuwait,' where the dictator, Saddam, was burying babies in the sand. Imperialism also learned to avoid conscription and only use soldiers who volunteered to join the military whilst at the same time creating paramilitary organisations like Blackwater, Inc. to further their geopolitical interests. This is where the first big change occurred. Imperialists adopted the Kurds in Iraq for their own geopolitical interests, i.e. to weaken the integrity and viability of the Iraqi state after they had used them in the war against Iran's revolution. That did not imply that the West had suddenly become pro-Kurdish independence, but they adopted the Kurds as an issue and ensured tens of thousands were given refugee status in Europe. First they came across Turkey to Greece and then they moved further north. [v]

Once the Vietnamese took control in the south of their own country a massive wave of migrants started. It is clear beyond all reasonable doubt that the first wave was comprised of direct collaborators of the US occupation. The second wave was made up of people who were generally small businessmen, probably with a reactionary outlook. None of those that left Vietnam were progressive one iota. The third wave consisted of those returning back to Vietnam from the West.

American leftists were clear at the time and an excerpt from a zero refugee campaign regarding 'welcoming Vietnamese Refugees' is cited below:

"The big Vietnamese war criminals and mass murderers were spirited out with the aid of their U.S. masters right after the fall of Saigon in 1975. We were utterly opposed to giving any kind of sanctuary to these butchers, declaring, "No Asylum for Vietnamese War Criminals!" The wave of Vietnamese "boat people," which came somewhat later, originated in a social layer which included former petty traders and entrepreneurs whose shops were nationalized. In the eyes of the U.S. and its allies, these would-be migrants were of marginal use and thus dispensable. At the same time, a racist outcry was whipped up against the "boat people."[vi]

Why is it today that all those that leave Afghanistan for instance, are progressive and not ultra-reactionary? Within the corporate media the Taliban are beyond the pale but the Occupation apparently is ok as it is …liberating women, whilst at the same time doing zero regarding the Bacha boys? Why is it British generals have led campaigns about importing Afghan collaborators of the occupation?

Social Imperialism in the Service of Neo-Colonialism

NATO had adopted the fake left theory of mass migration as a consequence of war, yet I have shown in just three examples that there were no mass migrations as a direct consequence of the war in the three cases mentioned. There was a mass migration after Euro-American colonial entities collapsed and revolutionary regimes took over. Not before. Now NATO argues that because of the Russian bombing of Syria, which started late 2015, Europe has had mass migrant flows despite the fact that they occurred way before the Russian bombing. So it appears everyone has a theory to justify their politics. If you are a globalist, it's just wars that create migrations so 'everyone is welcome.' If you are a globalist but anti-Russian as well, then it's Russia creating the migrant flows. Either way, it happens naturally, it's not organised and no single entity is inviting them in like Germany, in an organised manner. [vii]

The irony of history is that we have various globalists today like Eric Draitser of 'Stop Imperialism,' Sukant Chandan of 'Sons of Malcolm' or various 'Solidarity with Refugees' movements who support and promote the hyper-globalism of Wall St. and the City of London (re-location of peoples to other continents erg. Afro-Asian

continents to the EU) and act as if the various Left parties in the centres of imperialism were actively involved in the liberation of the colonies when nothing is further from the truth. Yet this is the tradition they defend in totality today. Let no one be fooled with the labels or the titles. They are a globalist smokescreen much like Syriza, with the 'radical left' label branding by the corporate media, if not something more sinister (Chandan has been in joint publications with ex-Afghan CIA station chief). [viii]

Where were the solidarity movements when the struggles of the colonies were actually going on in the Left Parties (communist or social democratic)? A whole raft of countries had brutal wars for national liberation - Vietnam, Algeria, Kenya, Cyprus, Yemen, etc. There were no solidaritymovements. There were paper declarations. But more importantly, where there was influence in Parliament the votes were always with the powers that be (PCF voting record during Vietnamese and Algerian Independence Labour Party during Kenyan, Cypriot Independence struggles), just like they are today (Syriza supports NATO operations the world over and its Foreign Minister Kotzias was seen singing songs with the other NATO members). [ix]

It's no coincidence that in a broadcast once more on RT on George Galloway's programme, which invited Sukant Chandan (of Indian descent)[x] with the misnamed title of "Sons of Malcolm," Chandan pretends that he agrees with the Mau May resistance, and George Galloway, a staunch Labourite, almost had a heart attack, which is obviously logical as the Labour Party never had, nor ever created a solidarity movement in any parts of its Empire. One cannot find one

big solidarity movement for Indian, Kenyan, Cypriot, or Yemen independency from the British Empire. Throughout the present day, mass population movements are presented as if they are part of a global conflict with imperialism. How come those that left Cuba,

Algeria and Vietnam were never involved in any subsequent left movement? Why is it in our time 'solidarity' movements have emerged by the kilo for 'refugees,' supplemented by hundreds of NGO's? Even Generals are now on board in solidarity with Afghan 'refugees' (read quislings).[xi]

Hyper-globalists are nowadays two for a penny and are quick to draw conclusions that imperialism organised the Arab Spring, overthrew all the regimes (that had been in power for decades), and everything is controlled by Washington, but mass migration (isn't this how the USA was created?) apparently isn't a US sponsored and engineered event, but is solely the by-product of turmoil, economic dislocation and invasion. In other words, if there were no turmoil there would be no mass migration. So what explains the arrival of 1 million Albanians in the 1990s into Greece or the 3-4 million Poles in the UK? Cheap travel? Or the bosses' desire to replace indigenous labour? The whole of the Arab Spring is orchestrated from Washington, but mass migration is its natural offshoot. To put it more succinctly, Washington is able to command such day to day micromanagement in distant countries, but it cannot control migration flows. They occur solely as… blowback. This is the type of nonsense that inaugurated the Project for a New American Century and the fake 'war on terror.' Allegedly, Saudi hijackers blew up the three skyscrapers in New York and Afghanistan and Iraq paid the price, whilst recently a New York judge ruled Iran has to cough up the cost of the damage to the tune of $10 billion. Shades of Lockerbie again, on a grander level. The fake Left has been selling this line for over a decade. It no longer washes; in particular, with state infiltration of the events around 9/11, which has created an industry of doubters (truthers).

With no class analysis of capitalism in decline, which has features of mass unemployment, mass disparities in currencies, the breakdown of permanent unionised labour, the rise of the black market in labour, the fall of profits by bosses in western countries, etc. and the turn by the ruling class of each country into importing the US model, i.e. migrant labour, we must understand that what is happening is not classless nonsense about a 'Global South' (a Kuwaiti oligarch has nothing in coming with an Egyptian labourer other than they are both Arabs). A Russian oligarch arriving in London to recycle stolen booty in the banking and property sector isn't a political refugee we must 'all welcome' despite that being his official status. Now deceased Russian oligarch Berezovsky comes to mind as an example.

Current 'solidarity' movements, which adopt a classless approach to mass migration alleging they are all war torn refugees or economic migrants due to imperialist dislocation, justifies all, and that is precisely what their purpose is. Anyone raising objections to the process is branded with the modern fascist 'antifascist' stick of racism. Seeking to maintain national independence and integrity is perceived as being reactionary, but those who seek population movements like those of the old British Empire (of Indians into Africa or of European Jews into Palestine) are considered progressive.

Up until the mid-1970s, many working environments had closed shops. One had to belong to a union in order to work there. Now it's a globalist free for all; a musical chair for labour with conditions akin to those shown in the film of US Dockers 'On the Waterfront' with Marlon Brando in the 1950s. This is the actual present that the hyper-globalists want extended into all the areas of social life. That is their political mission whether they are paid or not. They are the 'left' promoters of the NWO.

However, history never remembers the turncoats, the quislings, the collaborators, or the defenders of regimes in disarray. Neither will it remember those like Syriza's Tsipras, who recently stated that "national rights cannot supersede the rights of the EU." If history is any guide to action, then the current migrants in a situation of severe economic crisis will be isolated and looked down upon as societies descend into an economic free-for-all for non-existent resources.

The extent of this globalist stupidity and the most extreme example in the EU is the idea that they will park a few million migrants in Greece, subsidise them with free housing, food and money whilst the indigenous population languishes in dire poverty and unemployment, and is made homeless due to rapacious banksters. This whole process is a recipe for social conflict and disaster, and as the referendum on Merkel's policies have shown in three states in less than a year, things will get much, much worse before they can get better.

[i] https://www.marxists.org/archive/trotsky/1940/xx/jewish.htm

[ii] https://www.marxists.org/history/etol/document/icl-spartacists/vietnam/trotskyism.html#en22

[iii] 'Those that Leave' http://classicalmarxismvsimmigration.blogspot.co.uk/2016/03/those-who-leave-on-vietnamese-boat.html

[iv] **Kos** http://www.newsit.gr/topikes-eidhseis/Kos-Andras-ton-MAT-se-katoikoys-THa-sas-gam-oloys-Xaos-sto-nisi-KSylo-dakrygona-kai-syllipseis-VINTEO-/571483

[v] Jeffery Archer Tory Chairman and the Kurds
http://www.theguardian.com/uk/2001/jul/26/iraq.archer

[vi] http://icl-fi.org/english/wv/1083/immigration.html

[vii] Manual for Migrants W2EU
http://news.sky.com/story/1551853/sky-finds-handbook-for-eu-bound-migrants

[viii] http://www.conflictsforum.org/index.php?s=sukant

[ix] http://www.hurriyetdailynews.com/video-turkish-greek-foreign-ministers-sing-for-peace-with-nato-head.aspx?pageID=238&nID=82392&NewsCatID=359

[x] Sukant Chandan on RT with George Galloway
https://www.youtube.com/watch?v=3Y8ESCNtHqQ

[xi] Afghan Interpreters getting asylum in UK
http://www.dailymail.co.uk/news/article-2512612/Up-600-Afghan-interpreters-council-homes-serving-British-troops-UK-asylum-deal.html

Greek Women against the Mass Importation of Cheap Labour Migrants

Interview with **Aliki Papadaki** Citizens Committee Member of Ag.Panteleomonas (central Athens District)

Introduction

Between 2000 and 2008 the square in Ag Panteleomonas was occupied by a multitude of migrants from every quarter of the planet but primarily from Albania, Pakistan, Bangladesh, Afghanistan. The square was divided into various ethnic squares where each ghetto went about their business, ie. drug dealing, gambling, boozing, sexual activity at night, urinating, defecating etc. The situation became so bad that citizens of the area felt under siege as they couldn't go about their daily business. Citizens on an individual basis complained to all official bodies in person or in writing from the local councillors, to the police, to their MP's, to the political parties present in the area. No one listened and they organised themselves in a committee which had a majority of women.

Women bore the brunt of the situation as they were either robbed for their handbags or sexually molested whilst going near or around the square. As the migrants were many and operated as such individual resistance was futile as one was outnumbered. Particularly obscene was the victimisation of old people and targeting their pensions from ATM machines. Anyone who witnessed first hand the situation could not but feel for the plight of Greek citizens.

For a two year period there were demos after demos, counter demos by the so-called anti-racist fake left and the square received national prominence in particular as this was the area that led to the electoral growth of Golden Dawn and the teargassing inside a Church of citizens who continued to protest against becoming a minority inside their own country and being unable to operate as they had before. The economic crisis of course hadn't fully arrived but the arrival of continuous numbers of migrants. The square became synonymous nationally with everything that was wrong with uncontrolled migration and remains imprinted in the national political psyche in particular now that migrants have been dumped in tens of areas around Greece and protests against their presence has occurred almost everywhere.

The fake Left having abandoned Greeks to their fate has written its own death warrant as a political force and it will suffer the same fate as all the other political forces that tied their economic coattails to mass migration and cheap labour, let no one be fooled. Allowing an economic free for all in any type of migrant to arrive and live against the citizens of the country without their advance knowledge or even minimal approval is a recipe for civil war.
Van Gelis

Committee of Citizens in Ag. Panteleomonas
   1. **What issues gave rise to the creation of a citizens committee in Ag Panteleomonas?**
      After the fall of the Soviet U immigrants started arriving in Greece. After 2000 many migrants started to live in the square. All day long they were in the square, the Albanians had created a ghetto and the square was nicknamed Tirana square and they played on wooden boxes and they gambled with dices. Many had taken out Greek OGA (Organisation of Agriculatural Development) pensions being declared fake Greeks from Northern Ipirus (Southern Albania). The Polish were workers, but many spent all day drinking and fighting and there were no public toilets in the square and they smelled of urine. It was impossible to make criticism of Albanians as they said we are 5k people and we will cut you down. In the meantime many houses were burgled and in particular as there were many unemployed and in Crete where I gathered olives every season robberies were immense as everything was stolen.

      At the time we had dogs but the Albanians bought pit bulls and they had dogs which fought for money and drug dealing and many shootouts amongst their community. There were also many fights amongst Albanians and Georgians (initially women arrived to look after older people) and deals that went wrong. Drugs were mostly in circulation and all types of drugs controlled by gangs from all of these ethnic groups. A mini USA in an Athenian square which boasted one of the largest Orthodox Churches in Greece.

The priest in the main church on the square gave to the Georgians a small side church facing the square (old believers in Orthodox Church) and another ghetto was created around the Church as a focal point, they started to open their own shops with special dispensation for (illegal) migrants who can set up shop in one day as opposed to a Greek who takes up to six months.

Most of the shops don't even have a VAT receipt and if anyone rings the Greek tax office they only turn up for Greek owned shops as they don't bother with migrant stores. Most Greek women who crossed the square had their bags stolen and my mother had her money stolen from the ATM at least three times when she went to take her pension. A few days ago a man was fixing his sign outside his shop and migrants climbed up his ladder when he wasn't looking and entered the flat above and robbed it and left by the entrance as gentlemen. All Greek women were harassed sexually. What led to the Committee being created were two incidents that were beyond the pale:

The First Incident
The situation deteriorated when Pakistanis and Afghanis arrived as they had weird traditions mostly being famers and many being gay and the story is they brought live sheep for their Ramazan festival, slept with them and then killed them on the roof (arab style) and they ate them. They used to throw the rubbish from the balconiesin black bags which split and rotted leading to a health situation and people took photographs and took it to the local council.

In the square the on one side the Afghani, Pakistani and Bangladeshi muslims had taken over a part and had turned it to their own special UN ghetto and it was impossible for a Greek woman to enter. They would touch up every woman as she passed, and during this period there is a famous video of Greek women during New Year celebrations in Sindagma square being sexually abused and manhandled.

The Second Incident

At the time an Albanian girl was raped at the age of 14 by what appears to have been a muslim of Pakistani, Afghan or Bangladesh origin as recounted by the girl. The state did not take any reports or interviews from the Albanians. A few of them came to our committee and reported they would handle the matter internally ie. take measures against the Afghani Pakistani and Bangladeshi people in the area. Inter ethnic ghetto conflicts ensured.

2. **In what way were women a catalyst in setting the agenda of reaction to the presence of multitudes in the public square of Ag Panteleomonas**

Greek women started the protests in the Ag. Panteleomonas area to regain control of the square. They were under total attack and had never encountered such behaviour in their lives and in the trolley bus women would be manhandled at all times and raise their middle finger. Women from the ages of 40 to +70 were involved in the committee. We decided the situation was under total disarray we couldn't leave our flat and we couldn't enjoy the square which in the summer (+40c in flats) means we became prisoners in our own homes. In many flats there were flying body lice which became an issue for the whole area. People couldn't put their clothes out to dry. In many buildings there were over 300 people in a three story building and when we took a reporter there we saw two people sleeping in the small space above the bathroom where the hot water boiler is kept. An unheard of situation for post-war Greece.

We went to complain to all the official bodies, Mayor, Council, Police, Health service etc. and this led to nothing. So we decided to hold weekly meeting and then public demonstrations and the first person that came against us was Petros Konstantinou of KEERFA who threatened us with the migrants of Afghanistan and Pakistan who started to pray on the square and they started to throw stones and burn dustbins. Up until then GD did not exist in the area. In the first demo all the Greeks in the area turned up for the demonstration. Confronting them was KEERFA.

Looking back at the situation it appears KEERFA'S arrival was pre-ordained to defend illegal migration and the subsequent arrival of GD to taint the area as being ...nazi. There is a possibility they were working together as before 2008 Golden Dawns presence was less than 0.9% nationally and over a two year concerted campaign by KEERFA every protest against the arrival of migrants or turning squares into migrant dumping grounds led to Golden Dawn appearing to be the force that was against ...migration. It's funny as their star candidate turned MP who had a shop near the area Panagiotaros has left the area and moved to wealthier areas by the sea and wants nothing to do with the area. Politics in Greece is a just a career which opens doors to self promotion.

3. **Which forces in society were you up against during the protests in the square?**
At the time no one was with us from the major political parties and none of the Left were concerned. KEERFA[1] organised many support structures for the muslim migrants in the area and many were involved in the drug and sexual

favours trade in the main square and they exchanged goods for sex.

KEERFA is a front for illegal migration in close cooperation with bosses.
Both New Democracy and PASOK encouraged mass migration into Greece and sought to arrest the collapsing rate of profit by employing migrants with no insurance in a range of industries: farming, tourism and industry. In no sector of the Greek economy is their presence not felt.

Throughout the early part of the 2000 decade a mass propaganda campaign occurred by the so-called anti-racists filling up all public walls with the slogan 'the bosses promote racism' when in reality we must have had the most anti-racist bosses on earth as they exclusively recruited migrants. When enough were recruited these slogans disappeared and they became chasing ...nazis. In the meantime Greeks became a minority in many workplaces and anyone opposing the unlimited arrival of migrants was now branded a ..'nazi' whilst Parliament pushed through anti-racism laws banning the criticism or talk about migrants in anyway whatosoever.

4. **How do you explain the rise and fall of Golden Dawn in the area?**
As all the parties had one line a political vacuum was created. Let us remember before *2008 they didn't exit.* What existed was LAOS a splinter group from New Democracy which allegedly took on board issues of migration. GD came to the square and used its appearance for electoral promotion. They no longer have an organisation in the area and the day GD's MP Kasidiaris last arrived in the area is the day Rouvikona and other NGOs arrived with their ...antifascist banners. They essentially go round the square targeting any young Greeks

who might happen to be visiting the area or passing the square but have insignia on them with the Greek flag. Not long ago these same NGO's as reported in the press targeted a Cypriot tourist unbeknown to them, who was in Exarchia with a Greek flag and beat him up so badly he ended up in hospital. We are dealing with globalist neoliberal scum who hate anything in relation to Greece as a nation.

5. **What is the situation now like and how do you see it developing?**

The situation is critical and I believe they will be a conflict. It is much worse and Greek houses are being repossessed and now migrants are filling up houses and their rent is being paid and they are being paid to squat. It is being organised by PRAXIS from the Mayor of Athens Kaminis. They are given a card to use in supermarkets. An indirect way to support big business.

No Greek card for the unemployed has been given. My friend who was fired and replaced by Pakistanis in the kitchens was paid in supermarket vouchers as compensation. No health checks are carried out when they recruit migrants. Its anything goes as it's a perpetual race to the bottom.

Houses near have been rented for Euro 3000 in an area where the cost of the actual flat is about Euro 10000 if it can be sold and they have placed around 20 people who smoke all day and do nothing. Allegedly 1400 flats have been taken over by migrants and if this situation continues migrants will no longer be in the squares but inside every building which has unrented property. No health and safety over the issue in relation to the overuse of dwelling space. In the building next door to mine over two flats have more than 30 people in them and taking into account many come from villages living in concrete buildings leads to a massive health and safety issue where fire could become inevitable.

All the new migrants are 110% muslims, mostly 99% men and they have one   woman with a child as a front to pretend they are from war ravaged communities. The agenda the government have is impossible to impose what they think is possible ie. replace Greeks in totality in their own country. It's basically a race against time us versus the new world order globalist agenda. Now the issue has gone national many will remember our battles, hopefully learn from them. One notices even today hesitation by governments of any political direction in allowing the squares to become giant squatter camps as before. The state is trying to avoid conflict, but conflict will not in the end be avoided.

1. KEERFA- 'Anti-racist anti-fascist' committee of Greece

KEERFA has led campaign after campaign against Greeks in Ag Panteleomonas labelling them all …nazis.

Saker Rant about a Stolen Europe

March 26, 2016

My latest column about Europe has elicited a lot of reactions, more than I expected, and I feel that I have to follow up by answering some of the comments made and by simply sharing with you not so much my thoughts as my feelings about Europe and her plight. Careful here, *this will be a angry rant, written with sadness and despair in my heart, and with no regard whatsoever for good manners or political correctness* (or spelling and grammar, for that matter)

If you offend easily, stop reading now. Same thing if you expect a carefully written analysis. This will be a *rant*.

You have been warned!

For those who might not already know this, I was born in Switzerland in 1963 and, as most your Swiss people do, I traveled all over Europe for many years. My favorite destinations were mostly in the South: Greece (Athens, Aegina, Aghia Marina), Spain (Gran Canaria, Andalusia, Madrid), Italy (Ansedonia, Rome, Milan, Aosta), France (Creuse, Corrèze, Vercors), but also in the *real* "Central Europe" of Switzerland (Berner Oberland, Graubunden, Val Poschiavo), Germany (Bavaria), Holland (Amsterdam, the Hague) and Belgium (Brugge). I even has some wonderful trips to Ireland (Dublin, Donegall, Connemara) and I loved it all. I loved the languages (I speak Spanish, German, French, Italian), I loved the beautiful diversity of people, the music, the food, the landscapes, the accents and beautiful buildings as witnesses of the past reaching as far as antiquity – all these were joys to my heart and food for my mind. I absolutely LOVE Europe, and not only because by ethnicity I am half-European myself (my father, who did not raise me, is Dutch) but because most of my life was spent there and no matter what Europe will feel like home to me.

[Sidebar: when I say "Europe" I mean Western Europe, the real Europe, the one which was occupied by NATO, not the eastern part, occupied by the WTO (Warsaw Treaty Organization, it was never called a "Pact" – this is US propaganda), which never was really Europe anyway. No offense to anybody, but for me the notion that Poland or Bulgaria are part of Europe is laughable. And neither are the Balkans for that matter, with the possible exception of Greece. I know, most will disagree and prove me wrong, I don't care. MY Europe will always be a purely western one, for better or, sometimes, for worse]

But that home was stolen from me.

First, that home was stolen by an EU project which from day one was anti-European. How is the EU anti-European? First and foremost, because it was aimed at unifying a beautifully diverse continent. What does a German and an Italian have in common. Let me tell you: exactly *nothing*. In Switzerland we used to joke that the border with Africa began in Carouge, a southernmost neighborhood of Geneva. If you asked a Swiss German from Zurich, he would say that the border with Africa begin just south of Bern, on the linguistic divide between German and French speaking Swiss. And, please, don't see that as a sign of anti-Italian or anti-French-speaking Swiss racism – it is not. It was a *joke*, but one which reflected real differences.

The Europe of my youth

There once was a real and viable European (as I said, every time I say "European" I mean "West European") core: Germany, France, Belgium, Holland and Denmark were fairly close to each other, with France being the odd man out (France is, at the very least, two countries: southern and northern France, glued together by history and language). Switzerland was politically too independent to ever join this "core" as for the UK, it was never European in the least. If anything, the UK was always anti-European and the worst enemy of Europe.

The EU went much further. It added Spain, Italy, Greece and Portugal. This was already rather crazy but, I suppose, painfully doable. But then came the deathblow: adding all of the former WTO countries in a suicidal expansion to the East. I don't feel like discussing what the central and eastern European countries ought to be called, maybe "eastern European" is okay, but they never were in any way part of western Europe. Yes, for political reasons, the Poles, Estonians and Romanians think of themselves as "European", but just like the Ukies with their ridiculous "Україна – це Європа!" (The Ukraine is Europe) they never were part of real Europe, not the one which used to joke that the European border with Africa beings in Carouge anyway :-)

The "New Europe"

The second deathblow to Europe came when the capitalists opened the borders of Europe to cheap immigrant labor for the south. Let me tell you, the first wave of immigrants, mostly Italians, Portuguese and Spaniards, could very easily be integrated. I went to school with roughly 50% of the classroom composed of these three groups.

Sure, they each had their own identity, language and customs – but they could really be integrated into the larger society. Then came the Yugolsavs and it was much tougher already. All of them –

Serbs, Croats, Albanians from Kosovo – had come from Communist Yugoslavia and while they definitely worked very hard, they never really felt at home in their new country of residence, and neither did the locals see them as their own. But then all hell broke lose with the arrival of the "Arabs" from the Maghreb (northern Africa) who were not all, or even really, "Arabs" but nevermind that, and sub-Saharan (Black) Africans. Can you imagine what it feels like to see *real* Africans in larger and larger numbers all over your home town when you used to joke that the border with Africa was Carouge (I repeat that example because I consider it very telling)? **It felt like a plague, even if nobody was willing to admit it**.

Now let me immediately get one canard out of the way. The issue of Islam.

French street thugs of the past

I submit that none of the Magbrebians or Africans could be really integrated into a profoundly West European society. But, and this is crucial, the Muslims, and here I mean the really religious and pious Muslims, were always respectful of the law and excellent neighbors. I know what I am talking about as I lived right next door to a big mosque myself, for decades, and that I know <u>for a fact</u> that mosque-attending Muslims are extremely courteous (more so than the locals, in fact) and that they are very careful about showing a refined, educated and proper image of Islam in front of non-Muslims. The real plague were the 2nd generation kids who were<u>neither Europeans nor Muslims</u>. Now those, especially the Algerians, accounted for the vast majority of crime and they were truly a horror to put up with: arrogant, loud, uneducated and <u>very</u> aggressive. These Maghrebians typically would mix with 2nd generation Black Africans and form the core of almost all the gangs of criminal thugs roaming around. And none of them, <u>zero</u>, were Muslims in any sense of the word, not religious not cultural. Again, I speak of long and personal experience, so please don't come tell me that I don't know Europe or Islam, because I do, very well in fact.[Sidebar: I cannot speak of Turks/Kurds in Germany simply because I have not spend enough time in these circles and I am not qualified to have an opinion about them]

So <u>my</u> Europe was stolen from me not once, but twice and while I weep over the Europe of my youth, I absolutely loathe the Europe of the European Union. Every time I see Hollande, Stoltenberg or Tusk, my stomach turns and I feel like cursing. They make me absolutely sick. I hate the Europe of Charlie Hebdo, of BHL, of Harlem Desir, the Europe of Conchita Wurst or of Dalia Grybauskaitė (there goes a typical European name, right?).

Street thugs in Paris today

London now looks like Karachi, Paris like Ouagadougou, Rome like Târgu-Mures. This is absolutely disgusting, revolting and suicidal. To say so has absolutely nothing to do with racism and only a person totally devoid from any real cultural roots can misinterpret the horror of those who see their cities and cultural roots being smashed by waves of non-integratable immigrants as a form of racism. You don't believe me?

Let me tell you this: in France there are a lot of Maghrebians who are now horrified to see their (usually poor) neighborhood being literally run over by Romanian Gypsies while in Switzerland you have more or less integrated ex-Yugoslavs who now watch in horror as their putatively "fellow" ex-Yugoslavs run the cocaine business. How many Swiss citizens do you think you would fine in a Swiss jail? Nobody knows, but my guess is less than 15%.

The worst part of it all is that both the Right and the Left are equally responsible for this state of affairs.

Lionized by Time, of course

Originally, the main impulse to bring immigrants to Europe came from the Right, from the organized corporate managers who wanted cheap labor at any cost. As always, if you look deeper, the force behind the corporations were the banks. It is of no coincidence that in France is all began with Georges Pompidou who, before being President, was a General Manager at N. M. Rothschild & Sons Bank. Pompidou, who came to power following the CIA's "color revolution" known as "Mai 68" succeeded a real French patriot, General de Gaulle, who had attempted to de-couple France from her AngloZionst masters and who was subsequently overthrown in a bizarre revolution which already saw Trotskists and CIA agents working hand in hand to achieve regime change in France.

All the French Right cared for was profit, profit and profit. The French workers were superbly unionized, they have achieved remarkable social and labor rights and the French capitalists simply could not turn them into the kind of right-less workforce they needed, so the imported them from abroad.

Bernard Henri Levi and Harlem Désir

As for the Left, it saw in this influx of immigrants a fantastic political opportunity to achieve the kind of societal change it always wants to achieve: a wholesale destruction of any form of tradition, national identity and religion.

The French Zionists, in particular, saw a fantastic opportunity to weaken the French national identity by branding it as <u>by definition</u> racist. This is how they did it.

President François Mitterrand wanted to split the French Right in order to win the elections, so he personally ordered the main French TV channel to make a long interview with the leader of the National Front, Jean-Marie Le Pen. This interview is what really put the National Front in the spotlight and the tactic worked. The French Right was split and it still is, by the way. The French Socialists joined forces with the Israel Lobby and created a movement called "Touche pas à mon pote" (don't touch my pal) headed by a guy called Harlem Desir (I kid you not!). Their mission? To fight the alleged racism of the French people. Sounds familiar? Create a problem and then 'solve it' ("Zionism 101"). This operation worked superbly and made any discussion of immigration tantamount to racism.

France: from King Clovis to this…

Now that the EU has replaced Europe, the Right and the Left have logically fused into what I call the "Extreme Center" – the same globalist model with, on one hand, wants to eliminate all the borders while, on the other, dismantling all social regulations protecting the working class from exploitation by the Capitalists.

Sorry for this long excursion in the past, but I want you to understand why I am always so angry when I write about today's "Europe": I am angry because I remember "yesterday's Europe" very well, because I saw it killed step by step before my eyes, because I personally lived through every stage of this slow murder and because I absolutely loathe the pseudo-Europe which the Zionists are building on the aches of the old Europe.

A few more comments:

Gladio: yes, I know about Gladio, I remember the bombing in Bologna and the kidnapping of Aldo Moro. Could the latest bombings be a Gladio v2? Yes, absolutely, but this in no way impinges in the fundamental thesis that uncontrolled emigration is a moral threat to Europe and an ideal vector for the penetration by terrorists. Just remember that Daesh is CIA-controlled anyway, and that whether the handlers are in Raqqa or Brussels makes no difference. The Takfiris have always been the CIA's footsoliders.

The US role: huge. The EU is essentially a US project via the Bilderbergers and the Zionist lobby in Europe. The EU today is run by a *comprador* elite which is totally subservient to AngloZionist interests. What real Europeans wanted was the "Europe des patries" (the Europe of fatherlands) which de Gaulle advocated. We all know what happened to de Gaulle for daring to oppose the AngloZionists Empire.

Russia: this is interesting. I see no *Schadenfreude* amongst Russians, none at all. First, most Russians simply like Europe, especially southern Europe with which we feel a much stronger connection. But we also admire the northern Europeans for their undeniable achievements. Furthermore, Russians know, through their own bitter past, that good people can live under a disgusting regime. This is also why Russians don't usually blame regular US Americans for the policies of the ruling 1%. But what bothers Russians the most is the abject servility of most Europeans in front of an abject regime. The great Russian philosopher Ivan Solonevich used to write that "the Germans are not better organized, they are easier to organize". What he meant by that is the be it under the Nazis or under the US occupation, the Germans would be exceptionally obedient and *willing to be ordered around.* In contrast, the Russian people are far more freedom loving and even anarchistic and they always rebel against any authority they don't respect.

[Sidebar: dubious about this? Consider this: the Germans actually elected Hitler and then obeyed him up until his death. In comparison, the Soviet regime came to power in 1917 but only achieved stability in 1946(!) after a huge civil war, many insurrections, bloody repressions, bloody purges and a terrible war which saw, for the first time in Russian history, millions of Russians switch sides. Even after 1946 – the year of the last big wave of repressions – the Soviets still feared their own population up to 1991, and for good reason, would I add].

I personally expect that the first explosion against the EU will come from France, a country which, like Russia, has a deep, almost visceral, attachment to freedom and which will, I am certain, eventually blow up. When that happens, it will be violent and bloody (alas, another French – and Russian – tradition). I think that the AngloZionists will go to unimaginable levels of depravity and dishonesty to prevent it, but my money stays on France as the first country in the EU to rise up against the Empire. Why? Because the other candidates, Greece, Spain or Italy, will always "look over the shoulders" whereas the French will simply explode in rage with no regard to the consequences (in that the French are much more like the Russians). Plus the French will always hate the Anglos anyway.

Islam: Fact 1: Muslims are here to stay. You can hate it or love it, but that is a fact. Fact 2: Islam, real Islam as opposed to Wahabi Islam, is categorically opposed to AngloZionism. I think that Islam will be one of the forces which will eventually help to "clean house" in Europe. Wahhabism on the other hand, will have to be completely and totally eliminated from Europe. This is a mortal threat to all of civilized mankind, a threat which cannot be negotiated with and which must be totally eliminated.

The Ottomans: Call me crazy, but I am coming the conclusion that Turkey, at least in its present form, is inherently a dangerous and non-reformable entity which must be beat back to a size and quality commensurate with the notion of "normal country". Just look at the past couple of decades. The Turks were involved in: Cyprus, Kurdistan, Chechnia, Bosnia, Albania, Macedonia, Crimea, Lebanon and Syria! How is that for a terrorism-support scorecard? Does anybody remember that Turkey does still occupy half of Cyprus and that the Turkish military has been bombing and attacking Kurds in Syria and Iraq for decades already. Clearly, the "imperial virus" has not been eradicated in this ex-Empire and this rot must be eliminated until Turkey finally becomes what all other former empires have become: a normal country, like Greece or Holland. By the way, the only thing which currently keeps Turkey together and gives it a kind of immunity is, of course, the protection of the United States, NATO aka the AngloZionist Empire. Get rid of one, and the other will soon follow.

The *real* Left: there used to be a real Left in Europe. And, unlike the modern 'caviar-Left' it was really patriotic. The French Communist Party leader Georges Marchais saw through the Capitalists plan to import masses of immigrants and he denounced that as a conspiracy against both the local French and the immigrants. Some of his speeches sound very similar to what Jean-Marie Le Pen has repeated for decades. The real left has now been completely eliminated from Europe or, if it exists somewhere, it is too small to make a difference.

The *real* Right: The National Front of Jean-Marie Le Pen used to be the real deal, even if it was carefully manipulated by the French Socialists. But ever since his daughter Marine came to power, the National Front has been totally co-opted by the Zionists and from a _popular_ and _labor_ movement it has now turned into the typical Capitalist pseudo-Right which is sold out to the system and unable to even peep a word against the Zionists. There is a real Right left in France, mostly around Traditionalist "Catholic" (Latin) circles but, just as with the real Left, it is too small to really make a difference.

Sorry for this long rant. My heart hurts over this topic and it is painful for me to write about. Please don't come and pester me about spelling or grammar or other inexactitudes. I wrote this in one shot, off the cuff, and at the kind of warp-speed typing I do when I am emotional about something (heck, I won't even bother re-reading it or check for typos). Though I will post this under the "analysis" section, I do that only because this is a follow-up to my analysis yesterday. But, as you can tell, an analysis this is not – this is just a frustrated and angry rant about what has been done to the place were I was born and which I still love.

To end on something personal and beautiful, I leave you with this GoogleEarth photo of the place in Greece where, as a kid, I learned how to free-dive (decades before the movie "The Big Blue" made freediving a trendy sport): the rocks near the village of Αγία Μαρίνα (Saint Marina), on the island of **Aegina**. I visited this place at the age of 12 for the first time and this is also were I spent my honeymoon, almost 23 years ago. This is also one of the places I call 'home'.

The Saker

Reaction and Resistance to Migrant Hotspots in Greece

One year on...

When it initially started most people assumed the media narrative regarding Syrian 'refugees' was real. The reason wasn't that they actually believed it, but essentially since the fall of the Soviet Union all mainstream political parties run the same political line. Even the alleged right wing populists such as Golden Dawn have abandoned the area (Ag. Panteleomonas Central Athens) that brought them to national prominence and gone on to new pastures waiting for electoral victories, not a struggle for power on the streets.

The big waves of alleged migrants as written in a series of articles in the beginning of this book came in through Turkey and by boats from Libya etc. The Syriza government unleashed its paid NGO's to lead a campaign of closing down migrant hotspots that had been set up by the previous governments of New Democracy as allegedly they were set up to hold migrants as captives. This was all a show to pretend they were closing them in order then to open around 80 up and down the country. Now they are talking of opening two migrant detention centres for those that get involved in outright gangsterism ie gang rapes, child rapes and body part selling.

Syriza has received EU money to house and feed all these migrants and instead of spending it has utilized the resources of the Greek state (army conscripts and army catering to deliver the food) and has pocketed the difference. Scandals have already emerged to that effect where blood relatives are given lucrative contracts for this process. Thousands of jobs have also been advertised to work on these migrant camps and of course Syriza NGOs and affiliates will have first priority. This isn't solely about work but a globalist NWO calling.

Shipowners moved in on a new profitable business shipping over tens upon tens of thousands from the islands to Greece and they found it extremely lucrative as they were according to reports paid a lot more for their journeys out of government coffers. After all this is a shipowners government and always has been since the mid-1960s when the corporates became embedded as part of the Greek state, all else like Parliamentary politics is just for show for the masses like the X factor.

Illuminating was the case of Odysseas Voudouris from the Migration Ministry who had the post called the General Secretary of First Arrivals and Registration as if we are dealing with the concierge of a luxury hotel who resigned after falling out with Mr Mouzalas Minister of Migration and the argument is over who spends what and where when dealing with the migrant wave. It was later revealed that 'EU' money in relation to migration would go 75% to NGOs and only 25% to the Greek state and to tap these funds Syriza members placed bids to get contracts like the daughter of the regional governor of Serres Mr Tapas despite the fact that she had no relationship to catering whatsoever, but having secured the contract she could subcontract it getting a hefty commission of which some would appear as legal and the other under the table (has been the norm of Greek ministerial contracts since time immemorial).
We will now look at a few of the islands in the Aegean and how the situation has developed and how reaction and resistance has progressed.

Kos
In Kos they landed thousands of migrant blow ins and the actual refugees are few and far between. Most migrants claim they are from anywhere and in Lesvos in the centre migrants have held up banners saying 'we will destroy the island'. No one arrests them, crimes are committed and none are prosecuted for anything. This capitalist anarchy inevitably leads to power vacuums and in almost every island after the first year Greeks have started to mobilise against the presence of migrants. The mass media of disinformation will not report any instances of resistance only reaction. They will promote all areas where they will show Greeks opening their houses looking after a distressed child but not show anything else, people being robbed mugged or raped. Bosses seek to replace and displace millions of Europeans.

Avramopoulos EU Commissioner had eggs thrown at them, Mayor of Lesvos said we won't hold elections, Kammenos Defence Minister had eggs thrown at them. No Greek or EU politician gets an easy ride on the Aegean islands any more. Illuminating is the fact that people said if no one is reacting then the government will get away with murder and manage to ensure that Greeks become a minority in their own country and an unlimited number of new arrivals come and no resistance occurs. Yet Kos set the stage of conflict and resistance, an island which has the fourth highest number of tourists but did not really have any militant past. People protested peacefully against the hotspot and the Syriza government reacted over the top sending in riot police from afar as Athens to crack heads open which they dutifully did. Problem is island communities are small and everyone knows each others business and their relationships with politics and the people organized themselves to counterattack back and they did. In one instance when the riot police was held up in a hotel the hotel came under a sustained attack by people using ship flares and according to reports the head of the police called for the army commander on the island to intervene but he refused.

These developments from Kos which occurred during the first six months of 2016 have now spread to Chios and Lesvos and there have been large gatherings of people with Greek flags demonstrating on the streets.

Now one cannot call the migrants illegal as allegedly no one is …illegal. In other words anyone who happens to find themselves in Greece has a right to be there allegedly by international conventions so the rights of sovereignty of nation states no longer applies as no measures can be taken to defend the population at large, imperialist humanitarianism has promoted the alleged refugee crisis to shift vast populations from various regions at whim. There are villages in

Greece which are surrounded by thousands of illegal migrants and if they aren't funded to survive at a basic level then conflict will arise and has arisen that may take on the form of a desperate population crushed under the IMF austerity in conflict with migrants in general. This wont be the first or last time as the ruling classes no longer have any allegiance to their own populations under globalization. Most work has gone offshore and now they are just involved in bringing on shore labour. The capitalist class owns the media, the NGO's and the political parties lock stock and barrel. What they don't own are the masses.

Lesvos
Is a large island with a turbulent history. It had a strong socialist movement in the 1920's centred around the Electricity workers and in WW2 it had a partisan war that continued after the official end of the civil war. Lesvos got a Syriza Mayor and the party came first in the elections of January 2015 and the next elections in September 2015. As such it became the epicenter of one of the largest waves of migration into its shores using closed down state facilities like the childrens camping sites that the Troika mothballed.

One of the famous incidents on the island was when NGOs took over a labour centre without asking its participants and turned it into a homeless shelter overnight and refused to leave. The local branch of the KKE (which in Athens is 'antiracist and hyperglobalist' took it back with a force of arms with the Athenian clique being forced to defend them. The NGO's then attacked on Mayday 2015 another group of globalist leftists in Athens allegedly mistaking them for the KKE!

The globalist corporate media made it an epicenter and soon thereafter all globalists visited it having conferences etc, and doing NGO solidarity tourism from Susan Sarandon to the junkie diversity globalist freakshow Angelina Jolie. All the great and the good arrived in Lesvos to praise modern capitalist slavery.

Although it took around a year residents started to engage in politics and they held many meeting in Moria (where they set up a migrant hostpot double the number it was assigned for) and an 85 year old farmer became famous when he dumped a lambs head on the table of the Mayor telling him we have lost all our produce.

In one of the last big gatherings in Lesvos banners were unhurled asking for Minister of Migration Mouzalas to take his NGO's and GO HOME. In one of these days after having attempted to get the NGOs and migrants alongside the anti-Greek riot police to attack the crowds failed, they decided to burn down the migrant centre of Morias and send all the migrants packing to a cruise ship off the coast of Lesvos.

Globalists have tried time after time to march with migrants against locals using the riot police as back up (what became characteristic in the all the street demos in Ag Panteleomonas-Athens when the fake Left branded the whole area neo-Nazi) under the ridiculous slogan 'Locals and migrants work together, Greeks and Turks on the same island' in other words inviting Turkey over to take control. But there aren't enough globalists either in Greek society or on the state payroll on these islands. Athens is a different kettle of fish as they have all the main fake Left parties, the headquarters of the NGO's and those directly on the police payroll known as agent provocateurs

Crete
Having realized they are losing control in the Aegean islands they have decided to shift thousands to Crete and set up many migrant hotspots there. So far they have avoided Crete due to its turbulent history but Crete is as good a place as any and they are setting up these reception centres. As every week goes by new announcements are made as a reaction to developments. Now detention centres are to be set up to house migrants who behave illegally (not of course anything to do with their arrival into Greece) and Syriza will pretend they have resolved another issue.

A big bust up has occurred in an area known as Oraiokastro Crete where the parents association has flatly refused to accept migrants children in their schools. The whole of the corporate media has rounded on them like they did years ago emphasizing an Albanian who held the Greek flag in a Greek school (it only transpired many years later after the Albanian in question ended up in America that he was the son of a secret service agent probably in the payroll of the USA). The epithet of racism is thrown at the parents for not wanting their children to catch diseases and put up with whom the powers that be label refugees when 9 times out of 1o they are migrants in search of a better life.

Whenever locals have protested over mass replacement migration after a while so as to brand them racists, Golden Dawn appears. Then on their heels the 'welcome refugee' globalist brigade. One could argue they work in tandem and divide up their roles. Let's not forget the 'nazis' allegedly killed a Greek rap artist Fissas (right under the nose of at least 30 police) and subsequently two Golden Dawn members were killed by 'anti-nazis'. The theatre of the 'extremes' fighting whilst the globalist core rules untouched dominates Greek politics. Left on their own the communities would win as they did for instance in Keratea (over rubbish dumping). You would't though have a raison d'etre for the globalists if Golden Dawn didn't exist, indeed they campaigned so vociferously for this party that they took it from 0.3% with no coverage in Parliament to making it the 3rd party.

Conclusion
The hatred of the Greek ruling class and its political representatives in Parliament to Greeks is *visceral*. One only needs to read what the political class wrote in 1992 regarding mass immigration into Greece as it included representatives from all the main parties to see how far down the road they have gone embracing globalism and using state forces to implement it. But having created a political vacuum by all singing from the same hymn sheet (open borders for all) they are being confronted by island communities whose history has always been one of foreign occupation and how they fought against it. Most people do not understand the scale of the problem or the agenda. They believe as long as it doesn't affect me directly and it only affects someone on the other side of Greece or the other side of Athens it won't involve them.

But this issue isn't going away. Trying to house and feed every last person that arrives in Greece whilst cutting back on Greeks welfare, making them homeless and rubbing into everyone's noses that we will continue to house and feed migrants at your expense and you cannot do anything about it is a recipe for disaster. Just as the Greeks destroyed their old established political parties and turned them into a rump so they will in practice the resolve the issue of replacement mass migration if they want to continue to live in the geographical area known as Greeks. Otherwise after becoming for the first time in history a minority in their own country they will end up having the same fate as American Indians but this time won't even have reservations to end up on.

October 2016

VN Gelis

Serres Syriza supplying food to migrants won by daughter of regional governor Mr Tapas…

http://www.kyrtsos.gr/content?nid=2510

Kos: Police Teargas migrants

British Trade Union Solidarity and Greece: Aiding Reaction Then and Now

"When you leave the people to die on the streets, to be psychologically and physically destroyed and then you assert at the right time you will carry out a national liberation struggle, then you are a conscious liar and a collaborator of the enemy. Its like saying you will put coffins infront to fight" (Dimitris Glinos 'What is and what does EAM want? Athens 1942

The historical roots of today's neoliberal globalists
Whenever British trade-unions have been involved in solidarity and Greece invariably they have served reactionary causes which are related to the political issues of the day. Despite the recent promotion of Greek solidarity via the TUC, Unite and trade union locals the reality is they have promoted a neoliberal agenda and are now seeking the globalist occupation of Greece by what are labelled 'refugees' but in reality are part of the 4th Reichs replacement of domestic labour via the tool of mass migration.

German Occupation of Greece
During the brutal occupation of Greece and the eventual armed resistance by Greeks creating a partisan army of 100k strong when the German front was going to fall as with other areas of the planet, Greece was to belong somewhere. In Churchills discussions with Stalin, Greece 'fell' to the West ie the superpowers handed over to where they agreed irrespective of the desires of the nation. Thus decisions were taken to disarm the Greek partisans which occurred in the Varkiza Accords by Theonas leader of the KKE, to then participate in a government of national unity. The leader of the Greek partisans Aris Velouhiotis disagreed but abided by party unity, without personally disarming.

During the occupation and whilst the German front was imploding a Russian army detachment left Bulgaria to pass on the message from Stalin that Greece would belong to the West. From a Russian point of view having been weakened significantly to the point of dissolution by the German imperialist war machine securing a peace which would allow it to recover was in its interests, but those interests weren't necessarily the interests of Greece for that decision sealed its fate and all decisions taken subsequently by the leaders of the KKE were to serve the West, a policy which they have dutifully adhered to until today.

The problem Churchill had was how to disarm the Left, ensure the Left made no demands on society and no retributions were taken against the nazi collaborators. What pushed Churchill in this direction was the fact that tunnels which were in existence had partisans going under them all the way to where Churchill was staying (Grande Bretagne Hotel, Sindagma Sq) and as recent reports by Manolis Glezos have stated, they had dynamite under the hotel and were ready and willing to blow it up but an order was given and they stepped back. On the back of this Churchill organised the December events in Athens where they British Army and Greek nazi collaborationists shot an unarmed demonstration and many died. This caused ruptures in the British Parliament as Churchill was still in coalition with the Labour Party and in order to minimise the issue they flew out the head of the British TUC on a delegation to meet with Greek 'trade union leaders', the opposition and to report back. There was no real substance to the delegation other than to alibi Churchill and cover for his pro-Nazi collaborationist leanings and the fact that he was preparing a civil war to crush the Greek Left for a generation, which is precisely what he did. When the coalition fell the Labour Party continued and started the Greek civil war proper and ran it until the end of 1947 when they handed over the reigns to US imperialism. Those were in leadership positions in the TUC (Walter Citrine) and the Labour Party (Bevin) at the time were real pieces of work having gone to the bourgeois courts in 1939 against the British Communist Party's daily paper (Daily Worker) and won a judgement against them, for daring to tell the truth about the TUC supporting the imperialist war effort and wanting and seeking wage restraint on behalf of the bosses thus changing the nature of the trade union movement into open lieutenant dogs of capital. Below is a recently translated document from the historical archives in Greece

TUC Delegation in Greece: 'Red Atrocities' or the Greek Katyn

Introduction
The streets of Athens and suburbs hadn't dried up from being awash in blood from the heroes, children of the people that fell to the barbarity of the occupiers and their collaborators. The road to Kessariani was filled by the blood from the first days of last May. In Kallithea, Kokkinia, Dourgouti and Kolono the fascist barbarities were fresh. German quislings had filled up all the sewers with bodies as we witnessed them floating past every now and again in particular by the General Police headquarters. Hangings witnessed by our brothers happened before our very eyes. German collaborators were baptised 'national heroes' inside the courts provoking the population and the worst black marketeers, rapacious to the end showed off their wealth made by the blood of our children protected by the Germans.

All of this element who are traitors to our nation, of crime and tyranny are the same people who organised the fascist coup of December and they attacked the peole of Athens with foreign weapons, fighting alongside the German quislings. These are the same cliques that have no intention of leaving the people alone and they continue quiet to hound with the most violent attacks on the patriots, those who fought for Greece and in order to hide their crimes and erase from peoples memory their violent acts, they found a method worthy of their cause. They tried to present a series of crimes which allegedly were created by EAM so as to cover their crimes with a black cloak.. This is the deeper meaning of the propaganda with corpses post-December events. All the circles of local and foreign reaction up until Sir Citrine arrived were mobilised to globally propagate about the "deadly crimes of EAM". Thus they attacked the heroic struggle carried out by the Greek people for their Independence and their Nation and Freedom and on the other hand they covered up their countless crimes, those which were carried out in the December days and the dark days of slavery. They concealed, thought they concealed them, but the blood that flowed was equivalent to a river and cannot be hidden.

Irrespective about this, it is time to be told the truth regarding the world renowned 'crimes' of EAM.

It is true that in our times the whole of the people, the real, the true, the much tortured people of Athens and Piraeus fought a valiant battle and uneven struggle, it is true that there were executions, either from being indignant in seeing that traitors remained unpunished and they regained their weapons. Any objective observer would understand inside the fire and brimstone of a severe conflict these would be unavoidable and there would be no means for them to not occur however much actions such as this damaged the peoples struggle.

But no executions occurred as presented by those who unearthed corpses and none of the vicious and disgusting acts occurred as presented by the organisers of the anti-popular campaign
Proving this truth is the purpose of this document. To show to every objective person the mastery with which these vicious stories, of torture, limb removals, blinding eyes and other such indescribably crimes were magnified. Proof of this will be demonstrated with

indisputable facts. We invite whoever doesn't believe our account to make their own investigations and cross reference what we say. The task of defaming every just struggle for the Greek nation must be uncovered. The truth can sometimes be blurry, but in the end shines more bright...

"How was the blasphemous campaign organised
The resistance of the armed population of Athens and Piraeus lasted for 30 days. In these 30 days there wasn't one time when the suburbs of Athens and Piraeus weren't attacked by planes, by cannons, by tanks. Thousands were its victims. They were buried in gardens, outside Churches, on sidewalks, in fields. When ELAS retreated and the British came all these countless bodies were unburied and put on trucks. They were found in Peristeri or Kipseli or the Turkmountains cut up without eyes and ears. Relatives were called to receive the bodies of the 'citizens butchered by ELAS' citizens. So for the mythology to work better they circulated that those who were killed by the ELAS partisans would gain a pension whilst those who were killed by accident (ie by planes, canons, tanks etc) would receive nothing. Thus everybody had an interest in appearing to show that his victim was a result of ELAS partisans. Newspapers were filled with names of butchered citizens and foreign correspondents and Sir Walter Citrine were called to witness at first hand the barbarities of ELAS. Thus the slanderous campaign was more successful.

If there was an honest person who didn't want to become an organ of the traitorous clique abusers – despite all the promises for a pension – they then threatened them with the label of being a member of the KKE! 'They need hanging' was the response by those who unearthed the bodies of dead victims and trying to promote them for political gain.

But it wasn't simply this: Whole units were organised which unearthed the bodies cut their eyes and their body parts and then showcased them so the 'barbarity' of the ELASites would be revealed. It's the most heinous crime which only the people that collaborated with the Germans, the dishonourable students of the SS could think and put into action.

These are the means they used. Now for evidence we provide a list of events that confirm what has been said above. It's impossible to write down all we have verified. But they are enough to give a final answer to the classical sycophants.

(A full list follows of Greeks known and how they died and where-translators note!)

We are dealing with Sir Walter Citrine who came to Greece allegedly to be involved with trade union unity. He became the main megaphone of the anti-EAM sycophantic campaign. The above give an answer to this gentleman. But let us see what was written regarding his role in the 'Daily Worker' of London in the issue 9th February 1945.

"The report by the delegation of British Trade Unions in Greece was based by evidence provided by Greek enemies of EAM, by the British Administration and British soldiers with immediate contact with the delegation itself ... At the Press Conference where Walter Citrine where he explained in detail parts of his report we found the new facts:

1. That mass arrests occurred of citizens in houses where sharp shooters functioned. The delegation must accept that there is a number of victims of innocent citizens that exist caught by the Plastiras government.
2. The delegation does not directly condemn ELAS that have murdered those whose bodies were found in Peristeri at the end of January.
3. The identity of those executed are unknown to the delegation"

This was promised by Sir Walter Citrine to the representatives of the press so he can clarify his report, thus indirectly allowing the world the impression that ELAS committed these atrocities.
This is how Tribune answers (magazine of the Labour Party) regarding the stance taken by Sir Walter Citrine in Greece (23rd March 1945)

"Recently Sir Walter Citrine gave a report on Greece in the best fashion as propaganda material for Mr Churchill and the Tories for a long time"

Sir Walter Citrine arrived in Greece to justify the most violent intervention in our internal affairs. But the British people who have respected the struggles of our peoples haven't fallen victim to this sycophancy with whatever dead bodies they unearth and whatever machinations are done with them...
Published by EAM 1945

Below is a large excerpt from an old deceased comrade Bill Hunter who knew a few things regarding Greece unlike todays know all know-nothings... regarding the Labour Party's imperialist role.

"POST-WAR BETRAYAL

In the closing stages of the war Bevin supported completely the attempts of British imperialism to establish the old pre-war corrupt, dictatorial and imperialist regimes in Europe and Asia. He played his most despicable role in assisting Churchill and the British ruling class in Greece.

The Greek organisation EAM — a coalition of seven parties including the Liberals and the Communist Party — had the mass support of Greek workers and peasants. ELAS, its military organisation, was the main resistance to the German occupation. The mass of the people were opposed to the return of the monarchy and the pre-war dictatorship. Eighty-five per cent of the Greek army had been interned by the British in Egypt because of its support for EAM.

British capitalism was determined to re-impose the rule of Greek landowners and capitalists under King George of the Hellenes. The British Military Government demanded the disarming of ELAS. Workers and peasants refused to give up their weapons while royalist officers retained their arms. In Athens on December 3rd 1944 there was a peaceful demonstration in support if EAM and in protest at royalist demonstrations in the previous days. The demonstration was led by women and children. British troops fired into the head of the march and killed 15 and wounded 148. A General Strike broke out throughout Athens.

In Britain, the rank and file of the trade union movement reacted with anger. Civil war began in Greece. A section of Ghurka troops in the British army deserted to ELAS. *The Observer* prophesied 'serious labour trouble' and said that even if victory over ELAS was won it 'might break the coalition'. Bevin and other labour bureaucrats worked might and main to prevent a condemnation of the coalition government being passed at the special Labour Party conference which was to be held later in December.

Bullock in his biography of Bevin writes:

To avoid the danger of the party conference passing a direct vote of censure on the Government and its labour members, the NEC put forward a resolution calling for an armistice, without delay and the resumption of talks to establish a Provisional National Government in Greece.

Bevin lined up the block votes to carry the resolution and Bullock remarks that Churchill never forgot the debt he owed Bevin for this. The Soviet bureaucracy pressurised the Greek Communist Party to accept an armistice. Churchill had visited Moscow the previous October and got the assurance from Stalin that Greece would be in Britain's sphere of influence.

Fifty thousand British troops remained in Greece. Workers and peasants were disarmed. By 1947 there were 14,000 Greek political prisoners living on the penal islands, half starved, without sufficient fuel, bedding and water. Court martials were working continuously, sentencing to death civilians as well as soldiers.

It was Bevin's 'belief that foreign and defence policy, unlike domestic policy, should not be a matter for party politics' wrote Bullock in *The Observer* of March 8th in an article on Bevin. Bevin clearly put the imperialist content of this belief at the special Labour Party conference of 1944, when he supported the repression in Greece.
'The British Empire' he said, 'whether we like it or not, cannot abandon its position in the Mediterranean. It is impossible for it to do so.'

It was the rapidly growing hostility to capitalist policies that ejected Bevin and the other labour leaders out of the War Cabinet. Eden, in his memoirs, reports a conversation with Bevin in June 1944 about continuing the coalition in the immediate post war period. The growing opposition to the political truce and to foreign and domestic policy of the Government and the massive desire for a change made it impossible for Bevin to fight for his plan of a continuation of the coalition.

When the Labour Party swept the polls in July 1945, Bevin became Foreign Minister. Attlee appointed him at the suggestion of George VI. Mark Stephens tells us that Bevin was very intimate with King George VI. Is this supposed to impress T&G members? Stephens quotes the king, writing to his brother about the new Labour Government: 'My new government is not too easy and the people are rather difficult to talk to. Bevin is very good and tells me everything that is going on.'

We find here that the 'tough' trade union leader who, we are told, was a champion of 'his people', has a deep and essential servility to the rulers of society and their institutions. The Jimmy Thomases and the Ernie Bevins love to drop an aitch in front of the monarch — but as one of his most loyal, hand-kissing subjects. The same loyalty and attention, of course, is not given to their trade union members. It would be quite against British tradition and constitution for workers to expect their representatives to treat them like they treat the rich, unelected monarch, and tell them 'everything that is going on' in the Government!

For a decade after the war 'Bevinism' was a dirty word in the British labour movement. Bevin was the arch defender of the interests of British imperialism and the alliance with America's rulers. He was one of the leading protagonists of the cold war.

SAVING CAPITALISM

Bevin is reported to have said during the war that he wanted to see a 'Peoples' Peace'. But what sort of peace did he and the Labour leaders fight for? With their help and that of the Stalinists in Europe the revolutionary wave after the war was defeated, workers and peasants disarmed and the old capitalist rulers firmly re-established. With those betrayals the choice of socialism or barbarism gained a new dimension — for the capitalism they saved now developed nuclear weapons. Bevin and Co. saw their task at the end of the war to maintain the basic capitalist imperialist relations existing in Britain and the Empire at the beginning of the war. Any role for the 'peoples' interests' in the peace came about when imperialism was forced to retreat before the strength in struggle of the colonial people and the working class.

There is the myth that the participation of Bevin in the war-time government and the presence of trade union leaders in war-time government committees represented a big step in the upward climb of trade unions to a powerful place in society. Here, things are turned on their heads. Bevin did not represent the working class in the council chambers of capitalism. He represented capitalism inside the trade unions. In his forward in Mark Stephen's book, Moss Evans declares:

'Ernest Bevin both developed and exercised power on behalf of ordinary working people for a long time.' The truth is that Ernest Bevin exercised power which came from the working class, but he exercised it on behalf of the capitalist class. That is the meaning of what Bullock tells us when he writes that in the War Cabinet Bevin put *'loyalty to the coalition before party interest, to the anger of not a few members of the Labour Party'.*"

Greek Solidarity by British Trade Unions: Neoliberal Syriza Roadshow

The close connection of associated and assorted disparate leftists with each other and the top echelons of the British trade union bureaucracy is well known and runs deep and has done for decades and does not really require documenting. A small group of people were present in Greece during 2012 from the UK (including the author of this piece) responding to a call made by the Spitha movement of Theodorakis about creating a solidarity movement with Greece. The origins of the British involvement were the Unite trade union, the Stop the War campaign, ex-Union chiefs like Paul Mackney and Labourite councillors alongside journalists like Paul Mason. The original aim was to publicise the Greeks fight against austerity, provide medical aid to much needed Greek hospitals ravaged by the IMF and to group together activists in the UK and Greece to publicise the situation of austerity.

Syrizas riot police attacking protestors against home repossessions whilst at the same time housing countless migrants for free

This same group of people became ***uncritical bedfellows of the neoliberal Syriza roadshow*** and have now fully degenerated into open supporters of the mass labour displacement of the Greek population by the mass importation of alleged refugees and the creation of 'migrant hotspots' all over Greece. They are now doing what their forebearers in the trade union movement did many decades ago, allying themselves openly with imperialist policies, *no questions asked*. Illuminating is the fact that they have fellow traveller trade unionist leaders who do all in their power to scab on their members back home, but who go to Greece to show 'solidarity' with people like Papandreou (who instigated the IMF genocide programme) like the leader of TSSA Manuel Cortes. Corbyn also arrived in Athens to take his photo op with Tsipras at the area which had protests for refuse dumping in Keratea. It has to be noted that Syriza refused to go there and only turned up when PASOK lost a battle by the concerned citizens who refused to agree to their area becoming a dumping site, for purely electoral purposes.

Manuel Cortes TSSA President, Varoufakis, Clive Lewis MP
In the summer of 2015 when Syriza was already in power hey spent time justifying Syrizas neoliberal agenda by alleging 'This is a Coup' as Tsipras was in a 17hour negotiating meeting with the Eurogroup, (he looked fresh faced when they interviewed him in the morning mind you!) they then spent time promoting pro-EU Varoufakis roadshow and now their only concern is how many migrants should arrive in Greece, *be fed and housed whilst ignoring the plight of Syriza's austerity on people*: pension cuts, farmers strikes and blockades, migrants looting and disrupting peoples lives in the Aegean islands.

It's no coincidence that the British TUC which has never once written a retraction in its despicable role during WW2 when it openly collaborated with Nazi Greek collaborators now has statements in support of… 'solidarity with Greece'. What they mean by solidarity is solidarity with the banksters, the Euro, the EU, the London based hedge funds etc. That is all the British TUC, the Labour Party and its associated bedfellows in Greek solidarity are concerned about.

British Parliament
One of the first meetings organised in the British Parliament regarding Greek austerity was attended by one Syriza MP Samos Samoilides and a Syriza trade union rep George Harissis. They were rounded upon by Dianne Abbot and despite not being in government were asked how migrants were being treated by the government. Not how can a small country cope with an endless number of arrivals. Nor any questions regarding hospital closures as Dianne Abbots official position at the time was Shadow Health spokesperson. Syriza MP did say we are a small country and it's very difficult to cope with all influxes but we want and seek a humane treatment for all new arrivals (by implication inhumane for Greek citizens!)
In another meeting once Syriza was in power it became clear their official position would be one of defending promoting and extending austerity in areas which had not been reached before. This meeting was organised by a Labour MP John Cruddas with the new finance

ministry (current) member Euclid Tsakalotos (it is ironic his uncle was in charge of the British-American financed Greek civil war General Tsakalotos) and it isn't lost on people that having handed over unpaid mortgage funds (by the millions of unemployed) to foreign funds Tsakalotos is attempting to evict tens of thousands of Greeks from their properties and create a homeless army, whilst at the same time using state funds to house and feed thousands of surplus labourers to displace Greeks fully and irreversibly for the current demands of globalism.

The globalism of the British labour movements organised sections is so deeply entrenched and so anti-Greek that they participated in a well organised global charade of labelling the retro fascist pro-EU, pro-Euro Golden Dawn clowns as the new Hitlers of Greece, precisely to prepare the groundwork to stop all resistance to the illegal occupation of Greece, by German imperialism, NATO and Soros sponsored NGO's. But as with all these pseudo globalist attempts they always never take into account the wishes and desires of the local populations.

Despite allegedly setting up Greek solidarity on the words of Theodorakis and Glezos, both of them have been sidelined and never heard of since and in particular Glezos statements on migrants presence in Greece which despite being translated into English would never be re-circulated only because it doesn't fit in with the globalism of the (anti) Greek 'Solidarity' Committee.
But then again why would it. Glezos had a real life fighting fascism not promoting it, having been imprisoned for it not basking in some bureaucrats wage or pension. Recently during the second election for Corbyn at the subsequent Labour Party conference Greek 'solidarity' invited a London based Syriza spokesperson Marina Prentoulis to waffle about the 'debt' and you guessed it…. Fighting austerity! By implementing the 3rd MoU or how the recent privatisations of Ports, Regional airports, Trains, Electricity and Water company are progressing. Syriza like the Heineken advert states reaches the (privatised) parts other (parties eg ND or PASOK) can't. A few days later from this 'dynamic' meeting, Greek pensioners were teargassed for marching…

Pensioners Demo Athens 2nd October 2016

The most right wing Labourite MPs like Clive (I love NATO) Lewis and Tottenham Harvard boy the MP David (I love the EU) Lammy have tried to be associated with… Greek solidarity. One flew to Athens and had his photo taken infront of migrants in Piraeus port looking sad they weren't all housed and fed by the Greek taxpayer whilst the other hanged around Soros boy Varoufakis and Papandreou. Why wouldn't you. It raises your fake anti-austerity profile and your globalist pseudo-humanitarianism

A

ll together now…they all met in 2015 after Papandreou had brought in the IMF in 2010 and inaugurated the economic genocide programme on Greeks leading to 30k suicides and 2m unemployed and 600k emigres.

True to form British 'trade union solidarity' has a (dis)honourable tradition, of supporting quislings of both the 3rd and 4th Reich. As such it should come with a warning like the one on cigarette packets *'Danger to Health'* avoid at all costs as before you know it they may have *displaced and replaced* you and sold you off to the highest bidder.

José de Sousa Saramago, the Portuguese writer and recipient of the 1998 Nobel Prize in Literature. Though written about twenty years ago it remains universally up to date:
"Privatize everything, privatize the sea and the sky, privatize justice and the law, privatize the passing cloud, privatize the dream, especially if it's during the day and open eyed. And finally, for the embellishment of so many privatizations, privatize the State, surrender once and for all their exploitation to private companies through international share offerings. There lies the salvation of the world… and, while you're at it, privatize your whore mothers."
Cadernos de Lanzarote (1994)

VN Gelis

 2015 You cannot get a bigger smile than that from TSSA President. Salivating over 'President' of 2nd International Papandreou Mr economic genocide himself….

Notes

Greek Katyn

https://athens.indymedia.org/post/571888/
http://hansard.millbanksystems.com/commons/1945/jan/31/tuc-delegation

Walter Citrine

https://books.google.co.uk/books?id=99zc3xpMdRAC&pg=PA13
8&lpg=PA138&dq=tuc+walter+citrine+and+greece&source=bl
&ots=kBPxLLd7Ho&sig=viT5U9-
9iVXRj5bvieNmCqWF2Ss&hl=en&sa=X&ved=0ahUKEwiApfS
h7ezOAhXLAcAKHQ02CbUQ6AEILDAH#v=onepage&q=tuc
%20walter%20citrine%20and%20greece&f=false

Red Atrocities ie the Greek Katyn

https://books.google.co.uk/books?id=bKafAAAAIAAJ&pg=PA3
34&lpg=PA334&dq=tuc+walter+citrine+and+greece&source=bl
&ots=XYVpNY2BNy&sig=OWveu4h5568-
ZUcj8kD1liEP_SM&hl=en&sa=X&ved=0ahUKEwiApfSh7ezO
AhXLAcAKHQ02CbUQ6AEILzAI#v=onepage&q=tuc%20walt
er%20citrine%20and%20greece&f=false

http://www.billhunterweb.org.uk/articles/Ernest_Bevin.htm
http://greecesolidarity.org/?p=2945

32billion Euros The cost of Illegal Migrants in Greece

Greeces Foreign Minister Kotzias stated in Germany last year:
For another time in an interview in Suddentsche Kotzias mentioned waves of illegal migrants towards Greece and that if there is a collapse of Greece "Millions of migrants will start coming towards Europe and no one knows what will occur"
Previously the ex-minister of (Illegal) Migration Chrostodopoulou stated in Parapolitika 90.1 that the "aim of the Ministry is to register all those that are present on Greek territory and according to some information we are dealing with 200k people"
How many illegal immigrants are in Greece therefore? That is why Syriza made a big emphasis on open migrant centres. So no one knows who is here and who isn't, who is coming and who is going.

According to Eurostat there were around 900k migrants who lived in 2009 in Greece who represented around 8.1% of the population. In 2011 once again based on official statistics (ie those who stayed somewhere and they remained to be counted) Eurostat stated there are 1.2million people ie 11.1% of the population. In two years we had a 355k people increase.

Now four years later officially and unofficially how many foreigners do we have in Greece?
Why are they coming to our country?

Let us clarify that the lie regurgitated by the 'solidarity' brigade with refugees who want to maintain the NGOs with state money is the myth that illegal migration is linked to war zones or social problems etc. This is pure nonsense.

In the 1990's decade Greece received no migration waves from war zones next to it in Serbia and Bosnia and in our days we aren't really getting a mass wave of Iraquis, or Libyans or even Syrians. Wars aren't directly related to migration waves as noted that in WW2 no Greeks went to Turkey, or French to Spain, or Danish to Sweden etc.

The Korean war provoke mass migration towards Japan, Taiwan etc. and the war in Iran-Iraq in the 1980s decade didn't lead to a mass wave to Europe as the 2006 war in Lebanon didn't provoke one either or the 1967-73 Arab wars with Israel.

As with the economic hemorrhage as expressed in Greece by the numbers of the Bank of Greece we see that Euro12 Billion leaves annually to go abroad by the migrants in Greece.

9 Billion Euros annual cost for loss of taxes and national insurance premiums by the black market in trade which is solely a function of (illegal) migrants.

2.7billion Euros the cost of hospitalisation regarding the uninsured illegal migrants. If one adds the visits to private health care centres that work with the state sector hospitals then this cost increases to 5-6.5 billion Euros (according to the the ex-Health Minister of PASOK Loverdos)

1.5billion Euros is the cost of policing the illegal migrants (these figures were provided by the Ministry of Internal Affairs regarding the extra cost for policing and everyone knows in Greek gaols the overwhelming majority are migrants)
7.5billion Euros is the income from the illegal trade of migrants and if we add the shops that are forced to close the amounts which the state is losing is unbelievable)...

Thus only the direct immediate economic cost of illegal immigration comes to the astronomic amount of 32billion Euros. The indirect economic cost (eg. increased cost of protecting borders) cannot be accounted for.

To have a measure of comparison based once more on ELSTATS (Greek Statistics Agencys) figures the deficit of the budget for 2012 where we were dragged into the 2nd MoU (Memorandum of Understanding) was around 25billion Euros.

By working backwards then the bosses have used the budget deficit to impose vast cuts and the mass importation of labour to extenuate the gaps in the budget so they are getting the best of both worlds massively reduced labour costs and vastly reduced social labour costs turning Greece into the first Asian country in Europe...

(http://www.bankofgreece.gr/Pages/el/Statistics/externalsector/balance/basic.aspx)

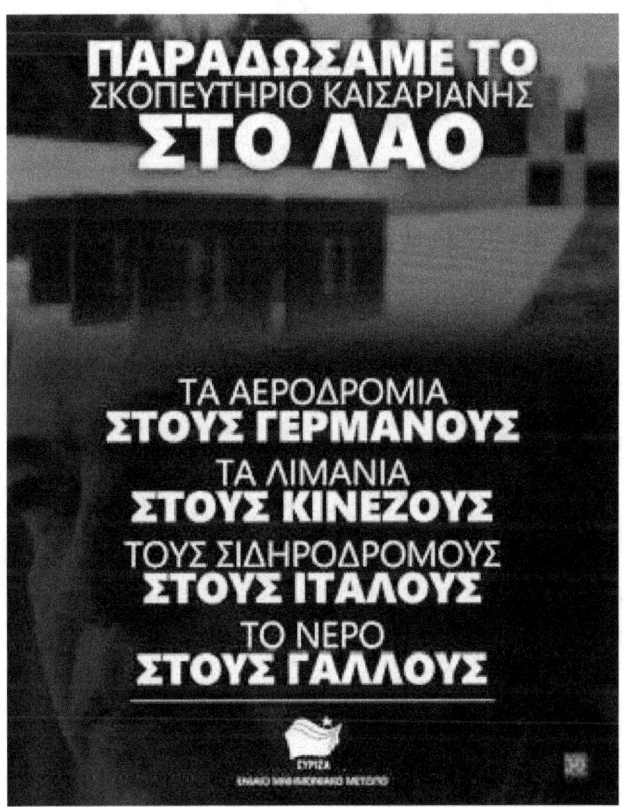

Syriza gave a park to the people (Kessariani where Germans executed many on May Day 1944)
The airports to the Germans
The ports to the Chinese
The railways to the Italians
Water to the French

Articles and Information on Population Substitution in Greece

From the Archives: Politicians Knew what was Going to Happen in Terms of Immigration
GREEK PARLIAMENT

Crossparty Parliamentary Committee
For the study of the demographic problem of the country and the presentation of proposals for their more serious confrontation:

CONCLUSION

Chairman Vasileos Sotiropoulos Argolida MP New Democracy
Vice President Vasileos Geratidisi Thessaloniki B' Constitutency PASOK
Secretary Manolis Drettakis A'District Athens MP, Sinaspismos

Athens
February 1993
The demographic Problem of Greece and the proposals for confronting it
Page 1
In our country which has one of the lowest birth rates the demographic problems takes important national characteristics which **may threaten our national independence and territorial integrity**

Page 2
In the National Committee we also discusses two further questions of Manolis Drettakis (12/279 and 14/2/86) plus proposal of laws of MP's of PASOK 'motivations for the confrontation of the demographic problem of the country' on 7th and 28th November 1991.

Committee Members
1. Σωτηρόπουλος Βασίλειος
2. Ανδρακτάς Παναγιώτης
3. Βαρδαρινός Βασίλειος
4. Γεωργολιός Κωνσταντίνος
5. Κανελλοπούλου Κρινιώ
6. Καραγκούνης Ανδρέας
7. Μπακογιάννη Ντόρα
8. Πάλλη Πετραλιά Φάνη
9. Παπαγεωργόπουλος Ελευθέριος
10. Παπανικολάου Ελευθέριος
11. Τατούλης Πέτρος
12. Χωματάς Ιωάννης
13. Γερανίδης Βασίλειος
14. Κρητικός Παναγιώτης
15. Κωνσταντινίδης Ελευθέριος
16. Μπαλτάς Αλέξανδρος
17. Παπαδόπουλους Βασίλειος
18. Παπαθεμελής Στυλιανός
19. Πάχτας Χρήστος
20. Σμπώκος Ιωάννης
21. **Δρεττάκης Μανόλης (EAP) Sinaspismos**
22. **Κοσιώνης Παναγιώτης (KKE)**

The members of the Committee Andreas Bakoyianni Dora, Palli
Petralia Fani were replaced later, due to them undertaking ministerial
duties from the MP's Theodoro Georgiadis, Dimopoulos Demetrios
and Theodoro Katsiki whilst the position of the recently deceased in
July 1992 Papadopoulos Vasiliou was received by the MP Skoulakis
Emmanuel.

Pg 15
The repatriation of political refugees and the mass arrival of
compatriots (Pontion and Northern Ipirus) with a correct political
intervention will have positive results. The state should help them
base themselves and work, not only in the city centres but also in the
agricultural and semi-agricultural areas and to provide a new

dynamic to many agricultural areas primarily in Northern Greece. The common cultural roots and Orthodoxy would help them adapt and assimilate into Greek society.

Particular attention should be place by the entrance and employment of tens of thousands of foreign immigrants legal (but mostly illegal) arrive in our country in the two last decades. Whilst the percentage of unemployment is around 8% in many sectors there is a lack of labour hands which has been covered primarily by foreign illegal immigrants.

With the illegal arrival of immigrants – mostly muslims from Afro-asian countries, Greece is being transformed into an area of receiving immigrants which creates social economic problems (conflicts in the labour market, increase in tax evasion with many consequences in the national insurance coffers, an increase in criminality, movement of drugs etc.) and they can't adapt to Greek society due to their totally different culture of Islam, which isn't simply a religion but a way of life

Page 24
-The distance from the traditional forms of life and the arrival of events of social decay with the undermining of the principles of marriage, family life and children have a significant influence on the demographic issues.

-The highest form of individualism, the weakening of morality, drugs, AIDS and generally the social undermining and the world insecurity influence negatively the demographic problem.
-Future population development of Greece

Page 27
If the demographic indicators aren't improved and the same indicators of birth in 1990 (1.4 roughly average children per woman) and if they don't develop significant events (war, immigration) then the total population of the country in 2015 will be reduced by

500,000 people from today's numbers. The increase in these demographic indicators which started in 1985 creates severe problems of population in our country. The empty spaces which are created cover by a larger part from Pontius and Nothern Ipirus but also from muslims from Asia and Africa and from others who illegally enter Greece (and remain with a variety of fake conditions adding new problems)
Social economic factors which influence the demographic problem
Demographic consequences

Page 30
Our country with the dramatic reduction of births in the last decade has the possibility of big dangers (which are being intensified due to the geographical position and the lack of cooperative peoples);
-The reduction of births in the 1980's decade whereby the indicators fell from 2.09 children per woman to 1.4 in 1990, **threatens quite severely the re-birth and continuation of our Greek race.**
-The demographic gaps which are created in various geographic areas (Aegean islands, Ionian etc) have as the danger to be occupied by immigrants (mostly Muslims) with sever endless consequences.
-In the armed forces we will create serious problems with the lack of numbers of those in the armed forces.

Page 31
If for the re-birth of our labour dynamic and generally the course of our economy and our social security we are based on the immigrants from Asia and Africa very soon we will have serious problems of social and national

Aims of Greek Demographic Politics - Proposals

Page 36
-To emphasise at every available moment Greek tradition and religious feeling (practically with proposals of the Church)

Administrative measures

Page 40

-The illegal and easy entrance of illegal immigrants from countries of Asia and Africa either directly or via other countries of the EU must be observed closely for many socialeconomic and national reasons. There must be severe control regarding the legality of the entrance in our country and the legal presence and employment.

Athens 10th February 1993

2m Greeks unemployed with no access to housing benefit or dole money. Syrizas Thessaloniki's programme was abandoned for the 3rd bailout and Merkels importation of migrants.

Greece Under the Path of the New World Order 1999

"Left-wingers", liberals and neo-liberals of every shade, are proposing a "humanist"-moralist approach to the issue of illegal immigration. This would perhaps be an interesting proposition, if the goal of socialism were to offer consolation to the dwellers of the valley of tears, promising heaven as a reward for their stoic patience. But this is the purpose of the Christian religion. The purpose of socialism is obviously to teach the poor, not to endure the miseries of life, but to change it. For this, they need to know the causes and the nature of social problems, like that of illegal immigration. Moralist approaches lead to contradictions and dead ends, and, as everybody knows, are often used as an alibi for the greatest crimes. It is in the name of moral principles and humanitarianism that the peoples of Iraq and Yugoslavia are being slaughtered, while NATO has turned these principles into an official alibi for its new strategy. For those reasons, we must be wary of moralists. In dealing with them, we should - to say the least - hold on tightly to our wallet. Illegal immigration is not an exclusively Greek phenomenon. Yet Greece has received an enormous number of illegal immigrants, out of any proportion with its size and resources. This fact is not unrelated to the infamous Schengen agreement, which defines

Greece as a country responsible for the initial reception of refugees - a door open for the whole of Europe. As a result, we have a dramatic rise of unemployment, and the modification of its nature. It is no longer conjunctural. It has become synonymous with the social marginalisation of the Greek worker. The destruction of his social conquests and rights. Of course the government and some of its fervent "enemies" are denying all this. But working people know very well what is happening, as they are the ones called upon to pay the bill.

Our fathers of the nation, first of all, maintain that illegal immigration has no significant impact on employment. Foreigners are employed in menial and dirty jobs that the well-nourished Greek worker would not deign to do. We read in the press recently that Spanish workers have equally aristocratic inclinations. That's why "their" government decided to bring within the next few years one million Romanians and Moroccans, to do the jobs that the locals ostensibly snub. It is to be noted that Spain has now officially more than 20% unemployment.

Here is what a father of the nation, a member of the great "anti-racist" family, has to say:
"All these conditions have created, as you have seen in the poll, in a great section of the population, the impression that foreigners are the cause of all the tribulations and disasters. This is perhaps the easy solution. We, who are always the same, are never at fault. It is always the others who are responsible. The others - who ?
The foreigners: dark-skinned, black-skinned, yellow-skinned, sometimes even fair-skinned - because of Germany. But the truth is usually different. The truth is that foreigners don't steal the jobs of our kids, instead they do the jobs that we don't deign to do, because we consider them to be below our social standing. Painters, garbage-collectors, housemaids, road construction workers, gardeners, agricultural workers."
Thus spake Yakoumatos, an MP of the New Democracy party, speaking in a meeting under the subject "racism and xenophobia - initiatives for the legalisation of foreign workers", organized by the

PASOK-controlled Athens Labour Council. A representative case of a political con-man - "anti-racist". He impulsively admits his class racism - the only racism that really exists. The honest jobs, that allow the drones of his clan the means to live in luxury, he considers below human dignity!

Following close, the groups of extra-parliamentary "left" - this substitute of western social-democracy, adapted to Greek conditions. They do nothing more than to serve the official sophistries, reheated. In one of the journals of this political milieu, we read:
"Most of the jobs occupied nowadays by foreigners, have been abandoned by Greek workers for years. Housemaids, gardeners, scrubwomen, nurses for the elderly ... land workers and shepherds, the rest in hard menial jobs, construction, quarries, and sweatshops" All these unrewarding and heavy jobs have been abandoned by Greek workers "for years"! It seems we didn't even produce stones. We used to import them!...

Further down, the columnist adds in petulant tone:
"Let all those ridiculous racists tell us ... the thousands of Ukrainian, Bulgarian and Russian women that are in the hands of ruthless procurers, whose job are they taking? (newspaper "Ergatiki Exousia" ["workers' power"]).

Is it true that the indigenous worker is snobby, that he considers some jobs to be below his dignity, or is there some other (well-known) secret? The chairman of the parliament, Apostolos Kaklamanis, spoke at least with more squareness to the journalist Yiannis Diakogiannis: "Cheap labour, not only for farm work, but also for the industry and the construction sector, has often been the ulterior unavowed aim".

A former cadre and minister of New Democracy, industrialist well known for his cynicism, Stefanos Manos is even more precise: "immigrants are god's blessing, we need them because they work with one third of a Greek worker's wages, because they cannot go on strike, they cannot form unions, they can do nothing".
So the foreigner is not for some "undignified" jobs, he is for every job, as long as he does it with one third of the wage, with no other rights, with the head bowed.

A natural law?

Another fairy tale widely circulated, presents the mass influx of illegal immigrants as a physical law: Wars and famines create inevitable waves of "economic refugees", that the state is unable to contain. It does its best. It organizes bodies of border guards, it buys speedboats, trains "Rambos" - all without result. Thus, since we can't prevent the phenomenon, we have to live with it.

It is of course a fact that there is misery in the world and that wars take place. But humanity has seen much worse, without these results. If capitalism didn't use the disasters it produces as an alibi for its policies, if the state did indeed want to stop illegal immigration, there are more simple, economic, civilized and effective ways to do it. Even the gentlemen of the extraparliamentary "left" can realize that the problem could easily be solved if the government prohibited employers to employ persons who are not legally in the country. A few heavy fines would discourage potential violators. There is no need for police dogs, live fences or machine guns. But the government doesn't want. It too is animated by "humanitarian" feelings...

Many are those who feign ignorance, but in fact everyone knows that foreigners are here not in spite of the authorities, but with their will, as cheap labour. As far as citizens of countries of the former "socialist" camp are concerned, there are also other expediences, purely political ones. Especially for Albanians. This doesn't mean that economic reasons lose their importance.

T. Krikellis, former MP of the New Democracy party, in a TV show hosted by a well-known journalist revealed that "In a meeting at the ministry of public order that took place in 1994-95 in the presence of three experts from the ministry of foreign affairs, the issue was raised of supporting Albania by showing tolerance in the issue of hundreds of thousands of illegal immigrants, because the neighboring country had made a definitive turn to the west and should be supported in this course."

Mr. Krikellis pointed out that there had been a related "message" originating from the U.S., addressed primarily to the New Democracy Party as the PASOK government had already accepted the propositions. In other words the U.S. want to pay their agents, in their efforts to resurrect capitalism in Albania (and elsewhere), not at their own expense, but with the wages of the Greek worker. Who doesn't know that the Greek consulate in Korytsa hands out heaps of visas? One of those suspect characters who have proclaimed themselves "representatives" of Albanian workers, speaks of 300 visas daily, in parallel with illegal entry. Foreigners not only enter with the indirect approval of the authorities, but are also subject to a selection process. No other country in the Balkans has suffered as many tribulations as Serbia. Besides the war, its people are tormented by an inhuman and long-lasting embargo. Still, there are no Serb illegal immigrants in Greece! You see, in Serbia they don't have their own people, Berisha or Maiko, to support. Instead there is the "last communist dictator", Milosevic, whom they want to overturn.

There are also many Kurds - but what kind of Kurds? Not the kind that are being persecuted by Turkish generals in South-East Turkey. These are few and, when they aren't being delivered to Ankara, they are getting shut in the camp at Lavrio. But we have many from the other kind, those who are under U.N. protection in the unofficially occupied Northern Iraq. Because there, there are also lackeys of the west, whom they want to support. Messrs Barzani and Talabani, who are being used against the other enemy of freedom, the "nationalist dictator Saddam Hussein"!

Of course all this doesn't look like a "law of nature", with which we 'll have to live, as we are being assured. But then, whatever serves the interests of capitalism is nature, whereas what protects the interests of workingmen is against nature.
Some will say: "but aren't immigrants workingmen"?
They are indeed, and the Greek working class has nothing to divide with them. But it has with the governments that are using the misery and pain of other peoples against it, embellishing at the same time their dirty policy with "humanitarian" pretexts.

This is a permanent tactic of imperialism. After WW II the U.S. took advantage of the persecutions and torments to which Jews had been submitted in Europe to gain the acceptance or the tolerance of public opinion to the uprooting of Arabs from Palestine and the creation of a "Jewish" state. They rounded up the more miserable Jews with the promise of giving them a motherland and used them in fact as cops of the region in order to continue stealing Arab oil.

Globalisation and Illegal Immigration

The phenomenon of illegal immigration has not occurred at a random moment. We live in the days of so-called neo-liberalism and of economic globalisation. In Europe, as far as tariffs are concerned, borders have been abolished years ago. Similar free trade zones have been established in North America and East Asia, while via the GATT (now the WTO) tariffs are gradually being abolished worldwide. At the same time, protectionist currency controls are being abolished and the movement of capitals is becoming totally deregulated. Under these conditions, it would be not only logically but also practically inconsistent not to release controls on the movement of the most important economic factor, namely of labour. So let them leave aside the sophistries about natural laws and snobby Greek workers.

The inconsistency of restrictions in the labour market has often been pointed out in the press of the extraparliamentary "left". In one of them, the columnist Th. Koutsoumbos writes on this issue: "Contrary to what was the case in the 30s, today "globalisation" knocks down the economic borders. Commodities move freely, and in unconceivable quantities due to the use of modern technology. (Only for the movement of people are "walls of shame" being erected (Germany), with electric fences and police controls...)" ("Nea prooptiki" ["new perspective"])

We don't know what happens with other categories of people, whether some countries welcome tourists and businessmen with "electric fences", but illegal immigrants are certainly passing borders (those remaining "walls of shame"!) in unconceivable quantities, and without the need to use modern technology!.. The fact that this is not being done in a legal way is simply a matter of political expediency. Governments don't want to take upon their shoulders the responsibility and the resulting political cost. They prefer to shovel them to the immigrants themselves and to natural laws. On the other hand, it is also a matter of price: Just as illegally imported cigarettes are cheap for smokers, illegal workers are cheap for the employers. Being illegal they are literally at their mercy.

The gentlemen of the extra-parliamentary "left", although most of them deny the very existence of globalisation and brand it a myth (Th. Koutsoumbos is still using quotation marks for it), at the same time become its proponents and apologists. Their slogan "borders open for the working class" is nothing but a formulation embellished with left-wing verbalism for the liberation of labour market. Not only do they recognize as progress the fall of the "walls of shame", but they outbid for the completion of the process. And how could one be for the liberation of the labour market without also being for the liberation of the market in general and thus for the globalisation - and the converse?

Yet gentlemen, you cannot be for economic globalisation, under capitalism, without at the same time supporting political globalisation, that is the abolition of political borders (the "walls of shame") and consequently of the national state. Without in essence pleading for a global imperialist power, that is for the new world order. In short without being, in practice, pitiful western-style social democrats, totally aligned in all important issues with imperialism and the Simitis government. The fact is not accidental that the extraparliamentary "left" had a despicable position on the question of Yugoslavia. That some groups openly supported the NATO bombings, while others did the same implicitly, by regurgitating the cadaveric literature of the CNN in order to persuade us that the "nationalist" and "genocidal" Serbs got what they deserved!
The liberalization of markets is a necessary adaptation of world capitalist economy to the phenomenon of the multinational companies, which initially appeared after the WWII and have seen a tremendous growth in the last two decades. The merger of capitals across borders and irrespective of their national origin is objectively in contradiction with the economic and political existence of the

national state. In this sense, abolishing the national restrictions to world trade becomes an inescapable necessity for capitalism. Still this has nothing to do with the much-advertised restoration of conditions of healthy competition. Quite the opposite is true, as protectionism used to dampen competitive inequalities. Now the law of the jungle is being imposed everywhere. In the market of commodities, as well as in the labour market. The globalisation of markets is the means for the conquest of the world economy and the abolition of labour rights by the big beasts, the multinational monopolies.

In the past, and even more so today, under conditions of a deregulated economy, competition forces multinationals to transfer more and more of their economic activities to regions that can ensure them competitive advantages. Wherever there are limitless supplies of "black labour", tax exemption and unaccountability. Particularly to South-East Asia, where wages are up to 45 times lower than the equivalent western-European ones. Also to countries of the former eastern bloc, and wherever else attractive opportunities for cost-squeezing present themselves.

This is a totally new phenomenon, even if the eyeless of the extra-parliamentary "left" fail to see it. They have their reasons for this. In the past, a North-American company would invest in Brazil in order to conquer more easily the Brazilian market. Nowadays, the target is the North-American and the world market. This leads to loss of jobs for the North-American working class. The same happens to each and every country where the hunt for profit drives capital to migrate.

But what happens to capital that, for various reasons, remains invested in the traditional industrial centers and their immediate satellites? It is obvious that in order to survive, in order to avoid massive bankruptcies in Europe and North America, this capital must make use in the metropolitan centers of exactly the same advantages that are available in the periphery. If Muhammad can't go to the mountain, the mountain must go to Muhammad. Governments take it upon themselves to import in camouflaged ways "black labour" into Europe and North America, which means at the same time importing third-world standards of living for local workingmen. This is the real reason and the aims of the deluge of immigration that causes a stir in the working class, in Greece and elsewhere.

The well-paid strata of labour aristocracy, inside which most of the so-called anti-racists find their supporters, believe they are safe. But the unemployment and poverty of masses causes the European and North-American markets, the two largest in the world, to shrink. It is not enough to produce cheap, one must also have customers to sell the products to. What seemed to be a way out for capitalism reproduces the old problems in a more acute form, worsening the commercial crisis. Competition becomes more acute and squeezing costs even further becomes a matter of life and death. The capital seeks even cheaper labour while at the same time putting in the crosswire of austerity new strata of society.

Computers and communications nowadays, among other things, are unifying the labour market. Since the borders are open everyone can, via the Internet, knock a door in any other place, especially when he is being prompted to do so. This has started happening in Greece too. "Imagine - tells us an MIT professor (with the belief that this does not concern him personally) in a Scientific American article - a doctor in Sri Lanka who makes $20 a day, administering health care to homeless people in Boston via a kiosk, equipped with a remote video and medical instrument connection and staffed by a nurse. The service might cost $5 a visit, and although not perfect, it would be superior to no health care at all."

Computer-related jobs are daily gaining larger percentages in the labour market, especially among younger people. Here too, in order to offer his services, one doesn't have to go to Boston. He can do it from home! "imagine - says the same professor - 1,000 accountants from Beijing doing accounting services for General Motors at $1 per hour."

Why "imagine" it? It is already happening. Swissair, for example, has already transported a large part of its accounting services to India.

All this, seen from the point of view of progress and technology, seems seductive. But on the basis of capitalism, it means the globalisation of Sri Lanka living standards.

Immigration during the 50s and illegal immigration.
Many are those who like to compare the current illegal immigration with the immigration of Greek and other South-European workers to the North of Europe, especially W. Germany, in the 50s. In this way, they want to silence the working class.

Why does it complain? And with what right? Didn't it immigrate en masse to Germany? But, what connection is there between that immigration and the one of today? Is really the difference that hard to see?

Then the capitalist world was passing a phase of great expansion, which created increased needs in working hands. Without these hands, what was called "the German miracle" would not have existed, nor would the equally impressive economic and cultural flourishing of the other industrial centers. Conditions of full employment and increased demand for workforce, dictated the establishment of bilateral state agreements under which specified numbers of workers were dispatched to specific industries. This was a legal and coordinated immigration. Immigrants were filling real and great needs in the labour market. They had the same wages and enjoyed the same rights with their local coworkers. The same labour legislation applied to all.

What is happening now? Capitalism is deep in the worst crisis of its history. Workforce requirements are continuously shrinking. Millions of workers are officially unemployed in Europe, and even more are unofficially so. In Greece, out of one and a half industrial workers, before the big immigration wave started, hundreds of thousands were already unemployed, "employed", "semi-employed", "employable". Illegal immigrants, who are another one and a half million, didn't come in order to fill some big or small needs for labour hands. The well-oiled door was opened for them in the middle of the night in order for them to elongate to an unbelievable degree the columns of the unemployed. In order for the battles for jobs to become even tougher, with full conscience that for the local labourer they would be lost in advance.

What should we say and what should the position of the left be, if Greek workers had gone to Germany, not under the conditions that they did, but in order to work with one fourth the wage of the German worker, without social security and working hours, because they could afford it and this was the only way they could find work, taking in this way the position of the German worker? Would the left approve of this? And would the German worker be a racist if he denounced "his" government for this under-the-belt hit? Or would those who blamed him be imbeciles, if not agents of the German capital?

In such a situation, the Greek immigrant would be no different than a scab that, forced by unemployment and misery, and because of his backward class consciousness, accepts work with a lower wage in order to take the place of his brother.

Foreigners, due to currency differences in their countries of origin, due to their way of life, due to the fact that they accept to live without modern amenities, to be packed 4 or 5 to a room, to live in a sweatshop attic, in a shed of a peasant, eating the food prepared by the wife of the peasant, in short due to their limited needs, can settle for a fraction of the average wage, on which the Greek worker couldn't possibly subsist and which he therefore couldn't possibly accept. Thus the modern immigrant, the illegal immigrant, doesn't take his place alongside the local worker. He replaces him. The indigenous worker doesn't just become unemployed. He loses all prospects of ever being reintegrated into the production process, especially when he isn't young and specialized.

Even if the Greek worker can settle, even temporarily, for the employment conditions of the foreigner, even if he gives up his habits and his way of life, with the hope of better days in the future, the employer will prefer the "illegal" immigrant, to the Greek who may in the future take him to a court to ask for his legal rights.

No wonder we are reading in the press news like this one:
Miracles don't happen nowadays in the Duomo. Executions do,
however, even if they are symbolic, like the execution of the
"Napolitan unemployed". The cathedral was occupied last week by
hundreds of unemployed people. The Italian unemployed then
marched to the embassy of Gabon. "We want an African
citizenship", they said, "because those from outside the [European]
community find work easier than the locals. We are not racists. We
are just demanding equal opportunities with the Africans"...In the
troubled archipelago of the unemployed of Southern Italy, a war is
looming among the poor. ("Ta Nea", 2/24/1999)

The modern world has never known a similar situation. The
governmental staffs of the new world order have managed, acting
under the sign of "humanitarianism" and with the good services of
the "left", to return society to an era lost in the depths of history. The
position of an indigenous worker nowadays can only be compared to
that of the free Italian worker under the Roman Empire in the epoch
of its decline. Then the massive use of slave labor made a pariah of
him - permanently unemployed, a parasite of society, who eked a
meager living thanks to the municipal mess and the state wheat
allowances.

But the foreign competitor of the indigenous worker also resembles a
slave more than a free immigrant worker. Is it by chance that his
transportation to Europe has been called slave trade? From the point
of view of his compensation and rights, his employment is nothing
but a modernized form of slavery. Moreover, this archaic
employment regime is not restricted to himself, who after all has
chosen it. Its scope is inevitably being extended to the entire working
class. That's exactly the point: using immigrants as a battering-ram
in order to eliminate labor rights that have been gained with
struggles over the course of an entire century.
Those who are now speaking of the equalization of wages between
foreigners and Greek workers, in order to eliminate unfair
competition for jobs, are mocking the Greek workers and the
foreigners alike. The equalization has already been accomplished.

Not because foreigners are now being treated as Greeks, but because Greek workers, in their overwhelming majority, are being treated as immigrants, and this only if they are lucky enough. How could things be different? When there is this inconceivable super-supply of workforce, wages are necessarily equalized at the lowest limit.

If some "leftists" don't have ulterior motives, and are just contemplating the Greek workers as a salvage vessel, they should at least remember the coast guard regulations: a boat designed to carry fifty persons, can take a couple more. But when another fifty climb in, and others are constantly being coming, the result is not that a hundred will be saved - they will all go to the bottom!

The union issue nowadays

"No", replies the "left" almost without exception, "calm down - Things can be fixed with united trade union struggle!"

Workers who hear this will smile indulgently. They know first of all how temporary and fragile are the gains of any trade union struggle. That in the end, the law of supply and demand is imposed on wages too.

Of course, for the union bureaucracy, trade union struggles are everything. But if things were indeed thus, if trade union struggle was not in the end, in spite of its tremendous importance, ineffective, the working class would not be drawn into politics, it would have no reasons to build its own party, aiming at the abolition of wage slavery itself.

But why not organize common struggles that could for a while (who knows how long?) improve the situation? For the aforementioned Th. Koutsoumbos, this is a panacea. In the journal "nea prooptiki", under the heading "racism in the epoch of globalisation", exposing a position almost the entire left shares, he lays on the shoulders of the Greek working class the duty to liberate every immigrant from the bosses' super exploitation!

"But", he writes, "the working class can't liberate itself without liberating every exploited section of society, without first liberating the Albanian workers and other immigrant 'foreigners' from the wild super exploitation of the bosses"

Koutsoumbos has read somewhere that Marx and Engels were saying something similar about English workers, and he believes he can apply the same formula to the Greek workers, banking on their prestige. Marx was speaking about the word-ruler England. Almost the entire world was its colony. It had the world industrial monopoly. From this position, its bourgeoisie was realizing enormous profits. Thanks to them, it could buy out important layers of workers who, according to Engels, "were enjoying in a state of bliss along with them (the bourgeois) the colonial monopoly of England and its monopoly of the world market". Only when England would lose its colonies, the monopoly of the world market, and the English workers their privileges, could they start to think and act in a revolutionary way.

As far as we know, Albania, Pakistan, the Ukraine etc. are not colonies of Greece. The Greek working class is not "enjoying in a state of bliss" the crumbs falling from the exploitation of foreigners. Other layers are enjoying them, and, by a devilish coincidence, they are all "anti-racists" and "anti-nationalists". The only thing the working class collects is misery. And, of course, it can't liberate foreigners for the simple reason that their exploitation goes on against its will, and their liberation goes contrary to theirs.
In reality, every working class can only be liberated in its own country, against its own ruling class. Fighting behind the "walls of shame", which can only truly fall in this way, and in any case not upon the heads of working people.

Beyond this, the integration of foreigners in the union movement presupposes their social integration. This last is not a technical issue. Foreigners must first acquire common experiences and the feeling of a common nation, which replaces the solidarity of ghettos. They must become indigenous, native. And this is not simple, not easy, and often not possible at all. But even when it is possible, it takes a long time, which doesn't pass easily and agreeably for everyone. First of all, a precondition for a common union organization is a common program of demands. The wage of the worker has an upper and a lower limit. The upper limit is determined by competition between capitalists. The lower, by the vital needs of workers.

Nobody accepts a wage lower than what he needs in order to survive. One prefers to die slumbering than working. Competition is not absent within the working class. But at this point it gets surpassed, and the common organization of workers becomes possible, in order to demand a common minimum wage which will assure them a decent life.

Certainly the equality of needs is only relative. Needs differ from worker to worker. That's why there are some relative measures in the minimum wage, which bridge the differences. But how can differences of the nature and size that separate the wage that the native worker can accept on one side, and the categories of immigrant workers on the other, be bridged? What will the unions demand?

It is the impossibility of fielding commonly accepted demands that explains the total failure of unions to organize immigrants, not the "racism" of labour bureaucracy, as the "sole consistent", ostensibly, "anti-racists" of the extra-parliamentary "left" conveniently assert. As a result, instead of organizing foreigners, the unions see even the Greek workers desert them, being unemployed or, at best, a small minority at the workplace. The only possible form of organization for foreigners is the solidarity of the ghetto. Of the many ghettoes, in fact. And this has worked in certain instances, for example in the brief strike of Albanians in Almyros. Thus the union movement has been all but extinguished in the private sector and, to the extent that the public sector becomes privatized and subcontracting becomes more common, the dissolution is spreading there too. And if we take into account the fact that unions are the antechamber for the political organization of the proletariat, it is no wonder that the "left" becomes depilated from working-class elements and becomes a current of petty-bourgeois intelligentsia. Unless this state is overturned, the spectre of a dismal future is visible in the horizon. The proletariat risks being reduced, from an organized class and a springboard for the development of society as a whole, to an amorphous, tame, wretched mass, with no present and no hope for the future.

The exploitation of "black labour" in the periphery, the creation in Europe and America of a workingman of "new type", with a humiliating wage, without working hours, who is not protected by any law and is at the mercy of the master, lacking any potential for resistance, have permitted the multinational monopolies to realize surplus profits, and for capitalism to restabilise the world monetary system.

A decade ago it would seem unbelievable that inflation in Greece would reach 1.8% annually, with a tendency to go even lower. Based on the new slavery and the barbaric regime the Simitis government has brought to the labour market, it can now brag that it has ascertained the ticket for entry into the EMU (if this land is finally discovered). Bourgeois and petty-bourgeois have found free labourers, free servants, gardeners, nannies, nurses. Pimps have found plenty of whores. Real estate owners found hefty, untaxed rents, for stables at which even oxen would look down with contempt a few years ago. Gangs of slavers found the new El Dorado. And, in this happy conjuncture, the stock exchange of course rises. While the working masses suffer, new parasitic sectors and new privileged strata are being created.

So how could those who rule us not care for those "human rights", how could they not protect this "internationalism" those who collect the crumbs falling from the overflowing table of the rich?
Only the working class is being directly injured and overpowered, that's why it is the only one that grudges and reacts to the insistence of the ruling class and its foreign patrons, to defeat it, transforming into their "multicultural" manor the country, and the whole of Europe. We have never before seen such "internationalist" fervor from the imperialists. Reproaches for "racism" are being addressed to the working class only, and only from those who have nothing to fear, or at least who think so. Even though extraparliamentarians are thundering against the insignificant "Hrisi Avgi" group and the "Greek patriots". Who dares not beat the donkey, beats the packsaddle!

Marx on the competition between English and Irish workers

The English workers who, as Engels said, were "enjoying in bliss" their share from the profits of theirs bourgeoisie's monopoly, were a privileged minority. The great mass was living in poverty. Marx, as a member of the General Council of the international, concerned himself especially with the antagonism that existed between the poor layers of English workers and the Irish workers, whom the bourgeoisie forced to migrate to England as cheap labour.

Marx in a letter to Meyer and Vogt (April 9, 1870) informs them of his related propositions to the General Council. The paper "Ergatiki Exousia" ["workers' power"], using the method of the guillotine, by pasting together two sentences from two different paragraphs, transforms the revolutionary materialist Marx into a mainstream liberal petty-bourgeois. We believe that the reader stands to gain by reading the entire excerpt that refers to the Irish question, which we cite here, underlining the sentences used by the "Ergatiki Exousia".

I had intended to submit further RESOLUTIONS on the necessary transformation of the present Union (i.e., enslavement of Ireland) IN A FREE AND EQUAL FEDERATION WITH GREAT BRITAIN. Further progress on this matter has been temporarily suspended AS FAR AS PUBLIC RESOLUTIONS GO because of my enforced absence from the General Council. No other member of it has enough knowledge of Irish affairs or sufficient prestige with the English members of the General Council to be able to replace me on this matter.

Time has not passed uselessly, however, and I would ask you to pay particular attention to the following:

After studying the Irish question for years I have come to the conclusion that the decisive blow against the ruling classes In England (and this is decisive for the workers' movement ALL OVER THE WORLD) cannot be struck in England, but only in Ireland.

On 1 January 1870 the General Council issued a secret circular, written by me in French - {for repercussions in England, only the French papers are important, not the German} - on the relationship of the Irish national struggle to the emancipation of the working class, and thus on the attitude the International Association must take towards the Irish question.

Here I give you, quite shortly, the salient points. Ireland is the BULWARK of the English landed aristocracy. The exploitation of this country is not simply one of the main sources of their material wealth; it is their greatest moral power. They represent, IN FACT, the domination of England over Ireland. Ireland is, thus, the grand moyen by which the English aristocracy maintains its domination in England itself.

On the other hand: if the English army and police were withdrawn from Ireland tomorrow, you would immediately have AN AGRARIAN REVOLUTION IN IRELAND. But the overthrow of the English aristocracy in Ireland would entail, and would lead immediately to, its overthrow in England. This would bring about the prerequisites for the proletarian revolution in England. In Ireland, the land question has, so far, been the exclusive form of the social question; it is a question of existence, a question of life or death for the immense majority of the Irish people; at the same time, it is inseparable from the national question: because of this, destruction of the English landed aristocracy is an infinitely easier operation In Ireland than in England itself - quite apart from the more passionate and more revolutionary character of the Irish than the English.
As for the English bourgeoisie, it has, d' abord, a common interest with the English aristocracy in turning Ireland into simple pastureland to provide meat and wool at the cheapest possible price FOR THE ENGLISH MARKET. It has the same interest in reducing the Irish population to such a low level, through EVICTION and forced emigration, that English capital (leasehold capital) can function with SECURITY in that country. It has the same interest IN CLEARING THE ESTATE OF IRELAND as it had IN THE CLEARING OP THE AGRICULTURAL DISTRICTS OP ENGLAND and SCOTLAND. The £6,000-10,000 ABSENTEE and other Irish revenues that at present flow annually to London must also be taken into account.

But the English bourgeoisie also has much more important interests in the present Irish economy. As a result of the steadily - increasing concentration of leaseholding, Ireland is steadily supplying its SURPLUS for the English LABOUR MARKET, and thus forcing down the WAGES and material and moral position of the ENGLISH WORKING CLASS.

And most important of all! All industrial and commercial centres in England now have a working class divided into two hostile camps, English PROLETARIANS and Irish PROLETARIANS. The ordinary English worker hates the Irish worker as a competitor who forces down the STANDARD OF LIFE. In relation to the Irish worker, he feels himself to be a member of the ruling nation and, therefore, makes himself a tool of his aristocrats and capitalists against Ireland, thus strengthening their domination over himself. He harbours religious, social and national prejudices against him. His attitude towards him is roughly that of the POOR WHITES to the NIGGERS in the former slave states of the American Union. The Irishman PAYS HIM BACK WITH INTEREST IN HIS OWN MONEY. He sees in the English worker both the accomplice and the stupid tool of English rule in Ireland.

This antagonism is kept artificially alive and intensified by the press, the pulpit, the comic papers, in short by all the means at the disposal of the ruling class. This antagonism is the secret of the English working class's impotence, despite its organisation. It is the secret of the maintenance of power by the capitalist class. And the latter is fully aware of this.

But the evil does not end here. It rolls across the ocean. The antagonism between English and Irish is the secret basis of the conflict between the UNITED STATES and England. It renders any serious and honest cooperation impossible between the working classes of the two countries. It enables the governments of the two countries, whenever they think fit, to blunt the edge of social conflict by MUTUAL BULLYING and, IN CASE OF NEED, by war between the two countries.
England, as the metropolis of capital, as the power that has hitherto ruled the world market, is for the present the most important country for the workers' revolution and, in addition, the only country where the material conditions for this revolution have developed to a certain state of maturity. Thus, to hasten the social revolution in England is the most important object of the International Working Men's Association. The sole means of doing so is to make Ireland

independent. It is, therefore, the task of the 'INTERNATIONAL' to bring the conflict between England and Ireland to the forefront everywhere, and to side with Ireland publicly everywhere. The special task of the Central Council in London is to awaken the consciousness of the English working class that, for them, the national emancipation of Ireland is not a QUESTION OF ABSTRACT JUSTICE OR HUMANITARIAN SENTIMENT, but THE FIRST CONDITION OF THEIR OWN SOCIAL EMANCIPATION.

As we see, Marx doesn't have recourse to the pseudo-theory of "racism" in order to explain the existence of two hostile camps inside the working class. He looks for the cause, not in the ideas of people, but in the social conditions that determine them in order to finally point out, as the only solution, the revolutionary change of these conditions. The priestly idea that the problem could be resolved with admonitions about the fraternity of all races doesn't even cross his mind. He sets off the material root of the division that was none other than the English occupation of Ireland. This is the ABC of his materialist method, of which many declare themselves to be supporters and experts - but this is not enough to transform into Marxism their various subjective conclusions.

Marx doesn't try to persuade English workers to accept certain fait accomplit, he doesn't attempt to surpass the division by throwing bridges of morality. Contrarily, he draws attention to the causes of the problem and calls on them to support the revolutionary struggle for the independence of Ireland. Thus would open the road for the economic and cultural development of Ireland, its workers wouldn't be forcibly uprooted in order to be used as cheap labour by the English bourgeoisie. The last would lose its ability to sustain a labour aristocracy and to control by this means the movement of the proletariat. Contrarily to Marx, our anti-racists do nothing else than to muddle the waters and to cover the real causes of the current divisions in the camp of workers. For them, responsible is "racism". There is no other issue toward which they would have to take position and fight!..

Of course Marx is dealing with different questions of a different era. It is impossible to mechanically transplant all his propositions to the present, and especially to Greece. To say the least, the countries of origin of the nations that live and work here are in no way Greek colonies or subordinate partners in a federation, as Ireland was. No part of the Greek working class is gaining from their colonial exploitation. What is timeless in Marx is his materialist historic method. And according to it, there is no possibility of a serious, stable and frank cooperation of the Greek working class with immigrant workers as long as they are being used to degrade the wages, the living standards and to destroy the social rights it had gained with struggles. And, whether we like it or not, immigrant workers, as long as they are in Greece in this massive and limitless scale, can only fulfill this role, willingly or not.

As a result, the Greek capitalists, thanks to the cheap wage of the foreigners, are able to stabilize their economy, to demoralize the Greek working class, dissolve its political and union movement, extending in this way the life of capitalism itself. At the same time, extending the life of restorationist mafias in the countries of the former "eastern bloc", financing their counterrevolutionary regimes with the wage of the Greek worker. Of course, the same is being done by the ensemble of the ruling classes in the countries that compose NATO.

Thus illegal immigration, this modern-day slave trade, of which the "left" leaderships are becoming, openly or in a veiled way, apologists and defenders, is nowadays the greatest obstacle to the social revolution, in the East and the West alike.

The scarecrow of racism
The state with its plans creates the conditions of the nationalist antagonisms and at the same time propagates the myth of 'racism' so as to strangle under the shadow of this scarecrow every thought and attempt of the working class to fight against its social alienation, to

fight against the absolutism of the new world order. We should not be amazed if tomorrow any protest against illegal immigration and the multi-cultural mutation of the country provokes the intervention of the courts with the accusation of stirring up racist and nationalist passions.

The myth of racism is used to obscure the true nature of the problem, presenting it as a psychological and cultural phenomenon. The immigrants are swindled and their relations with the Greek people are undermined as a completely perverted image of the real reasons of the resentment of the Greek working people is presented to them. When the myth of racism is also underwritten by the "left", great political confusion is created and the path to right-wing adventurism is laid. Every increase in right-wing bigotry is due to the result the sell-out by the "left".

Everyone isolates the problem to racism. Grigoris Felonis doesn't pretend to be a 'leftist'. He is an "honorable" member of the central committee of PASKE (the pro-government union bloc) and, as president of the Athens Labour Council, the main speaker in the meeting on racism. This heavy-duty labour bureaucrat is in full agreement with the demoralised 'left'. He too believes that there are no other reasons for the reaction against the mass use of immigrants by the bosses, besides racism, which according to his descriptions is: "The philosophy of the intellectually lazy. They believe they are unique on earth. That the other, the one different from them, is essentially non-existent, a humanoid. They believe they belong to a race privileged with higher spiritual and bodily forces, which are being bequeathed to the clear descendants of the race."

This is then the problem of the Greek workers. They are frightened lest their "Aryan" race be diluted!
In Dafni, a suburb in Athens with mainly labour population, we had one of the government organised 'brush operations'. There we had certain extra parliamentary leftists who demonstrated as 'multi-cultural' Greece was in danger. The local residents of the area deprecated them. Koutsoumbos, ostensibly shocked, comments in "Nea Prooptiki":

"Our cdes were provoked from people they didn't expect. Frightened housewives and pensioners, whose hide been tanned by the state and capitalists with poverty and super-exploitation, the silent 'populace', usually silent when facing smacks from those "higher up", suddenly raised their voices against those few who had the sensitivity to react to the barbarity of the police".

Concluding:
"we aren't dealing with the traditional phenomenon of racism. Something deeper but equally bestial is developing and embracing popular masses".
These people overflowing with intolerance and contempt for the 'bestial populace", who is only worth receiving 'smacks from those higher up', dare to pose as anti-racists! They pretend to defend, like Hercules, the true interests of the working class. The ones only they, not the "empty-headed" workers, know!
There, outside the public sports hall of Dafni, an anti-racist employer arrived with the same 'sensibility and courage' as the "far left". He was complaining because the police had (provisionally) deprived him of his immigrant employee. If anyone proposed to this gentleman to hire a Greek worker in his place, they would have had the opportunity to witness with their own eyes that the first victims of racist discrimination in Greece is the one against Greek workers. All others follow, however... the Polish worker is being replaced by the Romanian, the Romanian by the Albanian, the Albanian by the Pakistani and the Pakistani by the next cheap hands that will be discovered. Fortunately for capital, 'multi-culturalism' has still many reserves left...

Koutsoumbos believes, along with the rest of the so-called 'left', that the "Brush Operations" are a right-wing turn of Simitis under the pressure of the masses, which sent their message, with the results of the European elections! Thus for them Simitis stands to the left of the popular masses. They criticise the Greek population which, according to their claims, has pro-fascist tendencies, those self-styled endangered remains of democratic citizens!

It's not only in the electoral result that they recognised the stigma of fascism. Fascistic they had characterised the massive mobilisations on the issue of Macedonia, with which the Greek people declared its decision to resist the chicanery of the new world order in the Balkans.

Whatever is the political consciousness of the masses, one thing is certain: among them and the extra parliamentary "left" lies an abyss. On the question of the side of the abyss on which fascism lies, we ask the right to believe that, if nothing else, it isn't on the side of the masses.

The extra-parliamentary left characterises the working class as being inclined toward fascism, attempting to base their calumnies on skin-deep aspects of its spontaneous resistance. On its supposed racism and nationalism. But fascism doesn't simply consist of some external traits. It consists of its fundamental objectives. And these were not the transformation of Jews into soap, or the triumph of the Aryans, but the imperialist union of Europe under one centre of power. In this consisted the 'new order', which the Nazis also proclaimed. Today American imperialism has exactly the same aims: To unite the whole world under its own hegemony. The cadre of American imperialism don't hide their affinity with German fascism, borrowing from it the term 'new order', even the codename 'Desert Fox', of one of their great operations against Iraq. But conditions are totally different and the past could not reappear, as many imagine, in the exact same form.

The Americans aren't obliged to repeat the doomed in advance attempt of Hitler to militarily occupy Europe. They attempt to base themselves on the consent and collusion of their big and small allies, taking advantage of the common interests created by the multinational forms of composition of capital, from the end of the war until today. That is why their 'new order' cannot be based on nationalism and racism, but on fraud of 'human rights', multiculturalism' and the levelling of national resistance by the steamroller of globalisation. (From one point of view this constitutes an advantage for current imperialism, but at the same time its Achilles' heel. Every time it is forced to use violence, it cannot count on the patriotic enthusiasm of its armies, but only on the doubtful successfulness of a new technological fascism.)

We could suppose that the extra parliamentary 'left', is a victim of naivete and of its hereditary inability to distinguish internationalism from globalisation and the modernised form of the fascist new order. In a few cases this obviously holds true. But we cannot say the same when we judge it as a political current. Because these gentlemen are the exact same ones who cheered the desert storm against the 'Islamist dictator Saddam' and the storm in the Balkans against the 'Stalinist dictator Milosevic'. Someone who can't distinguish between the imperialist new world order and its victims, even at the time when they are bleeding, is not just confused but an accomplice. It is the person who supports imperialist violence and robbery of the people as the foundation of his own privileges and good life.

New World Order and Multi-Culturalism
Imperialism, while dissolving with fire and brimstone the multinational entities created by the course of history, attempts to artificially create, even with the use of violence, new multicultural communities. In Bosnia it holds the Bosnian Serbs in a 'federation', whilst in Kosovo it's trying to maintain the Serbian minority against the Kosovo Albanians. At the same time, the monopolies' Europe advertises its multicultural future.

Are these changes a step forward, a step towards internationalism? Our 'leftist' friends say yes. Some with a subnote, some without. The working class says no and is right. It a step backward. It doesn't lead us into the post nation-state era, but to eras when the nation state was the issue. To the feudal and slave-owning empires. The Ottoman, the Byzantine, the Roman. It isn't the actualisation of the socialist perspective but the political adaptation and servility of the planet to the needs of the transnationals.

Multi-culturalism under the iron cross of NATO is the tool for the dissolution of the nation state for the sake of the new order and globalisation. It not only doesn't bring closer the peoples, but it constitutes an attempt to sink them to the depths of national antagonisms and conflicts. To mutual neutralisation. It is an attempt at generalising the American multicultural model. The plutocracy of the USA is convinced of its functionality. For two and a half centuries now it exploits a whole array of racial and national antagonisms in order to guarantee the stability of its power. It is these antagonisms that have prevented the working class, despite its great strength, from acquiring its own political physiognomy and its own political party.

From this perspective the Greek people are right to be wary. In particular with the Albanian element. It has both an infallible instinct, and long historic experience. Of course the Albanian nation doesn't just consist of Mafiosi eager to get rich. It also consists of people of labour, of wages. But the collapse of the hated Hoxha dictatorship, which called itself communist, has propelled the political pendulum to the other extreme. The pro-capitalist and agent elements are at the top. For the moment Albania is the feared bulwark of American imperialism in the Balkans.

The mercenary coalition with NATO against Yugoslavia, the demonstrations in Athens with the Star-Spangled Banner and the burning of the Greek flag, don't foretell anything good. The stance of the government and the political establishment make the situation even worse. Of course, Andreas Andrianopoulos and the other 'internationalists' are reassuring! Unfortunately they are not trustworthy. Especially those promising to tame the conflicting interests with internationalist admonitions.

"PRIN" ["before"], the well-known product of stalinist abortion, makes fun of the worries of the theatrical writer Dialegmenos regarding the demographic change which illegal immigration is causing. They obviously consider without importance the history and traditions of peoples. So does the new world order, which wants to restart history from scratch. But the Greek people will never accept to have decisions on its future taken by national groups that don't have its history and experience and are still proudly marching behind the American flag. All of this belongs to the past for it and no amount of wretched invocations of internationalism can force it to go back to stages of its history, which it has long surpassed. That may be the objective of the new world order but it is in no way to its own interests.

Nationalism - not with the warped definition which cold war anti-communism gave it, but as a right of the peoples to support their national sovereignty, as a demand for the respect to national traditions and cultures - isn't opposed to internationalism, but its pre-condition. It is the irreplaceable vehicle of history, which leads towards internationalism.

Multiculturalism and internationalism are the vision of socialism, the vision of the workers. But this cannot be translated into the right of the capitalist in using 'black labour' so as to crush the domestic worker in every country, nor into the means for imposing the hegemony of the American superpower on an endless array of national minorities and civilisations with no ability of resistance. The abolition of states under imperialism is a totally reactionary perspective. It is equivalent with a return to barbarity. It promises working people nothing but the generalisation of misery. This can't be, and isn't, the aim of socialism. Its programme is the surpassing of the nation state by moving forward. It aims to generalise prosperity. Workers' solidarity cannot be understood as, nor can it be, the Christian cue of sharing one dish of lentils into fourteen portions, so the poor can survive and the rich get richer. It is the solidarity of the workers who fight first of all in their own country, for the overthrow of their own ruling class. The common and planned effort to overcome the uneven development bequeathed by history to different nations, as a necessary precondition for the abolition of national states, with the free will of the people and in their interests.

November 1999

Communist Internationalist League - KDE

Father of the nation: A term used, often ironically, to describe the MPs in Greece.

New Democracy: The right-wing bourgeois party in Greece, equivalent to the Tories in GB or the Republicans in the USA.

PASOK: The "left-wing" Greek bourgeois party, more or less equivalent to the Democrats in the USA.

Extra parliamentary left: The collective name used in Greece to denote the groups that claim to stand to the left of the "official" left (represented by the CP and its various splits).

The expression "the wall of shame" was used in Greece to denote the Berlin wall.

Black labour: The word "black" is used in the Greek language to denote unofficial, shady, illegal or semi-illegal dealings: "black market" has the same meaning as in English, "black money" is money received under the table, not declared to the IRS, etc. Black labour specifically, refers to illegal employment, in which the employed person is being paid in cash, without social security and retirement benefits, and without the safeguards provided by Greek labour legislation.

Hrisi Avgi: a totally unimportant extreme-right grouplet, which nobody would be aware of, if it wasn't for the "leftists" advertising it and using it as a fig leaf for their bankrupt policies.

Andreas Andrianopoulos: A former minister of the right-wing New Democracy party, one of the foremost proponents of "neo-liberalism" and deregulation in Greece. He is best remembered for abolishing state control on the price of gasoline, reassuring everyone that this would result in a fall of gasoline prices. Within a week, the price jumped from 80 to 200 Drs a litre, and remained there since. He too is an anti-racist, of course.

Street art in Athens.

'Brussels is one City'

Debate on State of Greek Labour

2004 Olympics Bonanza

'Ergatiki Exousia' (Workers Power)-Globalist 'Anti-Racists

Editors Note-'Workers Power- Globalist Leftists (Ex-Morenoite Affiliates) who disintegrated soon thereafter and joined one of the many groups who ended up in Syriza.

It's a stupidity to be a Volunteer Anti-Racist when Around you Millions are being given by the EU...

It's difficult to start to make an analysis for the positions of 'Ergatiki Exousia-Workers Power' around the issue of racism, as the class perspective is totally missing from their perspective. They are just trying to theoretically justify (if we can call it a 'theory' the eclectic and contradictory combination of ideas where they try to make things black and white) so as to propagate the policy of Open Borders which is being followed by the imperialist EU, from a 'progressive' perspective. The labour movement is being obliged to adapt to the policy of the EU and thus must sit at the desk of 'Ergatiki Exousia' so as to be taught manners and to be educated in an anti-racist manner.

In their paper num 76. July-Aug edition they publish an article on racism where without understanding what they read and write they use a section from an Essay of the Greek TUC which states the following:

"The entrance of the new labour movement which covers now around one third of the total number of labourers who are occupied in Greece".
(Greek TUC Report)

In other words 33% of the working people are immigrants. From this they conclude that the borders of Greece are hermetically sealed. Greece is a Fortress inside a European fortress! Someone could ask them what percentage should the 33% of cheap labourers be so as to theoretically accept the borders are open? 100% of all labourers, 200%, 500% an endless figure? Not that we expect a reply to this question.

"Whoever continues to talk about open borders is either consciously lying or doesn't have a consciousness of reality" they state in their paper the volunteer anti-racists of Ergatiki Exousia. Just think about it. More than 2million (and more) immigrants who live in Greece, a percentage which represents 20% of the total population are a 'conscious lie'! Whilst truth is that Europe closed its borders a long time ago, stopped immigration, became a Fortress. The simple Greek worker who believes in the opposite doesn't have a "consciousness of reality"! As this reality isn't one which he witnesses daily in his journeys on public transport, in factories, on ships, on building sites and public works, but that which exists in the pages of Ergatiki Exousia.

Do Foreign Workers Take any Jobs?

Nah!...No jobs are taken we are told by the open eyed volunteer anti-racists. Greek capitalists didn't bring them to replace the more expensive and demanding Greek workers but for them to do the jobs which the well fed locals refuse to do! The foreign workers who' "work in Greece occupy positions which are exclusively those of unskilled labourers such as cleaning duties, cleaners etc for women, or building work, agricultural work etc for men"...

The historical analysts of 'Ergatiki Drasi' after an intensive analysis of the history of professions in Greece found that in their

"overwhelming majority we are dealing with occupations which were created after the arrival of immigrants in Greece expanding the labour market"

As the 'reality' for which we don't all have a 'consciousness' is that before the immigrants arrived in Greece there were no *house servants, no building workers, fishermen, no one dug any fields or worked in making furniture!*

Let us not say that the ridiculous logic of the ahistorical globalist, who also wears the cover of the far-left anti-racist! Before 1990 the Greek worker didn't work. He knitted and waited for the arrival of immigrants to stand upright and become a... labour aristocracy. Now he has found a new occupation! A "manager of consumerism" avoiding every labour intensive activity, just like the writers of 'Ergatiki Exousia' avoid every intellectual activity, with the end result of filling up their paper with illogical lies.

The whole of the history of the Greek labour movement and for every country is based primarily on one-two militant sections with a history and tradition, with a socialist tradition and perspective for another world. The dockworkers and building workers before they were globalised were the advanced guard of class struggle. The example to be copied by all the other sections. Whoever sits to read a little history will see that the dockworkers and sailors were the first in Greece during the 2nd world war who created Workers Committees which decided and forced the shipowners onto their regime on the ships. They reached such a level of class militancy and dynamism that the bosses couldn't recruit or sack who they wanted when they wanted. Their fame spread in all the significant shipping fleets around the world and the dockers and sailors in many countries followed the example of the Greek dockworkers.

Greece occupied 25% of the shipping fleet of the Western world and it is no coincidence that the shipowners tried to break the power of the dockworkers and ships crews. This was finally achieved by the rise of PASOK in power and the policies of the Stalinists who wrote off the leadership of the dockworkers and supported the party of 'change' (how PASOK called themselves). The ship owners created schools of sailors in the Phillippines and slowly but surely started to replace Greek crews with hungry and subdued politically and educationally backward workers so as to escape from the high labour contracts, and the special provisions regarding in particular unhygienic and dangerous labour, pre-determined hours of work and to introduce on the ships a regime of the Roman galleys, once more.

The shipowners from their base in the City of London have in store a future identical to the one above for the whole of the working class. With the use of foreign crews they achieved what they hadn't in 4 decades. They gained from the paltry wages they paid and more significantly they achieved a significant strategic defeat on the whole labour movement in Greece opening the path for the subjugation of all sectors, using as a lever mass immigration. This task will be undertaken when every relationship with militant and revolutionary traditions of the Greek labour movement are broken with the replacement of the natural carriers of these traditions not by the 33% of the Greek TUC report but by 100% with the support of the 'leftists' of 'Ergatiki Exousia' ilk. Now I am thinking about it maybe they should be called 'shipowners power' as they attack all gains of the Greek working class and they try to defamate as racist and to fantasise against it for the benefit of the immigrants and the hordes of petty-bourgeois who even today swear against the high salaries and militant tradition of the Greek building worker. The building worker which they so hated as he was militant and wasn't easily subdued and they wanted to see him so.

'Ergatiki Exousia' doesn't ask to whom do the jobs belong. To Greek workers or their bosses? If the Greek boss had 5 Greek workers on an X wage and he sacks them recruiting 15 immigrants, he didn't create 10 new positions but divided 5 wages to 15 people. With such logic (if anyone can call it that) they claim with all honesty that unemployment in Greece has remained stable and during certain periods even been reduced!... What a nice picture for Greek capitalism, which the working people would appreciate if only they read Ergatiki Exousia!...

With 1/3 of the labour force being immigrants, with only 2,000 Greek dockworkers left out of an estimated 100,000 in 1970, everything is going fine. For whom isn't really the issue! We owe them a lot. Due to the immigrants the wages on the building sites –as everywhere else in the private sector – are now under the level of the 1980's decade.

Hours of work have gone through the roof. Thus the beggar became a 'strong Greece'. It's a fact. Not only told by Simitis. Also agreed to by Ergatiki Exousia. Greece from being at the bottom of the EU, due to the expansion is now somewhere in the middle. First among last. Great is its glory (but these borders keep on closing whilst the EU keeps expanding. Goddam Fortress!)

The use of immigrants we are told by Erg. Exousia hasn't occurred due to the collapse of gross sales by companies but because the expansion of the market. We needed immigrants in booming capitalism. You see without them the Greek worker would be lazying about. He wouldn't get off the couch to pick a grape (despite doing this for thousands of years) or to clean a hospital. Saviour for the ruling mafia always came from abroad. In the olden days with loans-neckbraces from the big powers, now with immigrants.

Foreign workers do not take jobs from Greeks states 'Ergatiki Exousia' as the market has developed and unemployment remained the same. But if the market truly developed would unemployment remain the same? The unemployed remain unemployed in a period of growth of the economy? So who takes all the new jobs (if they truly exist) as they aren't being taken by Greeks? Even with their so-called economic analysis 'Ergatiki Exousia' cannot be consistent. It is full of contradictions. Whilst they present a picture of economic boom of capitalism and the appearance of new jobs unemployment remains static. In other words development doesn't equal a drop in unemployment. Immigrants don't then take the jobs of Greeks. Or are they taking the new jobs and therefore a drop in unemployment is impossible, despite development?

Trying to justify the unjustifiable and to state that the presence of immigrants has no social, political or economic consequences, but only brings to the surface the racist nature of Greek people, the writers of 'Ergatiki Exousia' are being led by mathematical precision into the camp of the apologists of capitalism, in its greatest crisis in

history, which is attempting to survive transforming the planet into an arsenal of racial conflicts and planetary slavery. The industrial bourgeoisies in globalised capitalism will try to replace the hands it uses with cheaper and cheaper pools of labour, using the endless pools of illegal labour wherever it can on the planet. Not to improve the standard of life of the hungry and dispossesed but to destroy whatever was achieved by struggle by Western workers and to globalise immiserisation.

Imperialism has already moved far along this path due to the good services of our current social betrayers. 'Ergatiki Exousia' appears to be on this camp already. It wants (alongside the bosses) for the building workers who remained unemployed and their wages were attacked in the 1990s to not fight back exploiting the opportunties given by the Olympic building programmes and all the other public works and to remain on the sidelines as the ruling elite guarantees immigrant labourers to the sub-contractors with ridiculous wages allready moved far along this path due to the good services of our current socialbetrayers. 'Ergatiki Exousia' appears to be in this camp allready. It wants (alongside the bosses) for the building workers who remained unemployed and their wages were attacked in the 1990s to not fight back exploiting the opportunities given by the Olympic building programmes and all the other public works and to remain on the sidelines as the ruling elite guarantees immigrant labourers to the sub-contractors with ridiculous wages.

Our so-called anti-racists think they live in the old good days of the British Empire when the jackboots of the Victorian era brought Indians to Africa to build the railways as the locals were truculent, couldn't be trusted and indigenous. As they see in globalisation (and multiculturalism) the lesser evil, confronting the threatening Greek plebs and because they believe that the imperialists will finally pass

 onto public opinion their 'anti-racist' propaganda and that they will be saved from the slaps they will get from the Greek populace. In such a manner also thought the pimps and contractors who worked for the English around the world. Without though being saved. Even their last remnants in Africa in our days are bleeding. The same will happen here when the governments try to turn the 33% to 60% or

80%. When you make accounts without the customer being present, anything may happen. You will not avoid this fate adopting the propaganda of the tv media networks and the paid journalists who swear at Greeks on a daily basis.

Bosses hand over their jobs (as they belong to them) to immigrants for many and varied reasons:

First and foremost for cheap labour.

Secondly because of the low pay and bad conditions which the immigrants are forced to accept creates a division in every workplace.

Thirdly the appearance of many immigrants from many different nationalities creates the impression that the old immigrant can easily be replaced by much cheaper more pliant labourers. Ergatiki Exousia has another opinion with respect to the above. Allied with the ruling elite and its hatred towards Greek people it states the most amazing thing here:

"The most oppressed part of (Greek) society we can find the most prejudices and backward views. They read 'Eleftheros Tipos' (Daily Mail) wanting it for the presents it provides and at work they are the spies of the bosses"

This part of the people according to 'Shipowners Power' is uneducated as it belongs to the 45% of people that haven't finished the 9 classes of compulsory education! Whilst the Bangladeshis who worked on the Olympic games construction sites as well as others had university education! The problem though isn't the bourgeois education of workers, Greek or immigrants. Uneducated and oppressed peoples the world over when they had honourable

leaderships have written with courage and heroism history and these features are few and far between the higher the bourgeois education of social layers. The problem is elsewhere. The immigration policies of current imperialism we are witnessing the destruction of the gains,

the unions and the political parties of the working class, instead of them spreading in the rest of the world. This doesn't concern the article writers of Ergatiki Exousia. Their stance truly makes an impression and they have the audacity to call themselves 'workers power'! Someone may ask what is it they represent. Their passion is akin to the passion of anti-communist labour aristocrats who witness with pleasure the Greek working class sinking under the conditions of the immigrant cataclysm.

This pre-planned and directed by the imperialists new world order. The talk about 'racism' and 'anti-racism' are just the pseudo-cover, a fake camouflage of a truly anti-working class and anti-communist stance. Not even the most ardent English imperialists, Hitler's death squads or the American torturers of the Abu Ghraib prisons have such hatred from the depth of their soul for a peoples and in particular for its most oppressed part! This stance transfers with the cover of the 'left' the policies of the big bourgeoisie which finds a welcome mat in some sections of the pettybourgeoisie, the enriched part as well as the lumpen parts who consider the Greek working class responsible for its state. They follow the path opened by the shipowners and the big developers. The main responsibility lies at the hand of Stalinism which aided the first government of PASOK to break the dockworkers union and the later leaderships of the KKE which helped to break and dissolve the union of building workers transforming it into a business for sub-contractors and gangmasters of immigrants. 'Ergatiki Exousia' doesn't say a thing about these issues, neither does it concern them. Like a madam in a brothel which isn't concerned by the entrance of immigrant prostitutes to the profession as long as prices are lowered and custom increases. They don't think that the whole of society will be transformed into a brothel, as long as the madam has a plate of food to eat. Such a future Ergatiki Exousia is being prepared for itself …

*For the reader to get to grips with the countless contradictions and illogicalities of Ergatiki Exousia one only has to read the following excerpts of their paper.

"There is no doubt that Greek capitalists need foreign workers in Greece. One could therefore be led to the conclusion that Greek capitalists aided immigration…"

"Categorically No!" they inform us. Consequently Ergatiki Exousia doesn't do the job of the capitalists who on the one hand want the immigrants, but say "Categorically No" to immigration! Ergatiki Exousia wants them and stated Categorically YES! Now as all of these appear and are contradictory, they categorically inform us that they aren't. For the "very simple reason": Greek capitalists want immigrants only to be illegal.

"Capitalists require the entrance of the immigrants but only as cheap replaceable labour. They only require them as workers of second choice. To live and work illegally or semi-legally with the permanent fear of expulsion".

As the Greek capitalists want illegals and they would logically encourage the illegal entrance into the country legalising with green cards the illegals they do everything in their power to block illegal immigration! If this seems a paradox learn the truth from Ergatiki Exousia, which much better than the simple Greek citizen has a "consciousness of reality". Here is what they say:

"That is why they don't 'open the borders', but instead have recruited more than 100,000 special border police so as to stop illegal immigration. They have land mines in Evros, they sink ships

VN Gelis
August 2004

Racial disturbances broke out in Greece in the last week of August with many injured and immigrants being killed

The delights of globalisation Imported women line the streets of Athens looking to make a buck. What the Greek labour market was lacking alongside street beggars, car window cleaners, muggers, thieves etc.

The End of Greece

Cultural Identity

During the recent immigrant ghetto insurrection in France, Fukuyama posited a new perspective on such events. Whilst most analysts focused on the economic causes of the phenomenon - unemployment, poverty, bad conditions of sustenance - Fukuyama emphasised the cultural identity of European nations. These nations, he stated, have identities which are based on history, blood and soil, 'strong' identities one would say, in which the foreigner is unable to participate even if he wanted to. These possessors of European Nationality, but without a true nation - apart from the global community of the followers of Islam - are the cornerstone of terrorism which is being exported to America. He saw the issue as being one of the European nations readjusting their national identity – obviously retreating from their blood, land and history – so that the 'immigrants' can fit in. A model for this bed of Procrustes is the great exemplar of nations, America.

Fukuyama proposes even harsher oppressive measures against extremists claiming that if this doesn't occur, Europe will have a problem with democracy and will continue to export terrorism. This analysis differs from that of economists in that it explains why 'immigrants', who are not all 'poor', rebelled in France. Beyond this, we have the observation that democracy doesn't function in heterogeneous societies, only in those which are homogenous, a thing which is ignored by the fervent supporters of 'multiculturalism'. That is why ancient Athenian democracy placed so many barriers to those who sought the status of citizen. But if the national identities of the Europeans lose every essential element which ties humans together, if their countries become a folklore museum of 'globalized' society composed of 'citizens' without qualitative differences, if the system of nations is replaced by the system of a massive multinational market, will democracy then be viable? Or will we have a dictatorship? This hasn't been analysed enough.

Fukuyama in his small piece doesn't explain how Europeans are going to accept the necessary repression of the globalised regime, which requires them to forget their national identities in order to live peacefully in their lands with all the new arrivals. But we can suspect the answer to this burning question if we turn our attention to a small European country beyond the common borders of Europe: Greece.

 Yes Greece has to show 'progress', in the direction of political-social globalisation to place it in the spirit of Fukuyama, as a vanguard within Europe. Let's look at the objective elements:

Firstly: Greece has subsumed in a small period of time, 15 years - in relation to all other countries **double** their number of immigrants - whilst for other countries, the comparable period would be: for Germany, 50 years, and for France, 150. Obviously we know that in Greece we don't receive honest statistical figures with respect to the number of immigrants, as can be seen by the latest research of Panteion University, Athens. According to the specialists this was quite problematic due to the research methodology: e.g. we don't know how to categorise anyone as an 'immigrant' after three contradictory legalisations. So, in the end, we ended with a number double the official figure, i.e. 1.5 million. That is 1/6 of the Greek population of 9 million in pre-immigration Greece. We will not be surprised if in the future we are informed that the true number is indeed much larger.

Secondly: Greece constitutes a case of 'hard' national identity, as from 1922 onwards it maintained a homogenous population with Greek identity, which, apart from the language, 'blood' and 'history' (Fukuyama), also was unified by the Greek Orthodox religion (important according to Huntington as one of the elements of identity). Greece therefore contains as historical survival two strong founding symbols of European civilisation: 'Athens' and 'Jerusalem'. Such a strong identity constitutes - in the spirit of Fukuyama - a provocation directed against the experiment of 'multiculturalism'. If Multiculturalism is achieved here, the lessons and perspectives opened up by this achievement are of great importance.

An historical 'experiment', by its nature cannot be fully controlled as in natural science. Control of the issues is nevertheless very advisable. Luckily for Greece, given its extreme geographical position and incomprehensible language we are guaranteed of this, of a small vision of what is happening. It is a purer reflection of the general European public opinion, if not the centres which make decisions in Europe and America.

Subsidised multicultural ideology

How are they to 'reorientate' the national identity of a country so as to make it fit for Multiculturalism? A study of recent Greek history confirms the importance of a dimension which we all suspect: Education: in particular, the weakening of all the elements of Greek history which today might disturb the 'neighbours' of Greece. Of course these same neighbours in their schools, in their textbooks, maintain to the limit the view of Greece as an historic enemy which stole their national lands (Tsamouria, Macedonia, Western Thrace, Eastern Aegean), Alongside this are the historic crimes committed against the Greeks, whilst on the contrary, in the name of objectivity, they condemn all Greek issues, or Greek heritage: pride and love for the country and they condemn it as Nationalism and an abuse of the similar Greek ideal of Pan-Human Solidarity. Finally the subsidised programmes of Multicultural education in the secondary schools, where the Anglosaxon ideas of Political Correctness dominate, with its democratic insistence on the equality of all civilisations.
Here an important point, which was emphasised by Castoriadis: that the privileged work occupation of the person for his own civilisation, does not necessarily equal a denigration of non-Greeks, but is legalised absolutely by the necessity of self-knowledge.
Note: It is a simple inference from Castoriadis' notion of 'civilisation as is a privilege' to multi-civilisation as a privilege of the second order.

Of course the spreading of Multicultural ideology isn't intensified by school education only, but also by what goes on outside: the Mass Media is able to influence very broad layers of the population.

Further, the messages from establishment politics teach that the idea that Greece belongs to the Greeks is a racist idea, whilst in the widespread consumerist sphere, what is at stake is the cosmopolitan 'lifestyle' for the rising petty bourgeois with broken English who years ago fantastically left village Greece for Beverly Hills. The slogan for a 'Multicultural Greece' contributes to the desired goal of finally dominating our hinterland as in the 'rest of Europe'...

The occupation of national space
As more immigrants come to be "citizens", we distance ourselves from the stigma of poverty, and of provincial, village, Greekness. The fact that the wretched immigrants won't finally bring our desiring cosmopolitans closer to Paris and New York, but to the Balkans under the Ottomans: they will not teach them English or French, but Albanian, Bulgarian or Swahili. And instead of turning Athens into a city with English parks and German neoclassical villas, are transforming its old petty bourgeois areas into grey impassable refugee zones where one hundred and one barbarian practices occur. Our cosmopolitans will suffer their deserved fate, when, at the end of the process, when the bank has taken away their flat, their credit card, they end up homeless on the streets seeking work from their new Balkan bosses.

The brainwashing via the education system, which first of all influences easily led youth, and secondly, the rest of the population, doesn't immediately guarantee the success of the experiment of nationicide in a country where it will take many years for the new 'cosmopolitan' youth to assume power. Therefore there are limits to the power of simple propaganda to change established opinions. To enforce the change of the nation state to that of a Multinational state, it is of course necessary to create the conditions of finalised events, such as the occupation of the national terrain with millions of immigrants: 'Greece, from a country which exported immigrants, has been transformed into a reception centre for a massive immigrant wave which inevitably transformed its personality, giving its national homogenous character a 'multicultural dimension' (Vradini on Sunday-Newspaper 13th Nov. 2005 p. 6-7). To achieve these aims within the framework of a well organised state with secure borders, internal policing, a legal regime, historic frameworks and material infrastructure it is necessary that the will and energy of administration is paralleled by a passivity of the population. Only in the case of the collapse of a state as result of war, revolution or extensive natural destruction, is it possible that, without the consent of the indigenous, can they wipe out the mechanisms of unity and defence for the self preservation of an organised society. Without the collapse of a state, only an extensive conspiracy from the centre of the state apparatus can ensure the erasure of the Nation-State. If this aim is being supplemented in part by the unclear project of globalisation, the necessity of the appropriate means for the achievement is becoming understandable. Thus in small Greece, on the outskirts of Europe, the agreement of the cadres of the majority of the political spectrum from right to left towards achieving Multiculturalism is impressive and surpasses as far as we know the rest of Europe. In particular, we see this occurring in the context of the rising doubts towards Multiculturalism in Europe. They state that 'Greece isn't France' (Metro 17th Nov 2005 p. 5) but have never claimed that there is peaceful coexistence between Greeks and other nationalities on our 'privileged' lands. It is not like Holland either. Greece isn't as liberal as the most liberal country in Europe but they constantly calls for immigrants to settle here whilst Holland is already reeling from their flood and seeking a solution of zero immigration.

But Greece isn't France, Holland or Germany. Nor is it Europe in general. How could it be? Immigration to Germany has occurred with democratic openness, with ceaseless public dialogue between all political parties and organisations on the subject under the prism of national interest. In Greece the largest resettlement programme of recent years in both city and countryside of non-indigenous peoples occurred immediately, automatically, without a political debate, without discussion.

Unanswered Questions
The Lecturer of Political Economy, Theodoros Lianos asks that the following basic questions be answered in order to create an immigration policy which will serve Greece:
Do we need immigrants? If yes how many?

From which countries? Do we need a big concentration of immigrants from one country with hostile politics? Is it dangerous for the Greece that Albanians constitute 55% of the total?

Which occupations are required and consequently what type of education is required of immigrants?
How do we choose immigrants? Is there a system of points which selects or refuses those who have certain characteristics (e.g. education, age, sex, religion…) or are we accepting immigrants purely by chance or in some other way?
For how long would a work permit be granted or would we grant residency? Do we want seasonal immigrants or do we want them for a greater time?
What do we do in the case of those who are here with their families including children in Greek schools? Do we provide permanent residence or do we provide temporary protection?
Replies to these questions must be based on a stable orientation: in other words on the basis of the interests of this country. This must be emphasised as there are many who see the existence of immigrants as a philanthropic issue and consider us obliged to receive immigrants, a thing which is of course absurd and dangerous. The immigration policy of our country must guarantee its interests, national, cultural and economic for the present and the future."
(Theodoros Lianos, 'A bomb in our hands' To Vima 28th August 2005)

Whilst in a European country like Germany the arrival of immigrants leads to organisational forms and criteria which ensure national interests: if those criteria aren't met they are expelled. But in Greece this year 90% arrived illegally and their right to remain has been registered in law! Whilst the biggest section, if not the totality of our political forces from the extra parliamentary left up to a section of the right and the representatives of our cultural elite, like the Greek Citizens Advice Bureau, unanimously and indiscriminately demand the 'legalisation' of illegal immigrants. A letter to the President of Parliament Anna Benaki the lawyer from the Ctizizens' Advice Bureau, Lecturer George Kominis emphasised the 'contradiction of the event from one side so as to settle matters of all the immigrants who can be proven to be living in Greece in the last year with the event that they have been characterised as sole manner showing this period or recognising the date of entrance in the passport as the application of this change would preclude a large number of immigrants" (Eleftherotipia 7th July 2005, p. 48).

Wonderful: the Citizens Advice Bureau proposes to legalize all illegal immigrants, thereby destroying the laws of the country: coming in without a passport or passport controls! Why should one be confused when the Lawyers Union of Greece in a Press Conference on the same day condemns the partial legalization of illegal immigrants as 'discrimination' against immigrants? (From the organisation of 'Forum Immigrants' 'Coordinating Committee of Anti-Racist Organisations and Communities' , 'Greek Social Forum' trade union left organisations and Youth Against Racism –)Eleftherotypia 7th July 2005 p48)

Recently a high ranking cadre of PASOK in presenting his argument on immigration called all Greeks who refuse nationality to immigrants 'fascists' whilst concurrently the same cadre recognised that the riots in France were the work of immigrants who already had French citizenship.('Eleftherotypia' 16th November.)
Here we have the nationality of immigrants, not overturning but concretely enabling, anti-national actions using their granted legal cover.

Despite this the 'correct' move for Greece is proposed by the PASOK cadre. Why? So that Greece will 'integrate' three times as many immigrants into its society, without France's problems. How could this be? With Greece's greatest benefits on offer being poorer than France: with higher unemployment, worse education, lacking social protection etc! Do we Greeks need this logic? But that is what the leader of PASOK believes is the essential 'integration' of immigrants into Greek society of second and third generation. It 'constitutes a basic precondition for the safety of all the citizens' (Kathimerini 13th November 2005, p11)

The politics in support of an immigrant cataclysm are discerned by means of a revealing logical and factual shoddiness. They constantly provide half truths like: we need immigrants, as Greece is suffering from a lack of births. The whole of Europe is suffering from a lack of births - like Germany which has an 1.4 births per thousand and hasn't decided to import - at a pro rate - 20 million immigrants in a population of 82 million so as to cover the gaps in labour. Despite it not being difficult for anyone to see the lack of logic in these arguments supporting an endless number of illegals, Greece dares to follow this PASOK 'counsel'.

The right of presence of illegals doesn't presuppose issuing passports to all those who demand asylum, or to all those who have been condemned by a court as underage citizens. The green card and total health cover for all the immigrants in Greece, the only country in the European Union available for free.

Eyewitnesses have condemned the fact that that immigrants receive priority in IKA-Social Security Medicine as well as the privileged service for immigrants as well as the organs of the state for misdemeanours.

Overturning Reality
Greek senior citizens experience dangerous situations both on the streets and in their own houses. Their property is as insecure as their life, phenomena related to immigration and the lack of police presence. The calm talk and analysis of politicians and criminologists is mere fantasy. The mass media is allegedly responsible for over-promoting the criminality of illegals as is of course the 'racist-frightened' character of the Greeks. Where then lies the truth? This could be ascertained by an independent investigation at source: from the police, where the depositions of those who have fallen victim to crime are to be found. But so that the 'xenophobia' of the Greeks not be increased, no such investigation will see the light of day...

Recently an investigation by the newspaper 'Kathimerini' showed that the views of Greek citizens and the authorities regarding criminality are diametrically opposed: citizens declared that there is a very real, constant and increasing threat and that this is much greater than what is presented by the mass media which is constantly undermined by the Ministry of the Interior and the Police Service. A majority of citizens also believes there is a lack of policing, whilst they don't want an increase in policing as they believe it undermines individual rights ('Kathimerini' 20th November 2005.)

The above investigation doesn't analyse the subject of criminality as it merely compares the fears of citizens with the affirmations of the authorities which, as usual, don't pin the blame on immigration. But it indirectly shows who citizens are more frightened of.

Another investigation by the Polytechnic of Crete disconnects fear of foreigners and racism, thereby showing that it isn't the race, language or religion of foreigners Greeks fear, but the dangers provoked by the permanent residence of immigrants in our country with the perspective of gaining Greek identity and political representation at the highest levels ('To Vima' 20th November 2005).

That which we already suspected is now proved by independent investigations: the characterisations of 'racism' 'fanaticism', 'conservatism', 'fear of foreigners' with which the political and academic elite lightly dresses up and embellishes as earmarks of the Greek people, lacks a scientific basis, has no empirical roots and is, in the best case, just the waffle of bankrupt parrots who show a hatred against the country that gave them birth and of a nation which feeds them. In the worst case scenario it is a globalist conspiracy against the Greek nation with the aim its weakening and disappearance.

The Greeks: foreigners in their own country
The Greeks are going to become immigrants in their country and the immigrants masters of their country. Whoever disputes 'multiculturalism' is a fascist. The concerns of citizens are

responded to from a position of superiority like the wailing of a child. The aim is for Greece to become one large market of twenty million souls with no identity. The worst thing of all would be for the Greek people to be consulted by referendum. The settlement of Greece is presented as an inevitable fact. It's a function of the 'stable functioning of the era of globalisation' ('Vradini on Sunday' 13th November 2005). The foreigners must not be foreigners in the land of Foreign Zeus. Of course not! They must become owners: owners of land! In 2004 the President of Property Sales in the Attiki region, uncovered on TV that in the previous year 1/3 of the purchases of property in Attiki was by Albanians. It's also well known that the Albanian mafia spends money via the route of property purchases solely for Albanians. The average bank deposit of Albanians is double that of Greeks. It's important to remember on this specific issue a significant part of the Palestinian problem.

When Palestine was still Arab but and under British jurisdiction, Jews were purchasing land and property from the Palestinians at above market prices. The Palestinians finally realised their mistake when the new owners reached the critical mass so as to impose themselves politically, founding the state of Israel. That's how the occupation of Palestine occurred: with purchases. They must have citizenship, nationality, full political rights. So as to grant the wishes of the globalists, the Greeks must provide Thrace to immigrants who want it, without having lost a war. First the Greeks commit suicide as a nation from despair at the hungry of the earth from the Third World. Then, due to their philanthropy, they get cut off from their history and lose their land. They leave their country as immigrants (1.5million), so double that number is imported, to cover the gaps. To these foreigners they will show all the compassion they refused their own compatriots born around 1960 as they were hungry. The same fate befell Greeks in 1955, 1949 and 1922 when, being chased by armies and police forces, they were forced to emigrate from the areas they historically occupied.

The 'impartiality' of the 'progressives'
What fate did the Greek from Pontos exiled to Russia have when in 1990 they decided they wished to come to Greece? Who cares today about the 90,000 Greeks in Northern Ipirus where they are living

under Albanian occupation? Who cares for their survival guarantees of which Greece has never received any guarantees from the Albanian authorities, Greece doesn't grant them Greek nationality so they can become part of Greek society ('Elelftherotypia' 11th November 2005) Our progressive Greeks ask for solidarity towards the nations of Palestine, Kurds, Iraq and South America and the Indians against globalisation and imperialism. It's only the Greek nation that they don't defend. That would be Nationalism. They may also assume that Greece isn't threatened by anybody. But they are mistaken. Greece is under threat both internally and externally. It's a country that has been ravaged and indebted, which is neither respected by its enemies nor its friends, nor itself. Its neighbours are waiting like vultures to fall on its carcass once it has reached its nadir. Remember the words: Tsamouria, Macedonia, Eastern Thrace, Eastern Aegean, Cyprus ... "its truly unbelievable" it was stated eloquently that we "have the weakening of the reflexive pro-fatherland and collective dignity of Greek society today" (Christos Giannaras, 'Kathimerini' 5th June 2005)

For now our 'progressives'are organised in common demos with the immigrants who will ask for new rights and more State funding. In the meantime the grandparents of the progressive youth are demonstrating on their own. No one is concerned for the pensioners who are hungry...

The collapse of the social fabric
Globalisation predicts great movements of impoverished masses in answer to the demands and desires of multinational capital. The creation of a reserve army of unemployed lowers the wages and other rights of workers. Marx himself spoke about immigration as a weapon of Capital in the 19th Century. But current globalisation doesn't stop there. With the slogan of 'Multiculturalism' of 'Human Rights' and 'equality' it disrupts the social fabric of societies which are organised around common institutions, history, religion, language, heritage. The violent arrival of heterogeneous races and cultures, suddenly called to live together because of blind economic necessity, is a shock which tests to the limit the strength of nations.

Where we don't have homogeneity of the community and a lack of common goals the result is the collapse of democracy ('Where people have the same vote but not a common origin, each looks after his own interest' Thucidydes)

But when democracy is abolished, what is left? Dictatorship. Therefore Fukuyama did not recommend that in the multicultural era Europeans accept the "redefinition of identity" and the establishment of institutions of repression.

Every ethnicity, as a living organism, seeks self-preservation. I cannot easily abandon collective memories, customs, religion, language. Nor is it desirable for ethnicities, for diversity, as the richness of expressions of the human spirit, to disappear. And the same goes for languages. Otherwise why lament species of animals and plants disappearing each day from the planet by human activity? Are nations of people less important than the animal species?

Multiculturalism means Ghettos
Multiculturalism as has rightly been pointed out, means the ghetto. The ghettos become a micrography of nations in the narrow geographical framework of one state, isolated, each with their own goals and interests, rather than united by democracy. Or to put it another way, democracy gives to the ghetto the weapon to achieve its aims which can well be against the nation state which has given them hospitality. In Greece, an issue develops when an Albanian student is called forth to hold a Greek flag. Think what might happen in the immediate future when Albanians with political rights want instead of holding the Greek flag to raise the Albanian flag: they will have the right under the framework of multiculturalism, of equal rights etc. to do so. Greece will be divided into 'progressives' who will be in support of the Albanian flag and the 'conservatives' who will be against. In the end there will be a compromise so no one raises a flag. Thus Greece will have to lower its flag on its own territory. A gain some will say as if it were that simple.
All of these are issues which demand thought and delicate distinctions. The Greek left is obliged to advance concretely to the critique of this ideology unless it wants to remain unconscious followers or willing accomplices of multinational capital and the imperial logic of the U.S.A.

The phrase 'smooth integration of immigrants' is used in all the conversations of those in charge of the discussions as well as during the mobilisations of the activists. Many interpret this 'smooth development' as the cultural assimilation of the immigrants to Hellenism! Things aren't like that at all. Article 66 of the new immigration law considers immigrants must maintain diversity and cultural specificities (!)"It disclaims the "…Greece of ... integration and aims solemnly at social inclusion as being the coexistence and harmonious concurrence of cultural diversity. The assumption, even partial, of Hellenism as being extrovert cosmopolitanism cannot but inspire feelings of optimism "(Nikos Dendias. (New Democracy MP) and a member of the Committee on Immigration of the Council of Europe." The new law on migrants' , "To Vima" August 7, 2005. It is clear that we have here an authentic sample speech of the 'supranational elite'. Regarding the above article we refer to the fact that in 2015, according to estimates of the UN, the population of Greece will reach 14.2 million. According to our estimates this number will be reached a lot sooner. The new law regarding immigrants is therefore applies very concretely to this reality, as it is absolutely impossible for Greece to 'integrate' such numbers of immigrants. It is therefore only with cultural hybridity, with various nationalities with their own flags will be able to share our national terrain and those under conditions of equality. These foreigners, to the extent that they have political rights, will not accept any privileges of Greeks in the country which is still called Greece. They will find themselves in the councils, in Parliament, in the army and in the police force. If Greeks go against this sellout, they will find themselves against the state ("Thus small Greece with its globalist outlook will be able to respond to the xenophobic syndromes which I am fighting against using as a base the large population centres of masses who aim to weaken law and order and to undermine social existence..." Further comments regarding the new law on immigrants by the MP Nikos Dendias ('To Vima' – Newspaper 7th August 2005) In the explosive mosaic society of multiculturalism, ethnic communities don't demand integration and assimilation but group rights, every community against all. (K. Vergopoulos

'Eleftherotipia'-Newspaper 11/11/2005).'The universal democratic system remains only in name. The equality of the citizens of the society loses its content, citizens are forced to unite on the basis of 'communal' elements like religion, nation, race, culture (K. Vergopoulos, "Eleftherotypia" 11.11.2005).

War against All
'Harmonious existence amongst 'culturally diverse' communities' isn't our future but a war of all against all, along with oppression as predicted by Fukuyama. The cameras that watch our every move in the streets and on the roads, the opening of our telecommunications data by the media and the state, the anti-terrorist laws, the future possibility of establishing praetorian bodies consisting of foreigners with traditions in paramilitary occupations: dictatorship is our future. With the erasure of the national character of the state and the co-domination of foreigners on our soil, Greeks will lose their freedom. The multicultural state is a mafia state. Desperate economic migrants don't simply come with their hands alone for personal salvation, but many are willing tools of the mafia which mobilises everything to its advantage, both humans and goods. A provisional investigation by the TV channel 'Antenna' (17th July 2005) in the evening broadcast showed that the Chinese mafia demands Euro 10K from every immigrant they bring to Greece from China, Pakistan and Thailand etc. This is confirmed by police reports. With violent force and torture they extract their 'dues' from their victims. Behind a large part of the Chinese commercial activity - the Chinese shops with their vendors-soldiers with the petrified smiles - hide money laundering. The 'Snakeheads' of the mafia not only traffic in illegal immigrants but also provide shops with goods and protection ('Kathimerini' 22nd May 2005 pg 26).

Chinese products along with the Chinese mafia have brought Greek industry to a cul de sac to a much larger extent than for the rest of Europe. Ten thousand Greek traders have gone to Chinese trade fares compared with only 5,000 German traders. But despite the mass purchases of Greek traders in China, they cannot compete on Greek soil with the mafia's Chinese shops with Chinese employees who offer even lower prices.

The difference between Chinese trading relationships in Greece compared with Europe is the human factor i.e. the mass entry into Greece of Chinese – and the mafia. The Chinese tried to do the same in Serbia under Milosevic in 1999 where they created in no time a China town of 35,000 people. But his successor Zoran Tindits emptied Belgrade of Chinese who came in 2002 via Albania and Skopje as he had promised. These Chinese went into unguarded Greece.

The second wave of Chinese into Greece came in 2003 from neighbouring Italy which decided to clear the country of Chinese ('Kathimerini' 22nd May 2005 p36. It is held that the centre of the Chinese mafia was thus transferred from Italy to Greece.
Prime Minister Simitis visited China in 2003 where he cut a deal involving the import of 120,000 Chinese into Greece. The Chinese, whose birth control policies are linked to reproduction and population control, are happy to go abroad and have children in our country of low fertility. Many times Greek traders demonstrated against illegal trading activities of the Chinese. In one of their demonstrations, the Greek police intervened and told them to disperse so as not to provoke the wrath of the Chinese mafia.
Apart from the Chinese we have other mafias, Albanian, Russian etc who influence and are influenced in turn by illegal Greek circles, embassy circles, policemen, lawyers, tourist companies etc. so as to share the wealth from the trade in illegal immigrants, the illegal trade in goods, drugs, and protection to foreigners and Greeks. The newspapers don't provide us with information regarding the interconnections between the mafias and the higher levels of Greek administration and the political elite. But we live in a country of multifaceted corruption and it would be absurd to believe it ends just where national interest begins.

Subsidised Immigration
Is the arrival of immigrants into Greece the result of pure philanthropy? Or we are to be informed tomorrow, after the natural resources have already been looted, that the last source of wealth that was left was migration and settlement of the lands that remained for

Hellenism. Here we will add another thought: the USA subsidises Mexico as a filter zone in its northern borders where immigrants congregate on their way to the USA so as to lower the pressure of the immigrant wave. The EU, acting on the proposal of the Minister of Internal Affairs, Schilly, does likewise for Morocco as a filter of African immigration towards the North. The Portuguese journalist Paulo Mousa, granted a prize for his reporting on the issue of illegal immigrants, talks constantly about the unofficial camps which have been created with the advise of the European Union.

'The Moroccan government has undertaken the role of a gendarme for Europe... Soon the amount of 250 million Euros of EU funds will be released to it for as technical and economic aid aiming to secure control of the European borders' ('Kathimerini' 23rd October 2005). Is Greece being funded under the table so as to play the role of immigration filter in the Eastern borders of the European Union? In relation to the last thought there is a serious component. Greece has co-signed the Schengen agreement. One part of it is the policing and anti-terrorist laws of the countries of Europe, the other the defence of the European borders from illegal immigration and the visa requirements for the entrance of immigrants. But it is well known that the greater part of the immigrants who arrive illegally in Greece not only aren't prosecuted or deported, but are legalised. Why does Europe accept this absolute contravention of its Schengen conventions if there isn't a secret agreement excluding Greece from this condition?

Greece has another peculiarity in relation to Europe: a great part of the immigration originates from countries which have common borders that have demands against Greece.

Albania has made a lot of money out of Greece in the last 15 years. How can we quantify the event in which 1/3 of the population of hungry Albania found work, free healthcare (special agreements between Greece-Albania for free healthcare of all the Albanians? A Greek citizen hasn't such special privileges without insurance contributions or is able to acquire significant property in Greece as well as Albania. In what other ways can we quantify the influence of Greek investments on the economy of Albania? Or the Greek support for Albania's aim of entering the EU? Or for it to build hospitals after the economic collapse of the pyramid investment schemes collapsed? Or Greece's support of the Albanian police? Or the supply of Greek tanks for the Albanian army? Greece also implements EU directive 109 regarding the family reunion of an immigrant after 5 years of residence in the country they are in. Whilst France doesn't permit residence of immigrants beyond four years so as to exclude them from this EU directive, Simitis' Greece does the exact opposite. The unification of families multiplies the number of immigrants and their relatives and this becomes a cornerstone for their permanent settlement and acquisition of political rights.

What did Greece get in return from the government in Albania in relation with the rights of Greeks, for instance in Himarra or Koritsa? From what we understand, zero.

Albanian provocations
The Albanian provocations against Greece were recently shown with the demonstrations against the Tsamidon against the visit of in Albania of Karolos Papulias. Papulias left Albania whilst the Greek government repeated the oft quoted poem 'Albania's position does not now represent its European direction'. The Greek government believes that Albania, like Turkey, will forget at any moment in time their national interests with the sound of the word 'Europe' - like Greece constantly does. But these countries, as Erdogan has unambiguously declared, don't sell out their national interests for the sake of 'Europe'. Not against Greece whose threats about using the veto have no weight whatsoever. Albania will not abrogate its vision of a 'Greater Albania' which now, with the independence of Kosovo, seems realistic, for a Greece, which everyone ignores, notwithstanding its claim to speak on behalf of Europe. Today's Premier of Albania Berisha, from 1990 on showed that he is a follower of the old Albanian dogma whereby Turkey is a friend and guard of Albania which oversees its integrity, that Greece is foreign territory and Italy a necessary guardian ('World of the Investo' Newspaper 5-6th November 2005 pg 14)

If today Berisha wears the mask of a lamb he will throw it away when he decides the time has come. After all, time is working for him.

In 1991 the Albanian Cham founded their own organisation whose aims are recognised officially by the Albanian government. These are: a) to allow the resettlement of the Albanian Muslims in Thesprotia (the part of Epirus near the Albanian border), for the Greek government to return all their property and to officially recognise them as an Albanian minority. A few years ago the Albanian parliament voted to recognise a day of 'genocide' of the Muslim Chams by the Greeks. The Vice President of the Democratic Party Azem Haintari declared that the Albanian flag will be raised in Preveza and Thebes! The maps of 'Greater Albania' show its southern borders on the Amvrakion gulf! Let us not forget, there are other maps from Skopje which contain Thessaloniki and Turkish maps with Greek Thrace and the Eastern Mediterranean).

The issue of the right of return of Albanian Muslims was put to Mitsotakis by Ramiz Alia ('World of Investments' 5-6th November 2005) Here we have something strange: Mitsotakis reacted by calling on the Albanians to come and work in Greece 'opening the borders'. From then one to one and half million Albanians came, left, came again, remained in Greece as they pleased. There are villages in the Greek countryside with two or three old Greeks and one hundred Albanians. At this moment Thesprotia and in the rest of the countryside and islands of Greece is populated by many Albanians.

The well known UCK
States with an increased proportion of Albanians in their population e.g. Skopje/FYROM, acquire an element of Albanian irredentism. Our well known UCK with its offshoots in the Albanian Liberation Army NLA and the Albanian Naitonal Army ANA which acted in Skipje and South Serbia – has four active divisions with agreed areas of activity in the lands of the Balkans.

The "Tsamouria" division is responsible for North Western Greece and is based in Preveza ("Investor's World" 16-17 July 2005, pp. 22-3)! According to unconfirmed reports, the explosives used in terrorist attacks in London were of a military type and originated in Kosovo. It is also well known that Islamist militants were present in the ranks of the Albanian guerrillas in Kosovo and that Al-Qa'ida started to be active in the Muslim populations in the Balkans. Countries like Saudi Arabia fund the spreading of the Koran and the rise of mosques in Albania. UCK like Al Quaeda initially were trained in the USA ('World of Investor' 16-17th July 2005 p23) The Greek journalists Demos Verikios on the Greek radio on 21st April said that Greek customs officials seized a truck coming from FYROM with weapons bearing the inscription UCK. Verikios, who has contacts in the Greek army, uncovered the existence of thousands of leaflets in Greece with which the National Liberating Army of Albania and UCK recruit members and propagandise on the national rights of Albanians: 'Greece is the next target' (From the German radio station 'Deutche Welle 3.5.2001 **www.politikforumde/forum/archive/22/2001/07/29304**)

The political representative of UCK in Macedonia, Ali Ahmeti, spoke on Radio Australia regarding the perspective of the struggle from Macedonia to Northern Greece. Ahmeti spoke of about one million Albanians who live in Greece. The Greek Minister Stavros Stathopoulos condemned the declarations of Ahmeti as bright fantasies and called on the international community to condemn them (Berliner Zeitung 31.5.2001). From the same internet source we find the directives allegedly circulated by the Albanian Liberation Army directing those who migrate to the neighbouring countries. It is allegedly a plan for immigrants in five stages:

1) Poor immigrant refugee
2) Establishes himself and has children
3) Demands human rights and undermines the country of arrival
4) Finds allies abroad
5) Liberates the country he is resident in with allies from abroad wiping out the locals

(28.8.7.2001 on the same internet place)

The allies will ensure these actions seem understandable to the public (28 7.8.2001 on the same website). Said to have been found in more than one case, storage of military equipment to Greece. The

Albanian factor given certain characteristics that gathers (geographically dispersed, many people outside the nation-state borders, irredentism on the rise, weak institutions, intense activity of criminal organizations and their involvement in politics) is available for use by third forces as a lever to destabilize border region and redeployment and correlations. The interface between extreme Islamist groups, which can act in other Islamic immigrant populations in Greece poses further risks.

Warehouses of military equipment have have been stated to have been found more than once in Greece. The Albanian factor has various characteristics: (geographically dispersed, many people outside the nation-state borders, irredentism on the rise, weak institutions, intense activity of criminal organizations and their involvement in politics. This is being used by third parties to destabilise the area for the reordering of borders and exerting of pressure on governments. Their connections with extreme Islamist organisations, which can act amongst other Islamist immigrants populations in Greece gives birth to new dangers.

Unfortunately, all indications are that the immigration issue in Greece will not only drag us into an economic-political-cultural odyssey. It will also have an impact on the national existence of our country.

There must be an immediate conversation and public plebiscite on the issue of immigration.

Albanians to this day continue to act as Americas/Turkeys fifth columnists in Albania pushing for a Greater Albania with made up demands

Citizens Campaign in central Athens Ag Panteleomonas Against Illegal Immigration

Using the Excuse of Poverty the World Over they want us to Commit National Suicide.

Enough is Enough, of the Illegal Immigrants in Our Country!

1. We are the overwhelming majority of the Greek people. We are all independent of party, betrayed by those who are alive and still fighting.

2. We demand the logical right of human life independently for all.

3. We demand the loss of our respect and self-evaluation.

4. Greece is our home and no one has the right to park themselves here without our permissions under whatever regime either the present one or a future one.

5. No to the new quisling blackmarket sellers of 'globalism' No political force, in power, oppositionist or extra-parliamentary has the right to **decide on our behalf without us**. To impose in our absence and against our will the settlement of our country with illegal immigrants without this ever having been discussed or this practice being implemented without even asking the Greek peoples.

6. One aim one goal. End the nationcide conspiracy. Our patience has limits and has expired. We aint going to become the Palestinians of the Balkans. **Greece belongs to the** Greeks.

7. Greek Jobs for Greek Workers. No to their replacement by cheap and docile immigrants.

8. No to the erasure of Greek industry and the agricultural sector by the Mafiosi transportation of Chinese products and the business cartels with the endless and untaxed importation of bad quality products which are produced cheaply by the violent exploitation of third world labour.

9. We want to be able to move about (us and our children) with safety in the streets and our parks and our squares. To expel once and for all the criminal elements which have occupied our country from every corner of our planet.

10. No to the multicultural transformation and erasure of Hellenism. One nation one country. Multiculturalism implies the end of every civilisation. It opens the gates to hell creating racially controlled ghettoes which occupy only themselves. In readily created racial interests in **a permanent war of all against all.**

Residents Committee Ag Panteleomonas- Wall Poster calling for Action 2009

Manolis Glezos:
The Left covers the Illegal Low Lifes

http://en.wikipedia.org/wiki/Manolis_Glezos
Interview with Manolis Kotakis
Newspaper 'Democracy'

Q: Dear Glezos, Athens is in turmoil after the murder by immigrants of Manolis Kantaris. The Left just as like in the pre-war era and the rise of fascism, doesn't seem to be expressing the citizens with what it stands for and they are looking towards the Far Right. What is at fault?

Glezos: This is a big problem. The situation in many suburbs is unacceptable. The people cannot live by being confronted by all this wave which exploits immigrants. The mafias of immigrants, the low lifes made up of immigrants, I do not shirk from saying it, are creating problems for the citizens.

Who is at fault for this? Let us see the root of the evil. All the European governments are at fault, in particular those which had colonies in today's under development countries (Africa Asia) which ceased to be colonial but continue to exploit these countries and don't allow them to develop. The cause are the ex-colonialists. The govt is also at fault as its subordinate to the demands of Dublin 2 and does not do what it must. They should get everyone ask them where are you from and if they answered for example from Algeria send him packing to France! Get France to pay for this cause. They should have provided them with the right documents and send them to the colonial countries. Thirdly why should only the citizens of Ag. Panteleomonas and Kipseli pay for this (immigration influx translators edit) and not Psihiko and Filothei (rich suburbs translators edit)? Another issue. The govt uses the police as an organ of oppression of social struggles, instead of an organ for the suppression of criminality. If it acted out the latter we wouldn't have so many crimes. They would be avoided.

Q: And the Left?
Glezos: What? I say it doesn't repeat! The Left takes uncritically the side of the immigrants without condemning the criminal mafias, who act amongst the immigrants and does not distinguish the issue. From there onwards is the ground on which fascism develops. I am questioning then. Where was the Left at fault to not be able to stop the rise of fascism in the pre-war era? The question is as valid today!

16th May 2012

Editors Note

The above was provoked by the murder of a Greek in central Athens by Afghan migrants. The expectant father Manolis Kantaris was going to a maternity ward with his pregnant wife just as her waters were broken and he had a video camera round his neck 5am in the morning when he went to start his car to bring his wife into it. On the way he was mugged and killed for a Euro 100 camera and his wife came out to see him in a sea of blood.

http://www.tovima.gr/society/article/?aid=399926

New Democracy Builds Illegal Migrants Reception Centres all over Greece

Riots over Illegal Immigration in Greece

What started off as small protests in central Athens by concerned citizens regarding the massive rise in illegal immigration has now spread to other areas of Greece with the 'pre-electoral' announcement of Hrisohoidis-Interior Minister that 30 Illegal Immigration Reception centres will be built all over Greece to house the officially arriving 300 a day from the non-existent borders of Greece.

This situation, 20 years in the making, has turned central Athens into a 'third world reception' centre with no infrastructure to cope with the mass influx. Not having colonies in the modern era of the rise of capitalism Greece neither has the schools, hospitals or the capacity to cope. Daily Greeks are robbed, killed or maimed in violent looting sprees which resemble the conditions of banana republics of central America, and Hrisohoidis pronouncements that he will 'clean up the centre' and tackle illegal immigration, are just pronouncements added on to previous ones, the arrival of Frontex or the building of a wall in Evros. All show and no content, the stark reality is that Europes porous borders (latest figures show that 68% of new arrivals come in via Greece) is a long term imperialist strategy for the promotion of cheap labour and the replacement of indigenous labour with globalised labour.

No one in Greece believes the governments any more on anything. Hence the reaction has been rioting in a series of areas against these so-called reception centres (essentially holding pens to spread round illegal immigrants as the centre of Athens can no longer hold). The fake Left, proponents of mass illegal immigration two decades now (KKE famously refused to unionise Albanian building workers instead becoming sub-contractors to this labour and their politics reflected this change) alongside the globalists of Syriza suddenly remembered this is a problem. Yet not once have they had a single demonstration in relation to this issue, not once have they protested about Greeks being murdered. As if in tandem they have left the door open to the 'far right' retro fascists of Golden Dawn and from the sidelines have criticised Greeks who protest as being ....fascist. Yet who agreed to the foreign occupation of Greeks by a multitude of arrivals? The Greeks certainly didn't and now there have been at least 5 large riots over the issue in a variety of areas where these alleged 'new reception areas are to be built.

One of the slogans of the participants is that the 'whole of Greece will be like Keratea'....where the PASOK government was defeated over its attempts to turn an area into a large rubbish dump without taking into account the wishes of the local people, and where Pangalos (the then Vice President) declared that PASOK lost the struggle on behalf of the Troika, in Keratea.

The irony on the whole situation is that there are still globalists who believe the Greek capitalist class is against illegal immigration and cheap labour at the same time as one of the reasons the Greek seafarers association is on strike is the abolition of indigenous crews (cabotage as it is known) in line with the previous abolition of Greek crews that happened in Greek shipping more than 3 decades ago.

VN Gelis
April 2012

WE HAVE BECOME IMMIGRANTS IN OUR AREA-

Leaflet for Street Closure and Demo
Central Athens 6th Arrondisement

"only if you are blind and you don't see the state of the city. Only if you are dumb and you don't hear the screams of the people who are in danger and are forced to live like animals inside previous city areas which have now become favelas. Only if you are stupid don't you understand what is actually occurring"…

Once upon a time our area was one of the best in Athens. This picture changed dramatically. In the last two years the citizens of the area are under pressure from the conditions of the ghetto which have been created. Our calls towards the Athens Mayor and the police just fall by the wayside. A few days ago the feeling that we 'can't go on as before' forced us to 'try and take the situation under our control'. The whole area is a ghetto from countless and non-registered Illegal immigrants, who go to the toilet wherever they can and do their other daily needs as well, in our squares, on our door fronts and they sexually abuse our women. There is a severe danger for public health. Every one of our paths, every one of our squares is their point of departure.

-We can't continue like this as we are observing unable to react to this savage event of the total and absolute degeneration of our area not having the support of any section of society.
-We can't go on as we can't leave our houses, without the feeling of fear.
-We can't go on as the issue of legality and what is rented and for what use has gone by the wayside.
-We can't go on as our properties are sold for a piece of bread
-We can't go on as we are living frightened for our daily existence depressed about our future.
-We can't go on as there are many underground churches of every religion and dogma and the transformation of rotten basements into muslim schools.
-We can't go on as there is a massive rise of criminality in our area which has seen a massive increase.
-We can't go on as they transformed our area into a 'dustbin' of the capital and all of them are served by the wall of silence.

BUT ENOUGH IS ENOUGH as we are decided to fight beyond the attacks which we are receiving that we are racists and fascists.
ENOUGH regarding the promises and cheap justifications.
WE DEMAND the immediate de-ghettoisation of our area, with the registering of all the immigrants and for their distribution to all the districts of our Borough.
WE DEMAND to co-exist with the immigrants and to not be held hostage.
We took the decision to shut down Aharnon and to notify you that the situation is dramatic and uncontrollable, that the absolute negation of legality is unbearable and all is hanging from a thread...

Friday 12th October 2012
Niovis and Aharnon 8pm
Citizens Committee Central Athens

Call for Action for the Unemployed
Co-workers women and men, unemployed

We are suffering us and our families. We are destitute and in desperation whilst we are millions, when we are the power and in our country we should have the most powerful and dynamic movement of Greek unemployed. No one cares for us, neither parties nor unions. The Greek worker has become rubbish in his own country. The country for which generations have toiled and fought in wage slavery, has thrown us out.

We know there is an economic crisis but the only ones who don't have responsibility for this are ourselves. Others govern and others have enriched themselves from our work and sacrifices. The thank you offered by those who have profited from our own sweat and thrown us into a workless and socially isolated environment and to use in our position cheap imported slaves. So as to impose a regime of generalised slavery. They believe this is their interest. But the ridiculously low wages and the destruction of all workers rights weren't limited only due to cost. **THEY KILL** the market with the result being Greek unemployment increasing like a snowstorm and consumption to constantly fall with the result being the general dissolution of the Greek economy.

The situation can't go on any longer. As unemployed we have an obligation to organise ourselves and to fight for our rights for our families. For the rights of our country. We are the country first of all. We are raising the alarm. Rise up, organise. Come into contact with us. We are the power. It's time for the oppressors and traitors that rule us to realise our punch. We can change the country and our lives.

Citizens Committee 6th Arrondisement Central Athens

Greece: A Nation State in its EU Death Throes

Having fought an election on the platform that 'there is money' PASOK's American born leader, ex-Premier George Papandreou, fiddled the books and ensured the Greek budget deficit became larger than it was for Eurostat so that Greece could enter the IMF's bailout programme. Three years down the track, the aim is becoming increasingly clear: to create a new, tax-free, offshore, non-unionised region of the EU in the geographical territory that was Greece.

After 30 or so years of EU membership and a decade of Euro membership, for the last 5 years of which Greece has been in recession, GDP has collapsed by 25%, unemployment is officially around 25% (56% for youth, 33% in the private sector), soup kitchens and suicides (3,000 so far) are the only growth areas of the economy and the centre of Athens is starting to resemble parts of Detroit.

The last package of cuts—which cut by 50% wages for those still lucky to be employed and pensions by at least 25%—have the aim of dragging wages down to E300 and pensions to E100. The 'minimum' wage has been reduced. In the private sector, where workers are begging for work for as little as E10 a day for 12 hour shifts, 6 days a week, the minimum wage now stands at E580. Unemployment pay, which only lasts for 12 months maximum, stands at E360 with no housing component. This means that Greece is fast on the road to matching Asia in wages so as to become the EU's role model for the future of the new regions the EU wants to create, which are to be run from the centre with new EU gauleiters in every ministry and every public institution (hospitals, universities and council offices administration), who will dictate budgets and cuts and have overall control, thus superceding both the Greek constitution and all local decision making.

As if to rub salt in the wounds, Greece has had the arrival of Germans, which is of course deliberate and conscious, to ensure the wounds of old (occupation of the 3rd Reich which led to 6-700k

Greek deaths) are repeated in a new form. The purpose is the **total fire sale** of all public assets, bigger in form than anything that has hit the Western world—including in countries which are or were the poster boys for neo-liberalism, Chile and the ex USSR—with the eventual aim **being** the takeover of all public services in a deregulated, post-unionised, contract-based, private company paradise where will be employed workers willing to work always for less and less.

The process **by** which the Greek nation state is to be torn apart **involves a changed** electoral system under the Kallikratis Plan now being implemented. The plan created **13 regions of Greece** with their own separate tax and spending powers and merged all councils and town halls subordinate to the 13 regional governors who will decide policy directly for each region. Germany recently proposed to allow German companies to employ Turkish citizens in Western Thrace (Greece) by allowing the relatives of those expelled in 1923 under the Treaty of Sevres to settle there, thus creating a new Kosovo in Greece.

Depending on the resources each region has, privatisation lists are being drawn up. Assets are to be sold to transnational corporations for peanuts. For example, Skouries, in Thessaloniki, sold the rights to a Canadian gold mining company for a few million Euros, it was then listed for hundreds of millions in a foreign stock exchange. Thousands of local citizens have been resisting the arrival of lorries which will destroy their livelihoods by the underground drilling and the looting of national resources without any actual benefits to the citizens of the country.

Despite over 20 general strikes—a genuine mass movement of occupation of city squares in the summer of 2011 involving millions of Greeks in over 30 cities—the ruling elite proceeds apace to impose EU directives as though they are confetti and **to descend lower than** even the minimal alleged 'EU social charter'. This is permitted because **there is no minimum barrier for standard of living, health care or education.**

The enforced integration of Europe aims at creating one European government. This can only be accomplished by the abolition of the nation states, the centralisation of the banking system (three or four, controlled from the centre, will remain in Greece). Thus, the formulation and implementation of policies of indigenous national development cannot occur. The implementation of the Bolkenstein directives ensured illegal immigrants worked on the building projects for the Olympic Games and that Greeks never got a look-in. Over E10 B are exported to other countries via Western Union outlets as there are no capital controls.

Now that 95% of all building work has collapsed we have just the public sector left, which is the target of the large transnational corporations.

We have arrived at the stage where it has become clear that, instead of Greece's entry into the EU heralding development mirroring that of Germany, it has become de-industrialised and has lost nearly all its agricultural production due to EU directives and the open borders in the importation of agricultural goods with zero tax, setting it on a path much closer to Bangladesh. The perpetual race to the bottom has only one outcome. The effect will be to create the EU's first direct colonial region as **the shining path** for all others to follow suit—Portugal , Ireland , Spain.

VN Gelis (Democrat Magazine)
November-December 2012

Vietnam: Those Who Leave

(The 'Problem of Vietnamese refugees')

Thousands of people are leaving Viet Nam seeking to settle somewhere else.

Who are they?

Why are they leaving?

How to settle the problem?

It is clear that a problem of this kind, owing to its human and
political implications, cannot be treated in a simplistic way by means
of a few humanitarian tirades sprinkled with political slogans on
human rights. It can only be grasped within the present context
of Viet Nam, which is facing multiple problems left by several
decades of war and more than a century of colonisation; it can only
be solved by taking into account certain exigencies and restraints,
some related to universally accepted principles, others connected
with concrete historical and social circumstances.

1. THE HISTORICAL CONTEXT

How did Viet Nam appear after the historic date of April 30 1975
when Saigon and the whole of South Viet Nam were completely '
liberated — a liberation which put an end to 30 years of continuous
warfare?

For the first lime since 1945 — in fact since 1939 the country had
peace — a peace which was only relative, as everyone knows now.
For long years every Vietnamese had lived under the constant threat
of bombs or shells falling on his house, his garden, his children, of
foreign soldiers or local mercenaries coming to kill, burn and rape.
At last, he can now live in peace and devote himself to peaceful
labour. For the first time since 1859, after 116 years of French, then
American colonisation, the country was at last free and independent.
Free to build a new life, to exploit its natural resources for the sake
of its own people, not just a few multinational companies; free to
live its own way, not according to norms and patterns imposed by
foreign conquerors. Last but not least, for the first time in 21 years,
since 1954, North and South were reunited.

Another' nightmare had-also ended. For 21 years, American imperialism, having at its disposal colossal technical and financial means together with sophisticated mass media and other means of propaganda and ideological poisoning, and created enormous military and police machine which had turned many Vietnamese into torturers of their own compatriots. Worse still, within a given family, father and son might find themselves in opposite camps, and a man might be the murderer or torturer of his own brother. Now, those tragedies which had happened every day inSouth Viet Nam under American occupation, ceased to occur.

Peace, independence, reunification, liberation — perhaps one has to be a Vietnamese to feel the whole depth of the feelings that animated our people in those historic days. Millions of people were at last able to meet again their parents, husbands or wives, children friends, col-leagues. The people as a whole, even those who had not taken part in the struggle, were proud to be members of a heroic and indomitable nation.

Man, however, does not feed on sentiments alone. After those years of war, the country was but an immense expanse of ruin and misery. Let us quote a few figures, already known to all but which some are trying to erase from the memory of men.

Fourteen million tons of bombs and shells dropped on the country — 22 times the tonnage used in Korea, not counting napalm and phosphorus. About 25 million bomb craters: in many regions not a single roof was left standing, not a splint. Here is an example: in Nghia Binn province, 2.5 million coconut-palms had been destroyed by defoliants, bombs and shells; on liberation day, there remained (inly half a million palms in the whole province. You can imagine what had become of villages and people under those coconut-palms.

Jf one adds up the areas of cultivated land hit by the bombs and especially by the sprayings of defoliants, account being taken of successive sprayings, one finds the figure of 10 million hectares. Five million hectares of forestland were affected; large expanses of forest were burnt by napalm following defoliation. Hillsides denuded of vegetation by defoliants were brutally eroded by tropical rains and as a result several million hectares of land were lost, in many cases defini-tively. About a million head of cattle — buffaloes and oxen — were slaughtered: the American command, repeating a practice initiated by French officers, massacred these animals with a view to driving the rural population to famine.

In the South alone, 9,000 hamlets, out of a total of 15,000, were damaged or destroyed. In the North, material damage was not less. The American general Curtis Lemay recommended that every indus-trial installation, every factory be destroyed and that this destruction be continued until no two bricks were left that were still joined together. All industrial establishments in the North, and all rail and road bridges were repeatedly bombed. All cities and towns were damaged, and some, like Vinh, Hong Gai, Dong Hoi, and Phu Ly, entirely destroyed; two-thirds of rural communes were affected; 1,600 water conservancy works, which irrigated or drained hundreds of thousands of hectares, were wrecked. So were 1,000 stretches of dyke which protected the country from river Headings and prevented the intrusion of sea water into rice fields. Sixty-eight out of 70 state farms were hit, as well as nearly 3,000 schools and colleges, 350 hospitals, and 1,500 village infirmaries-maternity homes. The great leper hospital at Quynh Lap (2,500 beds) was razed to the ground.

In February-March 1979, Chinese aggression upon the six provinces along our northern border caused considerable damage; four towns seriously damage, 320 rural communes affected, the Lao Cai Apatite mine wholly dismantled, and 904 schools, 691 day nurseries, 430 hospitals and health stations and 42 logging-camps destroyed. Fifteen per cent of the cattle were killed or taken away. Let us note that in both North and South, American ordnance continues to maim peopf e. The tonnage of unexploded American ammunition left in our country is estimated by American experts at between 150,000 and 300,000 tons. Every day, children at play or peasants at work in the fields are wounded or killed by a mine or some anti-personnel device. In three years, there were 3,700 victims in Quang Nam province alone. Material damage is not the only sequel of wars. Even more serious are the human losses and the social and moral upheavals. On liberation day, hundreds of thousands of people werefreedfrom jails — sick and disabled. In the South alone, war invalids numbered more than 360,000. The number of civilian victims for the period from 1965 to 1973, when the American troops were directly involved, is estimated at 1.5 million. Again for the South alone, the war left 1 million widows, 800,000 orphans and children abandoned by their American,

Korean, Filipino soldier fathers. On top of it all, American strategy spawned a large number of 'uprooted' people — the key problem of post-war years.

Unable to conquer rural and hill-forest areas, the American command had recourse to the policy of forced urbanisation'. Repeated bombings of villages and chemical sprayings of crops ended up driving 10 million rural people (figure supplied by American services) from their villages and fields. They flocked into the towns, cities and regrouping centres under American control.

What was to become of those uprooted country people who over-night found themselves stranded in towns and cities where there were no industries to provide them with jobs? When the American war began in 1960, South Viet Nam, like other under-developed countries, had 15 per cent of its population living in towns and the remaining 85 per cent in the countryside. When the war ended, only 35 per cent of the population were living in the rural areas, the remaining 65 per cent were concentrated in overcrowded cities and towns.

The American strategy aimed at killing two birds with one stone: on the one hand, to weaken the Vietnamese by 'draining away the water', i.e. the people; on the other, to turn those same people into mercenaries of Washington. For those men who roamed the pavements of the towns had no other recourse than to enlist in Thieu's army and police. In this way 1,200,000 men were pressed into that army and police commanded by more than 50,000 officers, well-trained, indoctrinated and supervised by tens of thousands of American advisers. If one adds to these numbers the civil servants, political agents, and leaders of various anti-communist parties and organisations, one will find that at least 1.5 million people were living from salaries paid by the American budget — not to mention the taxes paid by the local population.

To serve that war machine, a whole commercial network — especially to import the luxury goods consumed by the Americans and the privileged strata and a 'tertiary' set-up: banks, insurance companies, coffee-houses, bars, hotels, brothels, drug traffickers — mushroomed. On liberation day, 300,000 Saigon households were registered as 'traders' at least twice the number of factory workers. American military aid averaged 1.3 billion dollars a year, economic aid 600-800 million dollars; not to mention the on-the-spot expenditures of the American expeditionary corps and services, the CIA for instance, which maintained at least 30,000 'pacification agents', not to mention, too, aid from other capitalist powers: France, Japan, Great Britain, West Germany. All that money — 2 billion dollars a year on average — allowed several million people to live without participating in any productive work. One understands why there were in South Viet Nam on the day of liberation:
— More than 3 million unemployed people;
— Several hundred thousand prostitutes and drug addicts;
— Several dozen thousand gangsters and other criminals, whose number later increased with the release of the former Thieu police, paratroops and rangers;
— One million tubercular people;
— Several hundred thousand people affected by venereal diseases;
— Four million illiterate people.

The former regime had wholly neglected social medicine; medical doctors cared solely for a rich clientele; endemic tropical diseases continued on the rampage, there being cases of plague and cholera in Saigon itself, malaria was wreaking havoc. In a word, one had to rebuild not only a country which had been ruined materially but also a society which had been completely perverted and turned upside down, in which millions of people had forgotten how to perform honest labour and had lost all sense of national and moral values. A society which had to be' remade; people who had to be reintegrated into the social community.

In French colonial times, the population of Saigon was 500,000. By liberation day in 1975 it had increased to 3.5 million. The city took 80 per cent of American aid; it was the hub of the former regime's administrative, military, police and commercial apparatus and also the main provider of its fleshpots. American aid in food — 300,000-700,000 tons each year — had been specially reserved for feeding its population. Immediately after liberation, American aid and that supplied by other western powers were cut off. Chinese aid to the North was reduced then completely interrupted. Right at the start of its immense work of national reconstruction, Viet Nam lost three-quarters of the assistance given to North and South in the war years.

Neither the Vietnamese people nor their leaders allowed themselves to be disheartened by the scope of the difficulties encountered. An overall line was quickly defined:
— Quick reunification election of a national assembly and a government for the whole country;
— Reconversion of the socio-economic structures of the South with a view to turning colonial andneo-colonial structures into national ones, and a gradual advance to socialism;
   Large-scale economic and social measures aimed at giving work to millions of unemployed people, rehabilitating hundreds of thousands of prostitutes, drug-addicts and delinquents, ensuring decent living and education to nearly 1 million orphans, quickly organising a health system capable of stemming endemic and social diseases, eradicating illiteracy in the whole of the South while developing the school system in the whole country;
— Strenuous efforts to develop science and technology, and a national and progressive culture while integrating traditions into this speedy modernisation of society and culture;
— Harmonious integration of about 60 diverse ethnic groups — ethnic minorities making up about 20 per cent of the population.

Let us give a broad outline of the achievements in those fields: quick repair of communication lines between North and South, which had been interrupted for 21 years; illiteracy eradicated in the South (in the North the problem had been solved 20 years before); educational development which made it possible for 15 million children and young people to go to school in 1979 (total population: 50 million) with help from the North, the South has set up a health system which reaches down to the village and set about eradicating endemic and social diseases. Remarkable results have been obtained in the medical and social rehabilitation of prostitutes and drug-addicts thanks to the atmcsphere of social renovation prevailing after liberation and the development of cadres engaged in this work. By helping clear large tracts of land of mines, the people's army has made in possible for many villages had to be rehabilitated and new ones to be built. The urban authorities, by setting up handicraft workshops and getting factories to operate again in spite of material shortages, have given jobs to hundreds of thousands of unemployed people. The people actively participated in the general and local elections, to the national assembly and the administrative committees of villages, town quarters, and towns and cities. By putting under crops land which had been devastated by war, building irrigation works, and reclaiming virgin land, about 1 million more hectares of arable land have been gained.

The champions of 'human rights' in the West, from Jimmy Carter to the correspondents of *Le Monde,* are apt to forget those results which have given back to millions of Vietnamese their human dignity **flouted by a century of French colonisation and 20 years of American intervention. Human rights in a former colony are first of all the right to national independence; the right to choose a line of development which does not sacrifice its natural and human resources to the greed of multinational companies, and that of a minority of landowners, capitalists and agents of foreign powers; the right to education, health care, work. Let us add that wartime destructions are not the only obstacles to the development of Viet Nam. Sine 1975 two more factors have contributed to aggravating the situation:**
— Natural calamities of unprecedented scope; and
— Peking's aggressive policy (in fact, that of the Washington-Peking axis).

In 1977 a great drought affected the whole country for several months resulting in a deficit of more than a million tons of rice for that year's crop. The year 1978 saw a series of exceptionally violent floods and typhoons, which hit areas with an aggregate population of 6 million. Three million tons of rice were lost, not to mention the washed-away irrigation works and bridges, the submerged orchards and drowned cattle, and the losses of people's household possessions and personal belongings.

But the major obstacle to the progress of reconstruction has been the aggressive policy pursued by Peking. Here are the main episodes:

Following Kissinger's visit in 1971 and the Shanghai Communique in 1972, Peking pledges itself to support Washington's international policy, with a view to bolstering its anti-Soviet position, emerging as the world's third superpower, retrieving Taiwan, and also gaining substantial technical and financial assistance. This about-face of Chinese international policy had manifested itself in Bangladesh, Chile, Iran . . . Starting in 1971, constant pressure was brought to bear on Viet Nam to compel its people to forsake all attempts to liberate the South, and moves were initiated to provoke a 'cultural revolution' in the country. In 1974, Peking resorted to armed aggression to occupy the Hoang Sa (Paracel) islands, which were then held by Saigon forces. This military operation was only possible with American assent.

In 1975, the Chinese government was not at all pleased to see Viet Nam win total liberation. But it would be difficult under the circumstances to launch a direct attack on Viet Nam; no Chinese soldier would have obeyed such orders. So Peking had Vietnam's South-

Western flank attacked by Pol Pot's Kampuchean forces, which were equipped by China and commanded by Chinese advisers. Immediately after the liberation of Saigon, Viet Nam had to face a new war. A war which compelled its government to evacuate

all villages located along the 1,000-kilometres-long border with Kampuchea, thus losing a not negligible area of cultivable land. The atrocities perpetrated by Pol Pot forces also compelled 300,000 Khmer and Chinese refugees to seek shelter in Viet Nam — a burden for the Vietnamese government.

The war by proxy made by Peking on Viet Nam by means of the Pol Pot forces was soon followed by a series of manoeuvres aimed at sowing trouble within Vietnam itself through the agency of the numerous Hoa community (people of Chinese origin) and through military pressure exerted on the China-Viet Nam frontier, ending in armed aggression on 17 February this year.

Economic or social problems were not the only ones, A very preoc-cupying problem was that of security, in other words, that of counter-revolution and civil war. Gerald Ford had announced in 1975 that there would be a blood-bath. Why should he have committed the honour of a President of the United States of America by issuing such an affirmation if he had no good reason to do so?

The rapid collapse of the Saigon regime was the result not of the extermination of the pro-American armed and political forces, but of their disbandment. After liberation there still remained, fully alive, 1.2 million soldiers and police together with more than 50,000 army officers and as 'many political agents. In his book *Decent Interval,* Frank Sneepp, head of the Analysis Department of the CIA in Saigon from 1972 to 1975, tells us that the CIA had left in Saigon, besides several thousand of its direct operatives, about 30,000 agents of Operation Phoenix, i.e. people specially trained for the assassination of revolutionary militants.

So Washington did not consider the loss of Saigon to be definitive, the more so since its collusion with Peking dates back several years already. Revolutionary Viet Nam, facing as it did enormous economic and social difficulties, would not be able to resist a two fold offensive — internal subversion combined with external aggression. Immediately after 30 April 1975, the counter-revolutionary networks installed by Washington started operating. Civilian and military cadres were murdered, factories and store houses set afire.

In those conditions, what was to be done about the 1.5 million soldiers, police, and civil servants of the former regime? Pol Pot had devised a simple solution which consisted in the outright liquidation of all those who had served the Lon Nol regime. It was clear that die Vietnamese government could not resort to this kind of action. All those soldiers, police, and civil servants who had had no important political responsibilities were quickly returned to their families, and the great majority of them were able to vote at the general elections of April 1976. But the army officers, the 'pacification' agents, the holders of important political posts, those who had ordered massacres, bombings, wholesale destruction of villages, torture of prisoners, could not be released immediately without creating the risk of a civil war. Those men, operating within a still unstable society, would not fail to fan up troubles. Those counter-revolutionary army officers were provided with shelter and financial assistance by Hoa traders of Cho Lon. The subversive network created by the Americans quickly co-ordinated its acdon with that set up by Peking with a view to sabotaging the Vietnamese revolutionary movement.

So the revolutionary government decided to keep those men in order to 're-educate' them. What does this mean? Kept in camps far from towns, those army officers and other responsible agents of the former regime were to participate in political discussions and take a look back over their past while careful investigation was conducted on what they had done under American occupation. The point was to assess whether so-and-so, if released, would join a counter-revolutionary organisation.

One realises that such an undertaking could be complex and would take time, that errors could be made and abuses committed.

That there should still be about 20,000 such men who remain obstinately counter-revolutionary, out of the 1.5 million who worked for the Americans, is a situation about which the revolutionary administration can do nothing, except wait until the time comes when, helped by the evolution of events, those men will eventually understand that socialist revolution is there to stay in Viet Nam and that it is utterly useless for them to oppose it. The concerted actions of Washington and Peking are certainly not designed to help those counter-revolutionary diehards change their minds.

And so, on three occasions, in 1954, 1975, then 1978-1979, imperialist and reactionary forces have availed themselves of difficult circumstances to provoke an exodus of refugees in Viet Nam. The aims have remained the same: to stir up and exacerbate serious social and economic difficulties in revolutionary Viet Nam; to weaken it from within, thus preparing conditions for renewed armed aggression. Aggression and the threat of aggression is a new factor urging people to flee. At present, the Chinese aggression of February this year, then the threat uttered by Deng Xiaoping to give Viet Nam a new 'lesson' and Chinese troop concentration along the Sino-Vietnamese border are pushing the Hoa into a new exodus.

Economic, political, social difficulties: for those who are not inspired by the will to rebuild their ravaged country, the only way out is to go away and try to find elsewhere a more comfortable life.

THOSE WHO LEAVE

The first population exodus of these long years of war took place in 1954. Under the terms of the Geneva Agreements the French expeditionary corps was regrouped south of the 17th parallel. About 800,000 people followed them south: soldiers and police, civil servants, businessmen, but mostly catholics (more than half a million) who had been living in villages put under ecclesiastical authority

That influx of hundreds of thousands of catholics from the North, conducted by aggressive priests, gave the South Vietnamese catholic church a strongly reactionary character. For a long time, the church was to be the main supporter of the Saigon administration and the most fervent advocate of American intervention. Diem and Thieu, the two presidents of the Republic, many cabinet ministers, army officers, deputies, senators, were catholics; the church was a real armature for the regime, a violently anti-communist church that even refused to follow the resolutions of the Second Vatican Council.

After the signing of the Paris Accord of 1973 and following the withdrawal of American troops, the American services, anticipating the defeat of the Thieu regime, worked out a plan for the evacuation of several hundred thousand people. This new exodus was to serve as a pretext for a political campaign to discredit the Vietnamese revolutionary government and would provide personnel for opposition movements in exile, or even an emigre government.

The rapid collapse of the Thieu regime and the lightening victory of the revolutionary forces left the American services little time. About 150,000 people were taken away helter-skelter in the last weeks by sea or air. Among that first wave of refugees there were: — Many generals and other army officers who had perpetrated often unforgivable crimes: Nguyen Cao Ky, the air 'vice-marshall' who had sworn to defend the country to his last breath against the 'communists', was among the first to fly to the United States. —i- The influential members of former pro-American Governments, first of all Thieu, followed by many cabinet ministers, deputies, high-ranking officials, leaders of political parties, politico-religious sects, rabid anti-communists.
— **Rich merchants and industrialists who had been able to buy then-places on the departing planes from American officials in charge of organising the exodus;**
— The staffs of many American services, including intelligence agents and torturers as well as cooks and maidservants taken to the States by their masters.
— **People who should have no reason to flee but who were seized by panic, on account of the terrifying rumours spread by American psycho war services:**
Those with money, gold, foreign currencies, diamonds could settle in the United States or France to set up businesses; technicians were recruited by the administrations or private firms of those countries; the others had to resign themselves to doing hard work or living from subsidies. In the United States in particular, the local populations did not give a warm welcome to those immigrants who, not knowing the language of the host country and lacking professional qualification, had to lead a hard life. The American administration, like the reactionary Western organisations, has been recruiting among those refugees agents who specialise in slander campaigns against the Socialist Republic of Viet Nam.

Some of the refugees, former officers and mercenaries of the Saigon army, have been receiving training in special camps. They are to be reintroduced into the three countries of Indochina in order to man the subversive networks there. Trained agents can come back quite easily to Kampuchea and Laos overland; in the case of Laos they just have to cross the Mekong river; and to Viet Nam by sea.

It would be utterly naive to believe that after their defeat, the American services have lost all interest in Indochia and will allow Kampuchea, Laos and especially Viet Nam to follow their destinies. The many counter-revolutionary networks set up by the Americans in Vietnam continue to keep in touch with foreign countries, mostly by -sea. The South Vietnamese coast, nearly 2,000 kilometres long, cannot be entirely patrolled by the Vietnamese navy.

This is the way things happen: a rich merchant wants to leave Viet Nam, against payment of a handsome amount of cash — 2,000-3,000 US dollars on an average —- a clandestine organisation will take him and his family to a coastal port where they will hide in one of the hundreds of fishing boats that put out to sea every day. At sea, they are picked up by ships which will take them to neighbouring countries. For an 'intellectual', especially a technician with good qualifications, the journey will be free of charge, for the point is to perform a 'brain drain' to the detriment of Viet Nam and simultaneously raise a political hullabaloo.

Let us point out that those with relatives living abroad, especially in France, and who submit applications to this effect, are authorised by the government to leave the country legally in order to settle abroad. From 1975 to 1978, there was thus a regular outflow, of limited scope, of emigres, both legal and illegal. It posed no serious problem either to Viet Nam or to the host countries. In 1978, a new element was to give the problem unprecedented gravity: the Hoa.

This is the designation given to people of Chinese descent living in Viet Nam and other countries of Southeast Asia: Thailand, Malaysia, Indonesia, the Philippines, about 1.5 million of them live in Viet

Nam, with two major concentrations, one in provinces bordering on China, the other in Cho Lon, a separate part of Ho Chi Minh City. The presence of Hoa people in Viet Nam is by no means recent, for the past 20 centuries, each time a particularly disastrous natural calamity, or a change in the political scene, happened in China many Chinese would leave their country to seek refuge in Viet Nam. The Vietnamese authorities would grant them permission to establish separate villages or town quarters. There they lived together, speaking the Chinese language going to work in other villages and quarters, mingling with Vietnamese folk, and would finally become Vietnamese. A large number of present-day Vietnamese are thus of Chinese descent, and the normal historical process was the gradual integration of immigrants into the Vietnamese national community. There never was any discrimination against the Hoa, who were called by the friendly and familiar appellation of 'Chu Khach' (uncle guest, uncle foreigner).

— In the 17th century there was an exodus of partisans of the Ming dynasty following its overthrow by the Manchus who founded the Ching dynasty. Those Ming partisans were authorised by the Vietnamese administration to settle in the Saigon are and in the

Western part of the Mekong delta. Side by side with the Vietnamese they reclaimed virgin land in Nam Bo and built the commercial port of Saigon. Their descendants were totally integrated into Vietnamese society.

— In the 19th century China was shaken by big peasant revolts, the Tai Ping movement in particular (18 50-1864). The failures of those insurrections and their savage repression forced large numbers of peasants to flee China. All along the latter half of the 19th century and the first half of the 20th, there were great upheavals in China: disintegration of the Ching empire, revolution of 1911, internecine struggle among 'warlords', anti-Japanese war, civil war between nationalists and communists. This gave rise to many waves of immigrants who were especially attracted by Saigon — Cho Lon, then in full development.

French colonisation, begun in 1859, brought about an important change in the economic and political status of the Hoa and iterrupted the historical process of their gradual integration into the Vietnamese national community. Following the classical method of conquerors, divide and rule, the French turned the Hoa colony in Viet Nam into a separate community. They used Hoa traders to collect rice in the villages with a view to export, and to retail industrial goods imported from France. Thus the profits drawn from that two-way trade were shared between French firms and Hoa merchants. A Hoa comprador bourgeoisie came into existence which, acting in concert with the French colonial administration, stemmed the development of a Viet-namese bourgeoisie. Solidarity between Hoa and Vietnamese workers was impeded by the special status accorded the former by the French, a status superior to that granted to the 'natives'.

American intervention, accompanied by an enormous inflow of dollars and goods, was a period of great prosperity of the Hoa bourgeoisie. It held the practical monopoly — at least 80 per cent — of all important commercial, industrial, and banking businesses in South Viet Nam. Many of its members became business 'Kings', reigning over such domains as scrap iron, cement sodium glutamate, barbed wire . . . Cabinet ministers and army generals allied them-selves with Hoa comprador bourgeois in order to get rich.

Liberation from the American neo-colonialist system completely upset the living conditions of the Hoa businessmen. No more US dollars, no more US goods, no more hold on foreign trade. The stocks of goods were quickly distributed to innumerable small shop-keepers and peddlers who took advantage of rhe scarcity of commodities and set the prices skyrocketing. An ubiquitous network of rumour-mongers in the immense city of Saigon-Cho Lon would at intervals create panics and provoke a rush on such or such commodi-ty. In this way fat profits were reaped. With the money thus collected, I he big Hoa bourgeoisie and its agents went to the countryside where they bought up as much as possible of the supply of rice, meat, fish and vegetables, which would be resold to the urban population at exorbitant prices.

This situation could not of course last forever. State stores and people's cooperatives were gradually organised and they narrowed down the field of activity of the traffickers. In March 1978, the big trading firms, whether owned by Hoa or Viet people, were ordered to close. The stocks of goods were purchased by the state and the big traders had to devote their capital to productive activities: handicrafts, agricultural or fishing undertakings . . . It is to be noted that this measure affected Viet as well as Hoa traders, but Peking nonetheless claimed it to be a discriminatory and xenophobic step aimed at the Chinese. How strange to see a government styling itself as a socialist one protesting against the suppression of commercial capitalism in another country!

Peking's campaign against Viet Nam concerning the Hoa question in fact started long before. As early as the last months of 1977, Peking agents, acting under the direct control of the Chinese embassy in Hanoi, were telling the Hoa community that Peking would soon make war against Viet Nam: that in these conditions the Vietnamese would certainly start massacring the Chinese; that the Hoa would be well-advised to leave Viet Nam as soon as possible and go back to China was only a few dozen kilometres away, and so many Hoa living close to the frontier opted for leaving.

When they arrived at the frontier, the Chinese authorities did not allow them to take normal passages for crossing, thus compelling them to ford streams and travel along jungle tracks: Chinese cameramen were on hand to film poignant scenes of exodus which helped the Peking propaganda machine to present the Vietnamese people to Chinese and world opinion as an ungrateful people who, forgetful of the great assistance granted by China, were now persecuting and expelling Chinese residents.

In 1978, about 160,000 Hoa people left Viet Nam, and more in February-March 1979. For, once back in China, large numbers of Hoa were given training and formed into special units specialising in reconnaissance, commando, and sabotage operations.

The precipitate departure of Hoa people threw the economy of some provinces into utter confusion. This economic dislocation was to become one of the targets of Peking, specially in Ho Chi Minh city where lived particularly large number of Hoa traders and workers. Clandestine Peking's subversive networks urged the Hoa population to engage in economic sabotage. The Chinese invasion of February-March 1979 and the subversive activities of on-the-spot Peking agents put the Hoa in Viet Nam in a particularly distressing situation; many decided to leave the country in order to avoid having to face agonising choices. Hence the massive wave of departures in 1979.

The impasse in the negotiations between die Vietnamese and Chinese governments and the bellicose declarations of Deng Xiaoping with regard to Viet Nam have given rise to great anguish among the Hoa community, the problem of leaving the country assumes special gravity. So long as Peking's warlike policy continues, it is to be expected that the exodus will go on.

POLITICAL PROBLEM, HUMANITARIAN PROBLEM

In the outflow of people leaving Viet Nam it is thus possible to make a distinction between those who are doing so for economic reasons and the Hoa, whose departure is based on much more complex factors. These departures give rise to two kinds of problems.

— Political problems: who is responsible for this human tragedy? What is at stake politically?
— Humanitarian problems: How to alleviate the sufferings of people reduced to leaving a country where they have been living for long years?

One need not be a learned scholar or a shrewd politician to see that the deterioration of the living conditions of people in South Viet Nam is not wanted by die revolutionary administration. The Vietnamese are not the only people in the world to recall the responsibility of the men who had sent their troops to Viet Nam: die Washington leaders, who are at present among those shouting the loudest at Viet Nam.

If the American government, and its allies, had contributed to the reconstruction of Viet Nam, this would certainly have spared many South Vietnamese the necessity of leaving dieir country. On 1st February 1973, the dien president of the United States, Richard Nixon, sent to Prime Minister Priam Van Dong the following message:

The President wishes to inform the Democratic Republic of Viet Nam of the principles which will govern the United States 'participation in th post war reconstruction of North Viet Nam. As indicated in article 21 of the Agreement on ending the war and restoring peace in Viet Nam signed in Paris on Jan. 27, 1973, the United States undertakes this participation in accordance with its traditional policies. These principles are as follows:

1. The government of die United Sates will contribute to postwar reconstruction in North Viet Nam without any political conditions.
2. Preliminary United States studies indicate that the appropriate programmes for the United States' contribution to postwar reconstruction will fall in the range of $3.25 billion of grant aid over five years. Other forms of aid will be agreed upon between the two parties.

Thus the American Government can use no pretext to evade the fulfilment of that written and formal pledge. And yet, for the past six years, Washington has not disbursed one single dollar for a country that American weapons had terribly ravaged.

Political obligation, moral obligation: any self-respecting American will think of the problem in these terms, the more so since the United States is the country which can most effectively help both in the reconstruction of Viet Nam and in providing the emigres with a decent livelihood.

Responsibility for the refugees thus should not fall on the countries of Southeast Asia, as is now the case, but on the United States in the first place.

As for the Hoa living in Viet Nam, who has driven them to the present tragic situation? As early as 1955-1957, an agreement was reached between the Vietnamese and Chinese Parties and Governments under the terms of which the Hoa would henceforth fall under Vietnamese jurisdiction and would be gradually integrated into the Vietnamese society. The Vietnamese audiorities did all they could to implement this agreement.

It is indeed strange that Peking should strive its utmost to denounce Viet Nam for persecuting the Hoa while keeping its mouth tightly shut when Pol Pot was massacring the half a million Hoa who were living in Kampuchea.

The two main responsible parties, the USA and China, having refused to shoulder their polticat and moral obligations, the considerable burden constituted by the refugees has fallen on the ASEAN countries. It is only legitimate that these countries should protest and ask to be relieved of this responsibility. (This is, however, no justification for inhumane measures).

If the Vietnamese regime were a ferocious one, comparable for instance to that imposed by the Shah of Iran on his people, how could one then explain the fact that the entire people rallied *like* one man behind their government and Communist Party against 600,000 troops sent by Peking? Why is it that the people, to whom the government had distributed arms in abundance, did not take advantage of the occasion to liberate themselves?

Could the Vietnamese Government find any advantage, economic or political, in this question of refugees? We can say this clearly and distinctly: The Vietnamese Government compels no one to leave the country; on the other hand it does not forcibly retain anyone who wishes to go and settle elsewhere. The outflow of refugees, among them doctors and engineers, disorganises the economy and disturbs social order. To think that the Vietnamese Government is forcing people to leave is to believe it masochistic.

The Vietnamese Government only wants certain principles to be observed:

— Those who leave should do so legally, after performing all necessary administrative formalities;

— Clandestine departures, organised en masse with the complicity of national and international reactionary forces, affect the security of the country, disorganise its economy, and infringe national sovereignty; such departures are therefore prohibited.

There may be cadres who have availed themselves of the situation to get their palms greased, but this is not government policy. Let us stress that while a number of Vietnamese cadres have allowed themselves to be corrupted, no senior cadre has ever been involved in such affairs for in Viet Nam no cabinet minister or army general keeps accounts in foreign banks or is connected with major foreign companies (Lockheed for instance of CF. Watergate).

The major political fact in this question is the vast and-Vietnamese campaign launched throughout the world by the mass media of Peking and the West in a well-orchestrated manner.

This campaign is no novelty. It has indeed started in Washington where the American leaders, unable to use Vietnam's tribulations to erase from people's minds the immense responsibilities of their government and stubbornly refusing to honour their aid pledge, seek to give a good conscience to the American people. Jimmy Carter has found the method: human rights. Viet Nam, the victim of American barbarity, will thus find itself in the dock while the USA will smartly join the ranks of the defenders of law and justice. There have been former friends of Viet Nam who have lent a hand to this legerdemain trick; some in good faith and without being aware that they are being-manipulated; others knowing^. The mass media have immediately supported the operation. On 27 December 1976, in the *Los Angeles Times* ran a big headline: 'No human rights, no aid!'.

From the USA the campaign has spread to Europe. Now, the Western and Pekingese press, radio and television are in a frenzy over the question of refugees. The American and European Governments are seeking to put the problem in tragic light and isolate Viet Nam from its Southeast Asian neighbours. All this concerted action has given rise to an atmosphere of cold war vis-a-vis Viet Nam.

This cold war may lead to a shooting war for world opinion is being conditioned for a passive acceptance of a new aggression upon Viet Nam. In the eyes of imperialist forces and the Peking leaders, this country is guilty of at least three 'crimes'.

— That of being the third-world country which stubbornly refuses to be integrated into the world economic system set up by the multi-national companies;
— That of being a socialist country; Viet Nam is considered the vulnerable link of the socialist system at present;
— That of being the major obstacle to Chinese expansion into Southeast Aia (in fact it has played this role repeatedly in the course of history).

It is no accident that while the campaign is being feverishly conducted, American and French military missions have made long stays in China to make a study of weapons to be supplied to the Chinese army and the strategy and tactics to be recommended to it. Although the failure of their invasion in February-March 1979 has seriously shaken the Peking rulers, their aggressiveness has not been damped down.

The same Western and Pekingese mass media that shed tears over the Vietnamese refugees are hushing up the fate of Palestinians forced into exile and have let the millions of victims of the 'great cultural revolution' sink into oblivion. Human rights are not their true concern. All this hullaballoo should not cause men of goodwill to forget that there is a human problem, a tragic one in certain respects, that should be solved and for which quick and appropriate solutions should be found. For several categories are to be observed among the refugees:
— The great majority have left Viet Nam for economic reasons, unable to bear the privations and having failed to find occupations to their liking. Among them are not only big traders and rich traffickers but also mere employees — bartenders for instance — whose trades have dropped out of use and who could not muster the courage to go and reclaim new land;

— Some are former war criminals or are now members of counter-revolutionary networks who feel they are about to be discovered;
— In the case of the intellectuals, there are various factors which combine in varying degrees.

All have experienced a serious drop in their standard of living; when a medical doctor who used to travel in a car and live in an air-conditioned villa becomes a cadre in a public hospital, his salary is barely one-tenth of his former income. To this is added the difficulty he feels to adapt himself to the new society, to the constraint of a revolutionary society which is, moreover, facing innumerable hindrances. It is with a heavy heart that those intellectuals resign themselves to leaving a country which, at bottom, they would like to serve.

Whatever category the refugees may belong to and whatever reason may be behind their departure from Viet Nam, the Vietnamese Government and the other governments concerned, together with the international community, must coordinate their action in order to resolve the problem.

The Vietnamese Government has agreed with the office of the United Nations High Commissioner for Refugees (U.N.H.C.R.) that the question be resolved on the basis of a seven-point accord which provides for the following modalities:

— Ah" those wishing to leave shall perform the necessary administrative formalities with the Vietnamese authorities;
— The Vietnamese Government shall hand over to the U.N.H.C.R. the list of would-be emigres so that the latter may approach potential receiving countries;
— The U.N.H.C.R. shall organise the journeys of those who will have obtained the consent of receiving countries.

All those who through personal channels have obtained the necessary visas from certain governments — this is the case of people with children or relatives living in France, Canada, Japan, etc. — can leave the country through the normal ways. As we said above, illegal departures, which may affect the security, sovereignty and economic stability of the country cannot be tolerated. Those who are standing trial before courts of law or who are holders of important economic and administrative responsibilities cannot leave. Obviously those who have left can return to Viet Nam only with the formal and individual authorisation of the Vietnamese Government. One should not forget that the Chinese Government which drove the Hoa into a massive exodus to China in 1978 is now demanding that the Vietnamese Government agree to the return of that mass of refugees who had left Viet Nam of their own free will. Such a massive return of those Hoa will give rise to innumerable economic and political difficulties.

The Government of rich countries, the USA hi particular, should give assistance to the countries of Southeast Asia on which the burden of the refugees, especially the Hoa, has fallen. To date the Governments of some of the richest countries have only picked technicians and intellectuals from the mass of refugees, abandoning the rest to the care of the ASEAN countries.

The Vietnamese people, fully engaged in healing the wounds of long years of war, fervently wish that this painful problem be resolved in the quickest and most humane way possible. Those who leave will remain for them brothers, friends, compatriots.

We earnestly call on people of goodwill throughout the world to
— Actively help the emigres to obtain decent living conditions in the receiving countries;
— Demand that the American and Chinese Governments fulfil their duty vis-a-vis people whom their warlike policies have uprooted and driven into exodus;
— Be on their guard against political exploitation of the problem with a view to preparing for war.

For its part, Viet Nam is resolved to cooperate with all international organisations to settle this problem in the most humane way possible.

(From a statement released in Hanoi on July 18, 1979)

US/British 'far left' and Greece

Just like they did nothing for the struggle of independence for Kenya prior to that what is it they did regarding Britain's involvement in fostering Greece's civil war and supporting the collaborators of Hitler?

The British 'far left' has always been in the overwhelming majority **pro-imperialist alongside their American counterparts.** Their support is always based on the 'ethnics' behaving themselves and following what the centre decides.

The **WRP-** Gerry Healy had an organisation in Greece which destroyed the first post-dictatorial printshop after expelling the majority of the organisation in a typical healyite frame up and shutting down all the bookshops. Throughout this period Bob Archer was with Gerry Healy and not only that, when their honcho in Athens (another self-styled fake jew Savvas Michael) was parading in Tehran and Libya singing the praises in order to get money from there we were supposed to keep quiet when allegations regarding rape and financial fraud were aired in public for the first time. I made a special journey to the UK to interview their Gestetner trade union rep they had called Richard Goldstein and translated the interview and with a series of reports, posters and adverts in Pontiki exposed the WRP and called for a Commission of Inquiry (as to whether they had handed over pictures of Iraqui communists to Saddam and taken money from the oil-igarchs) but the successors to Healy weren't interested only in trying to maintain Healyism without Healy. In the 90's Archers alliances with Slaughter were based on an anti-Serb venom paralleled only by Blair (who obviously had guns). There is a saying in Greek 'show me who your friends are and I will tell you who you are' fits accordingly with Bob Archer and David Walters. A marriage made in heaven.

The **Militant** had followers in PASOK who were in PASOK. One wing 'left' in 1991 another about three years ago. What discerned them was their slavish acceptance of PASOK as being 'social democratic' instead of pure capitalist (liberal centre party of Greek capitalism) and their careerist appetites. When things started to rock they jumped ship in order to find new homes (latest declaring themselves the 'communist wing in Syriza and supporting the Euro, EZ and EU!!) Those that joined PASOK or were allied to it did it for material gain, there wasn't much politics and there hasn't been much since. When hundreds of thousands hit the squares swearing at Parliament and the PASOK and ND MP's how did they cdes of Militant in Greece feel? Their whole lifetime in politics was geared around being in PASOK. Insofar as they marched in the 70's chanting 'US bases Out' 'National Independence and Territorial Integrity'' EC and NATO are the Same' Greece Belongs to the Greeks', they weren't racist or nationalist, but John Reinman http://oaklandsocialist.com/ ;if he was a member then forgets the 'sins' of his youth and in old age seeks revenge to those who remind him of his past. Now if they weren't the slogans being chanted confirm that with those who were there...

SWP Greece has been one of the most vociferous in gaining EU subsidies to promote 'diversity and multiculturalism' through their open border Soros networks (Athens Indymedia run on govt platforms from the Athens Polytechnic), language schools for foreigners, social forums etc and its no coincidence that when they were exposed way back in 2004 I was banned from even broaching the subject in their media. Half their organisation after the SWP UK touting it as being the biggest in Greece joined Sinaspismos to get an electoral subsidy and now in the leader of Davanelos they parade as being the 'left opposition' inside Syriza when they have been known to support every anti-Greek act by foreign US subsidised govts eg Skopje when they marched there holding up the flags of a foreign territory which has claims on Greece, over the issue of Macedonia. When hundreds of thousands of Greeks marched in the 90's against the USA's attempts at divide and rule they resurrected the hundreds of thousands who marched during the 3rd Reich (when it handed over a section of northern Greece to Bulgaria without fear for their lives and many were killed.)

They consistently campaigned against the citizens groups that sprung up in central Athens turning up with the riot cops to tear gas them and hurl abuse from 2008 onwards. GD turned up for the same reasons to pay lip service to the struggle of the residents in order to gather votes. Now because the SWP are the marketing agents for GD (they both call each other Bolsheviks and nazi respectively when they are nothing of the sort just two sides of the same globalist coin) they managed to help gain them votes from 0.29% to 10% in three years. A group which is so ridiculous allegedly against the Troika but for the EU and against Merkel but for her as they condemn the protests against her. Now the corporate global media jumped on the bandwagon of GD these votes hover around 15-20%. The system is creating its next fallback option in the form of Syriza or GD as players in any coalition that might be formed.

Left unchecked illegal immigration would be a ticking time bomb. Campaigning around the fake slogan of 'migrant rights' and calling for 'unity' among all and sundry may apply to imperialist centres which had colonies all over the world but does not apply to banana republics for the scale and volume of immigration surpasses the domestic labour force (Eleftherotypia-newspaper spoke in 2004 about the presence of 2.5m so has the Greek TUC research department INE-GSEE spoken about the presence of 40% foreign born workers in relation to the indigenous labour force). That is over a decade ago.

Campaigned pro-actively for a vote for PASOK in 1991...

Permanent Revolution- ex-Workers Power (another now disbanded group and the irony here is Walters always intervenes on the scene whilst groups are on the verge of disbanding) had a blog site. I intervened initially on topics related to Greece as I did with a series of letters in Weekly Worker regarding Greece. PR forecasted perpetual boom (instead of 'catastrophist theory'... as they labelled it) just as the EZ was going into depression and they asked for a meeting and a series of eyewitness reports from Greece. In the middle of one of them when we had a two day bombardment to destroy the occupation of the squares Walters appeared with his poison pen letters (not on the content of the material which was being uploaded by the way) to talk about ....gays and immigration. PR then blocked the second eye-witness report. PR who were an offshoot of Workers Power have known that I disagree with the Americanisation of politics in fields of sexual relations (its not the duty of labour parties to actively promote any sexual lifestyles) from the 80's. But as British they are in bed with the Yanks and kowtow to their every whim. In that they follow the political class that rules Britain to the letter. They are American poodles.

'Weekly Worker' or otherwise known as Globalist Weekly
When a book came out 'How the IMF Broke Greece' edited by me with contributions from others and was reviewed by an ex-British miner Dave Douglass, Walters appeared on the scene (without having read it to attack it!) and to say 'illegal immigration' is good for Greece as it has been good for... America. The irony now of the situation is that illegal immigration left unchecked has led to riots in many parts of Greece. We are now being told to condemn Greeks for rioting when Greeks are being killed by the local corporate media, the foreign corporate media (Paul Mason-Newsnight Channel 4 John Snow) in other words to accept their lot as no one can go against the 4th Reich (much like the ex-cdes of the Vitsoris group) for the arrival of millions in the territory of Greece is a natural phenomena ('migration theory,' 'human rights ' in the past it was just known as Lebensraum). Funny how Cuba closes its borders to 'gusanos' but Greece cant. So why does Greece have a navy, an army and a rail service? To ship them in by the kilo dump them without any means of support in a concrete mega city and then expect them to live like hippies (ie to molest no one, to commit no crimes to live idyllically by eating air and handing out flowers to each passer by in particular old ladies not living like animals in squares and using them as latrines in 40c heat) as if they are in Matala in Crete in the 70's.

Or let's put it another way. 15 million or so tourists visit Greece a year. Why not turn the tourist industry into just a reception centre of illegal immigration so no UN conventions on 'human rights' are breached. Ensure each new arrival is housed and fed to the standard of tourists in hotels and turn Greeks into waiters for this service so they can get some hotel work back as they have been made redundant from that as well. After all an 'open border' policy espoused by Greeks who were trained under Lyndon Larouche and happen to be the family that had the central bankster bros under Simitis who brought us into the Euro (and now pretend they are the rrrevolutionaries of Antarsya) are the direct connection between the British 'far left' and Greece.

But the fake left wont touch the topic as they don't want to go against the status quo. They are globalisations last vital bulwark. Hence when they look at Syriza they see 'success' and want to repeat it abroad as if the conditions are the same everywhere and the success of Syriza whatever that means in practice, is anything to look up to other than with they eyes of parliamentary cretins, just as the Greek parliament has ceased to exist.

There is no nationalism as yet of Greek labour. It has been decimated, de-industrialised and replaced by globalized labour which has no interest for Greece or the Greek nation. They are all there for their own individual ends not the collective ends of society as they can just up sticks and leave at any moment in time and aren't interested in society or social issues as issues. Hence one notices the total absence of immigrants from the globalist left and if they are there they are there for show like a flower on vase by the window.

But that isn't the issue with Walters. Walters does not seek debate just the closure of it by creating labels, latest one being I am David Irving when he openly supports the ethnic cleansing of Greeks. Well what label aspires to him? The only good American is a dead one? After all he is on record to not support the military conflicts arrayed against the USA from Afghanistan to Iraq... wants the mess that is the USA exported everywhere and assumes we have to fall for it.

The other irony is that all the parties of the official fake Left KKE-Syriza ask for illegals to leave Greece ie by overturning the Dublin 2 agreement and being given travel papers to go to northern Europe to alleviate Greece's problems. In other words they want Greece to be an open border arrival point, then processing and then movement up the chain. You don't hear Walters criticise them for being anti-immigration now do you? That is what Syriza and the KKE openly argue. Lets look at Lenin:

"What does 'Down with frontiers' mean? It is the beginning of anarchy.... Only when the socialist revolution has become a reality, and not a method, will the slogan 'Down with frontiers' be a correct slogan."

Lenin April 1917 on the National Question
http://classicalmarxismvsimmigration.blogspot.com/2011/02/lenin-against-open-borders.html"

I remain committed to the ideals of '**Greece belongs to the Greeks'**, '**US Bases Out'**, '**Greece must Exit the EU'** etc. even if Syrizas new found friends in the bankruptcy of the Anglo-American 'far left' have adopted the Brookings Institute, the London School of Economics and the world banks as their mantra and the evidence of it is that all talk of 'socialism' is in reality just talk about lifestyles (race or sex never about class). Hence there never was any 'debate' on the **WIN** site, just a concerted and united effort by Americans and their British toadies to state openly Greece should cease to exist. One does not debate neo-fascists, one exposes them openly for what they are, pure globalists whether of the 'open' or closed variety.

On neo-fascism...
I'll leave the last words to Lafazanis the leader of the Left Faction in Syriza with 30% of the votes at their founding conference:
"you want a procedure with Presidential decrees in order to avoid the control of Parliament – a control which is to be avoided only by non-democratic regimes. The two bourgeois parties have engineered a disgusting and to be condemned coup, blatantly, by using Parliament as a decoration"
2nd August 2013

Which leaves one with the obvious question if the Greek Parliament no longer votes on anything why does the Left still participate in it?

Much like the other question. David Walters alleges he has the same line as me on the nation state and he was criticised by Gerry (Hands off the US Ambassador in Libya!) Downing that he is a rabid nationalist and that a national question arises if the volume of immigration is such to question the identity of nations, but that this law is overturned if you are an imperialist country or sub-imperialist overturning Trotskys observations in 1940 that a national question may also emerge in imperialist countries if overrun by Hitler, he argues for the closure of borders in non-imperialist countries. So how come that doesn't make him a xenophobe, nationalist as Gerry alleges? So South Africa must have arrived at an imperialist level of development as well?

EU-USA=One World Govt
"The totalitarian state, subjecting all aspects of economic, political, and cultural life to finance capital, is the instrument for creating a supernationalist state, an imperialist empire, the rule over continents, the rule over the whole world."
Nationalism and Economic Life
-Leon Trotsky 1933

The centralising tendencies of global imperialism implies they no longer seek to have nation states with any role whatsoever. They are creating an imperialist unification based not on army invasions like Hitler (that happened with the defeat of Germany and Japan in WW2) but on NATO, WTO, central banks, IMF, common currencies leading to world currencies. By destroying nations or creating mini-USA's everywhere imperialism wants to create the old 'divide and rule' philosophy to control and contain all labour movements like what the British Empire did in Africa when it shipped Indians over and blocked the Blacks from working on the railways so they could not disrupt the Empire.

'Socialist' Discussion Site… WIN Ex Militant PASOK globalist lackeys now in **Left Unity**

I was on the site for one month prior to withdrawing. The eyewitness report from the ERT occupation affected the Syriza lackeys... on the site. Let's have a look at some of their comments:
'Greeks are 'primitive xenophobes' Dan

'*Apodidictic manner*' **Bob Archer Tradeunion co-ordinator Greek solidarity**

After explaining to me that Greece benefitted from the EU and EZ and the EU I am told...despite contrary information provided from a KKE source:
'I would be grateful if vngelis would take part in the discussion in a less strident manner.'
Dan

"The sarcasm in vngelis' postings is unpleasant and uncomradely. S/He is constantly trying to associate those who disagree with him as fake lefts, supporters of quislings or appeasers of fascism. This is not an appropriate style for this discussion"
Dan

Being labeled a terrorist here....
"Both sought to "expose" the true character of the "neofascist" state by provoking it into battles with the revolutionary brigades; both resorted to acts of individual terror, assassination and bomb throwing in an attempt to short circuit the process of winning the majority of the class. These were the Italian Red Brigades and the German Red Army Fraction."
Dan

"Sorry Comrade Gelis, I strongly disagree with your views. **If Greece is swallowed up by workers from across the world I will not mourn** but as Joe Hill put it: organize"
Stu

From a primitive xenophobe to whether I am ...Greek...

"I guess the question to Comrade Gelis and to all of us are you Greek (or wherever you are from) first or a communist revolutionary first? If the former than Comrade Gelis' comments fit and present a radical nationalist view. If the latter then we are internationalists and the borders drawn and maintained by the oppressors mean nothing to us."
Stu

"In some ways, there is a similar issue here in California, and we see it very concretely here in Oakland, where I live. My own neighbourhood, for instance, used to be 90% people born in this country; now it is a mixture of Asians, Latin Americans, one block which is primarily Iraqis, etc. (My own personal attitude is that this polyglot really makes things interesting.) Yes, there is competition for jobs. Also, I understand that some of the immigrants receive certain government services that native born people who are in equal need don't, and this does create some resentment. My attitude is that everybody should get these services.

If it is really true that Greece's economy is really, actually being strained by the numbers of immigrants, then I think the movement should demand that the EU help provide for them. But what I feel most strongly is this: How can any movement that is fighting for a better society take the attitude towards immigrants of "You can drown in the sea. You can go back home and be bombed to death. You can go back home and starve." No working class movement can take that attitude and move forward. It is inevitable that if it does, it will turn to nationalism and some sort of racism and/or sexism as well as homophobia, etc."
John Reinmann

"My son has worked on building sites in Greece where the lingua franca of the site was English because of the range of nationalities working there. The description of the working conditions was like something from a century ago. He is also scathing of the commonplace racism he experienced there."
Felicity Dowling – Left Unity Spokesperson

Walters other American friend a lawyer (Stephen R Diamond) who did a stint with Healy's outfit (under Wohlforth) in the USA prior to the Greenstein mob that took over and now prints the Financial Times for the USA has ditched the Trade Unions and on the WSWS website goes round attacking the nationalism of everybody, but not the American transnational corporations that rule the world… for which Walters has defended vociferously.

"A CAPITALIST WORLD GOVERNMENT IS A UTOPIAN ILLUSION, BUT IF IT WERE IN THE OFFING, IT WOULD PROBABLY BE MORE SOMETHING TO BE WISHED FOR THAN SOMETHING TO BE FEARED. YES, I VALUE THE ELIMINATION OF WAR MUCH MORE THAN THE PRESERVATION OF GREEK NATIONAL CULTURE. YOUR VALUES ARE FUNDAMENTALLY WARPED--IT GOES MUCH DEEPER THAN A MERE POLITICAL DIFFERENCE. "

SRD

US Imperialism a snake that cannot change its spots…

Weekly Worker (Globalists par excellence) in an ad hominem attack

Will the real Maciej Zurowski please stand up?
"If China," says Mr. Stapleton, M.P., to his constituents, "should become a great manufacturing country, I do not see how the manufacturing population of Europe could sustain the contest without descending to the level of their competitors." (Times, Sept. 3, 1873, p. 8.)

The wished-for goal of English capital is no longer Continental wages but Chinese."
Marx

Out of the blue the known globalist rag 'Weekly Worker' regurgitates old arguments on Greece not for the sake of a discussion as they have imposed a ban on responses from myself (after the last round of ad hominem attacks by David Walters, Gerry Downing with the respect to the book produced and reviewed in Weekly Worker on Greece) (1) and have now used the services of some unknown Polish journalist to promote the EU and the American NWO.

A search on the internet finds this character but he is now deceased. Our esteemed cde. assumes a name from the past (<ahref="http://en.wikipedia.org/wiki/Maciej_%C5%BBurowski">http://en.wikipedia.org/wiki/Maciej_%C5%BBurowski</a>) ...
Spitting on the past of the (19th Century) First International and the reason Marx created it (defend workers living standards and block the bosses ability of recruiting workers from abroad to break strikes) he pretends the First International didn't have whip rounds to repatriate workers, didn't agitate against 'free movement' and didn't realise early on that mass migration/emigration (controlled by the bosses) led to a perpetuation of slavery. (2) The reason he has such venum against the blog I have is that none of it is by myself, its what the classical Marxists wrote and that is what enrages him as anyone can read it and work things out for themselves.

Maciej isn't really interested in the 'debate' on open borders. Weekly Worker is imploding and one has noticed that they venomously allowed an attack on a Willie Hunter (paedophile connotations) an ex-cde of theirs being an anti-Semite (Ian Donovan) and now alleging I am a...Nazi. These tiny outfits act as vassals to globalism to ensure the flock return home (to Labourism) and they promote the EU above all else (repeatedly giving to the 'permanent boom of capitalism' lie in the letters of the buffoon Arthur Bough).

According to John Plant (editor of Revolutionary History), a Mike McNair was allegedly going to review the book produced in English 'Classical Marxism and Immigration' by myself and S Lawrence (3) but presumably this hatchet job from an anti-communist from Poland is the answer, in other words, mass immigration is here to stay, is positive the world over as it abolishes nation states and leads to a...post-capitalist nirvana, which raises living standards for the working class and does not reduce them to penury, as has happened to the Greek working class which has been forced to receive millions of illegal immigrants without being asked by the globalist Greek quisling politicians of the Fourth Reich. (Greek Cross Party Parliamentary Committee did look into it in 1993!) (4)
In the meantime in the real world, the EU instigated expansionist wars on the borders of the EU, starting in ex-Yugoslavia and ending in the Ukraine are events that are always supported by 'WW', the 'racism' of the indigenous nationalities (Serbs, E. Ukrainians) is always decried and the hyper-globalism of the City of London/Wall St always promoted as progress, precisely because they destroy working class living standards and create a globalised 'melting pot' so beloved by an 'educated lumpen petty bourgeoisie', current shock troops of the Fourth Reich, who move abroad in search of greener pastures like they change shirts and if an 'uneducated' barbarian from the 'lower orders' dares to complain about the EU and its four core principles (freedom of movement for capital, labour, services and goods), they bring out the big hammer of 'Racism' and for those who require special treatment, 'Nazism'. No wonder the rightists are sweeping the board clean (France, UK) and there is widespread popular venom against the EU.

Maciej wants to defend his Polish brethren in their mass movement West, (admitting by default that they are playing the role the Irish did in the Nineteenth Century in undercutting labour), but forgets to add that then capitalism was still expanding, in particular in the USA, whilst now it is declining and the jobs don't actually exist for population transfers of this gargantuan magnitude.

Recent surveys have shown for example London has 200,000 less school places and the use of the ambulance service has increased by 4 million in less than a decade whilst the actual service has been cut. Is this any wonder when the new arrivals have made no contribution to the capital cost, of this infrastructure?

Characters like Maciej want their globalist cake (unlimited mass migration) with no respect for the standards of pre-existing workers or the public services they were entitled to receive. But in reality this unceasing mass immigration becomes a harbinger of the third worldisation of all standards under the guise of 'working class unity' which dictates 'don't be 'racist' show 'class solidarity' and let it happen'. There were individuals like that in WWII who argued that one could not go against the occupation soldiers of the Third Reich as they were workers like us, and they were developing unity with them, borders were being erased, we were seeing the end of 'reactionary' nation states and so on, all this bringing the struggle for 'internationalist' socialism closer. They forgot to add that in the meantime the people were experiencing barbarism and they wanted to stop it, not encourage its further spread the world over. But since 1989 the old left has made peace with capitalism and not any capitalism in general, in any particular period of history, but US capitalism, the last global capitalism (that has used nuclear weapons and has the power to self-destruct) and it is to this type of capitalism, the bastard offspring of European capitalism, we must all bow down to.

The American Empire inaugurating its NWO destroyed the multi-ethnic state of ex-Yugoslavia in cahoots with German imperialism. Now it is intent on destroying the old nation states of Europe with the mass importation of millions of illegal immigrants, one of which

is Maciej himself. Some E European countries, like Albania, haven't even joined, but their population was one of the first into the EU. No host countries were allowed a referendum on the entrance of E Europe. This process has created multi-ethnic ghettos with no tradition and no history. In the field of labour we have had the emergence of zero hours contracts, the equivalent of these multi-ethnic entities could be characterised as 'zero history nations'. To this Maciej subscribes politically, but of course someone from 'WW' didn't tell him that he joined the 'party' just as it finished...
(Lehman's bros crash)

Stalinism, a cancer of the labour movement for a whole historical period, allowed the collapse of the British Empire to morph into the American one and get away scot free. Today the practitioners of the politics of globalism are everywhere defending and promoting America in decline, but nowhere more so than decrepit British Labourism and the trade union flunkeys that fund it and have made its politics indistinguishable from the Texas oil-igarchy.
On the other allegations which are the stock in trade of American globalists that there is only one holocaust ie the jewish one, (no Russian or Black or Armenian one) this obviously fits in with the adoption of cold war politics which sought to minimise the intra-european nature of WW2 (ie Russian, Greek resistance as a % of total population dead and in overall numbers) and elevate American storytelling that WW2 was only about the ...jews and if anyone was to question that they would join the ranks ...of 'holocaust deniers'. This type of garbage works well in academia or the 'legal marxists' (as Lenin referred to them in his days), but in the real world people just laugh. For deep down it's the politics of Hollywood, praising the US Empire even when we all know it cant fight (Vietnam, Iraq Afghanistan) or it joins wars right at the end to come on top (WW1 and WW2). Especially when we have current war criminals going about the business (Blair, Bush etc.)

Why the sudden interest in Greece? When Greece officially defaults and goes back to its national currency the whole EU project which was a political attempt at unifying the ruling classes will start to fully unravel. It is this event and this fact alone that massively enrages the pettybourgeoisie and they focus all their energies in arguing 'Greeks should be erased from history' (David Walters) (5) if that is to save the EU and condemning the nationalism of the Greeks (whilst at the same time defending the supra-nationalism of the EU, NATO, USA) or the hyper-nationalism of the Germans (whose sole claim to fame is that they bankrupt Europe time after time). The Pole Maciej is in good company. Having abandoned Russia and slavish subservience to Stalinism he has gone over direct from Warsaw without a stop straight to Washington and fully embraced globalism. If he was to be a waiter or even a doorman at the top table one could say good luck and good riddance, but I doubt if they ever even assign him a role in taking out the garbage, for which he has been trained (when he throws Weekly Worker into his own)…

For after all a so-called paper that prints attacks, but bars the right to reply is nothing better than the Murdoch press, a print medium they have more in common than anyone else. (6)

Part Two

Who runs Weekly Worker? Grandson of Neville Chamberlain ex-PM and Grandfater Secretary of State for Colonies?

That would explain why they are so pro-EU. They want it to reach New Delhi (Mode 4 agreement as highlighted by No2EU) and recreate the 19th Century Empire all over, not only does this run in their politics, it presumably runs in their veins...

VN Gelis
22nd October 2014

Notes

1. Dave Douglass Review of How the IMF Broke Greece: Eyewitness Reports and the Role of the Fake Lefthttp://imfoccupationgreece.blogspot.co.uk/2011/12/dave-douglass-reviews-vn-gelis-how-imf.html
2. 2. http://classicalmarxismvsimmigration.blogspot.co.uk/
3. 3. Book on Classical Marxism and Immigration http://classicalmarxismvsimmigration.blogspot.co.uk/2012/10/coming-soon-new-book-on-immigration.html
4. 4. The Left knew: Cross Party Parliamentary Committee on the Impact of Mass Immigration <a href="http://imfoccupationgreece.blogspot.co.uk/2013/08/the-left-knewparliamentary-committee-on.html">http://imfoccupationgreece.blogspot.co.uk/2013/08/the-left-knewparliamentary-committee-on.html</a>
5. 5. David Walters: An American Provocateur Proponent of One World Government.. http://imfoccupationgreece.blogspot.co.uk/2013/11/british-american-globalist-fake.html

6. Unpublished Letter to Weekly Worker
http://imfoccupationgreece.blogspot.co.uk/2012/02/unpublished-letter-to-weekly-worker.html

7. <ahref="http://www.google.com/url?q=http%3A%2F%2Fderekthomas2010.wordpress.com%2F2013%2F03%2F01%2Fwho-is-richard-seymours-friend-john-chamberlain%2F&sa=D&sntz=1&usg=AFQjCNGHG_OxS5g4yjIkh9mZ_LlFIVxTgQ">http://derekthomas2010.wordpress.com/2013/03/01/who-is-richard-seymours-friend-john-chamberlain/

Marx Memorial Library,

Complaint,

It has come to my attention after he was introduced to my Facebook site that you have held public meetings with a Sukant Chandan of a collective known as Sons of Malcolm.

Sukant allegedly wanted to know about the economic effects of the 3rd Bailout by Syriza for which I provided him information.

Subsequently not knowing who he is or what he stands for, I saw various posts he placed on his FB site. The main thrust of his argument is that *an unlimited number of migrants* have the right to come to Europe ie. Greece and that this is the right due to the colonial history of Europe. The fact that Greece never had colonies in the modern capitalist era but was itself like Serbia a neo-colony, was neither here nor there.

Subsequently Chandan appeared on RT and stated the following that **"black and Asian people should come here in the hundreds of millions, it's not right that in the last 500 years imperialism has looted our wealth destroyed our countries, we will come here we have been coming here and we will continue to come here in the hundreds of millions and like Gaddafi said until Europe turns black"**

https://www.youtube.com/watch?v=-HbS7EfFP1w
Whilst it's now fashionable on the so-called Left to spout genocidal nonsense about the elimination of nations the fact that you are associated with this individual and give a platform to such views makes you willing accomplices.

Serbs lost 75% of their adult male population during WW1 to gain independence from the Austro-Hungarian Empire and Greece had the 3rd highest casualties as a percentage of its population fighting fascism

The 1948 UN Convention on the Prevention and the Punishment of the Crime of Genocide. Article 2, section c states that genocide involves (c) Deliberately inflicting on the group conditions of life calculated to bring about its physical destruction in whole or in part.

If neo-globalist clowns like Sukant Chandan assume the rights of nations no longer exist and they have no say who comes into their territory and at what level due to some allegedly historic right of correcting the 'white races' genocide of colonial and semi-colonial countries, then giving a platform to such views characterises the Marx Memorial Library and all those who administer it.

Sukant Chandan wrote in Website edited by ex CIA Afghan station chief.
http://www.conflictsforum.org/.../secularism-and.../

VN Gelis

13th March 2016

Books in English about Greece published by VN Gelis

Classic Marxist Texts
on Immigration
(Marx, Engels, Lenin,
Luxembourg, Reed,
Kautsky,Bukharin,Trotsky)

New World Order and the
Politics of Mass Immigration

Edited by VN Gelis
S Lawrence

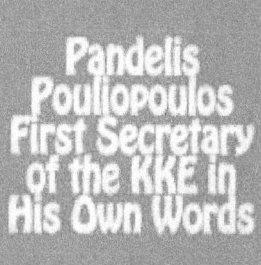

Pandelis
Pouliopoulos
First Secretary
of the KKE in
His Own Words

Greek Marxist in
the Inter-war Years

Greece:
Revolutionary
History

VN Gelis

SYRIZA BETRAYS
GREECE 'LEFT'
GLOBALISM IMPLODES

EYEWITNESS REPORTS

VN GELIS

www.ingramcontent.com/pod-product-compliance
Lightning Source LLC
Chambersburg PA
CBHW060241290526
45789CB00001B/144